Building Better Teams

The Facilitator's Guide for Building Better Teams: 70 Tools and Techniques for Strengthening Performance Within and Across Teams is available free online. If you would like to download and print out a copy of the guide, please visit: www.wiley.com/college/barner

Building Better Teams

70 Tools and Techniques for Strengthening Performance Within and Across Teams

Robert W. Barner, Ph.D.
Charlotte P. Barner, Ed.D.

Pfeiffer

A Wiley Imprint
www.pfeiffer.com

Published by Pfeiffer
An Imprint of Wiley
One Montgomery Street, Suite 1200, San Francisco, CA 94104–4594   www.pfeiffer.com

For additional copies/bulk purchases of this book in the U.S. please contact 800–274–4434.

Pfeiffer books and products are available through most bookstores. To contact Pfeiffer directly call our Customer Care Department within the U.S. at 800–274–4434, outside the U.S. at 317–572–3985, fax 317–572–4002, or visit www.pfeiffer.com.

Pfeiffer also publishes its books in a variety of electronic formats and by print-on-demand. Some material included with standard print versions of this book may not be included in e-books or in print-on-demand. If the version of this book that you purchased references media such as CD or DVD that was not included in your purchase, you may download this material at http://booksupport.wiley.com. For more information about Wiley products, visit www.wiley.com.

Library of Congress Cataloging-in-Publication Data

Barner, Robert (Robert W.)
   Building better teams : 70 tools and techniques for strengthening performance within and across teams / Robert W. Barner, Ph.D., Charlotte P. Barner, Ed.D.
      pages   cm
   Includes bibliographical references and index.
     ISBN 978-1-118-12726-1 (pbk.); ISBN 978-1-118-22488-5 (ebk);
     ISBN 978-1-118-23839-4 (ebk); ISBN 978-1-118-26294-8(ebk)
      1. Teams in the workplace.   2. Personnel management.   3. Performance standards.
   I. Barner, Charlotte P., 1957-   II. Title.
   HD66.B365   2012
   658.4'022—dc23
                                      2012011630

Acquiring Editor:	Matthew Davis
Editorial Assistant:	Michael Zelenko
Director of Development:	Kathleen Dolan Davies
Production Editor:	Dawn Kilgore
Editor:	Donna Weinson
Manufacturing Supervisor:	Becky Morgan

Printed in the United States of America

Printing   10   9   8   7   6   5   4   3   2   1

Table of Contents

List of Tools

List of Figures and Tables

Figures

Tables

Acknowledgments

WE WOULD LIKE to thank the following people for their willingness to contribute their valuable time and energy to make this book a success. This includes: Matthew Davis, senior editor at Jossey-Bass & Pfeiffer, for his partnership with us on a creative approach to a team-building manuscript; Michael Zelenko, senior editorial assistant at Jossey-Bass & Pfeiffer, for his helpful responses to our questions and offering valuable suggestions; Dawn Kilgore, our highly organized and flexible production editor; and Jennifer Reed, for her time and attention to detail on manuscript assistance.

A special thanks goes to the twelve contributors who volunteered their valuable time and experiences to share the following excellent team building tools and techniques: Ken Cloke and Joan Goldsmith for *Turnaround Feedback*; Samir Gupte for the *"Getting Naked" Session or New Team Assimilation*; Ken Ideus for the *Goals-Values Matrix*; Jonas Janebrant and Johanna Steen for *Stakeholder Hats* and *Idea Rotation*; Jim O'Neil for *Provocative Questions for Encouraging Dialogue* and *Guidelines and*

Questions for Engaging Dialogue; Chuck Palus and David Magellan Horth for *Visual Explorer*™; Daniel Rainey for *Asynchronous Work Spaces*; Mary Stall for *Mix and Max*; and John Sturrock for the *Human Due Diligence Audit*. Thank you all very much for your patience and assistance on this project. This book is a much more valuable tool as a result of all of your contributions!

About the Authors

ROBERT W. BARNER, PHD, is the associate director of executive education and a full-time faculty member at the Annette Simmons Caldwell School of Education and Human Development at Southern Methodist University. Prior to joining SMU, Robert held senior-level corporate HR positions at several companies, with three of these positions supporting global operations. These roles included responsibilities for career planning, executive development and coaching, the assessment and development of high-potential leaders, and talent management. Robert's work experience also includes management consulting to such companies as GTE, AT&T, Harris, Disney, TXU, Honeywell, and United Technologies.

Robert has published over thirty articles in such journals as the *OD Practitioner*, *Journal of Organizational Change Management*, *Team Performance Management*, the *Journal for Quality & Participation*, and *Career Development International*. He is the author of six books, with foreign language translations in Arabic, German, Norwegian, and Estonian. His most recent book,

Accelerating the Development of Your Leaders, was published by Pfeiffer/Wiley in 2011. Robert has also contributed to seven text anthologies, including three that are used in college curricula. Most recently he has coauthored two chapters for the *Oxford Handbook of Reciprocal Adult Development and Learning* (Carol Hoare, editor; Oxford University Press, 2011). Dr. Barner currently serves as a reviewer for the *Journal for Organizational Change Management* and is currently a reviewer for the *Journal of Management Development.*

Dr. Barner has presented to international conferences on the subjects of executive coaching, team building, and talent management strategy, including the OD Network Conferences (2006, 2008, and 2010), the 2009 International Conference on Collaboration and Innovation sponsored by Purdue University, and the SW HR Conferences. Robert holds master's and doctorate degrees in organization development from Fielding Graduate University, and bachelor degrees in education and psychology from Florida Atlantic University.

Charlotte P. Barner, EdD, has over twenty years of experience in the area of human and organizational learning and development. Charlotte is an executive consultant in the area of organizational effectiveness and is adjunct professor and student adviser for the *Organizational Dynamics* concentration within the Annette Simmons Caldwell School of Education and Human Development at Southern Methodist University's Master's of Liberal Studies Program.

Prior to joining SMU in 2010, Charlotte held senior corporate leadership positions responsible for creating and implementing human and organizational development strategies and systems. Most recently, Charlotte established and led the Organizational Effectiveness function for one of North America's top sales and marketing companies with clients such as Apple iTunes, AT&T, Best Buy, Cadbury, Disney, HP, Microsoft, and Wal-Mart, as well as all of North America's major movie and gaming producers. Charlotte was previously president and partner of a long-term, U.S.-based HD/OD consulting corporation serving such clients as AT&T, Disney, GTE, Harris Corporation, Honeywell, and United Technologies.

Dr. Charlotte P. Barner has authored articles in professional journals over the years, including coauthoring a three-part job-search series in *Wall Street Journal's National Business Employment Weekly.* Most recently, Charlotte has coauthored chapters for the *Oxford Handbook of Reciprocal Adult Development and Learning* (Carol Hoare, editor; Oxford University Press, 2011) and *Advances in Positive Organizational Psychology* (Arnold Bakker, editor; Emerald, in press 2013). Charlotte has served as primary editor on several books and journal articles. Finally, Charlotte presents at national and international HR and OD conferences, such as Academy of Management.

Dr. Charlotte P. Barner's doctorate is in Human & Organizational Learning from The George Washington University. Her master of education in Curriculum Design & Instructional Technologies is with honors from George Mason University, and her undergraduate degree in Business & Human Resources Administration is from Barry University.

About the Contributors

CONTRIBUTORS ARE PRESENTED in alphabetical order by last name. In addition to biographical information, each contributor's tools are noted.

Ken Cloke & Joan Goldsmith

Tool: *Turnaround Feedback*

Kenneth Cloke, JD, LLM, PhD, is a mediator, arbitrator, coach, consultant, and trainer specializing in resolving complex multiparty conflicts and designing conflict resolution systems. He is an adjunct professor at Pepperdine University School of Law; University of Amsterdam ADR Institute; Saybrook University, Massey University (New Zealand); and Southern Methodist University. He has done conflict resolution in twenty countries and is founder and past president of Mediators Beyond Borders.

Ken is the author of *Mediating Dangerously: The Frontiers of Conflict Resolution; The Crossroads of Conflict: A Journey into the Heart of Dispute Resolution;* and *Conflict Revolution: Mediating Evil, War, Injustice, and Terrorism.*

He is coauthor with Joan Goldsmith of *Resolving Conflicts at Work: 8 Strategies for Everyone on the Job; Resolving Personal and Organizational Conflict: Stories of Transformation and Forgiveness; The End of Management and the Rise of Organizational Democracy, and The Art of Waking People Up: Cultivating Awareness* and *Authenticity at Work.*

Joan Goldsmith (Santa Monica, California) is an educator, organizational consultant, mediator, and trainer, specializing in collaborative negotiation, high-performance teams, leadership development, and organizational change. She is a former faculty member of Harvard University and the cofounder of Cambridge College, where she is a life member of the board of trustees. In partnership with Ken Cloke and the Center for Dispute Resolution, she has been a mediator of community disputes and organizational conflicts. She is an international trainer in conflict resolution. She and Ken Cloke are the coauthors of *Resolving Conflicts at Work: 10 Strategies for Everyone on the Job* (3rd ed.)*; The End of Management and the Rise of Organizational Democracy; The Art of Waking People Up: Cultivating Awareness and Authenticity at Work;* and *Resolving Personal and Organizational Conflicts: Stories of Transformation and Forgiveness.* She is also the author, with Warren Bennis, of *Learning to Lead: A Workbook on Becoming a Leader.*

Samir Gupte

Tool: *"Getting Naked" Session or New Team Assimilation*
Samir Gupte is vice president of Enterprise Function Human Resources for Darden. In this role, he is responsible for leading efforts to build culture and talent for each of Darden's enterprise functions while also serving as their partner in driving organizational vibrancy and team effectiveness.

Ken Ideus

Tool: *Goals-Values Matrix*
Currently the founder and principle of London-based I-DEOS Consulting, **Ken Ideus**, EdD, has spent over thirty years working in a variety of countries and cultures around the world. His in-depth interest in collaboration began

in the early 1990s when working with multinational teams to help them collaborate more effectively through the use of virtual tools. This interest expanded into researching the impact of collaboration within multinational joint ventures. More recently, working with various tribes and constituencies in Southern Sudan, he was able to drive a countrywide collaboration effort for educating government employees in preparation for independence. Ken received his doctorate in education from Boston University and now resides in London.

Jonas Janebrant & Johanna Steen

Tools: *Stakeholder Hats* and *Idea Rotation*

Jonas Janebrant received his master of business administration from Lund University. He is the deputy managing director of MiL Institute, where he is responsible for tailor-made activities.

Johanna Steen received her masters of science of psychology degree from Lund University. She is the program director, facilitator, and individual coach, responsible for the Mentoring Programme at MiL Institute. She has directed scholarship within the MiL Research Foundation to research the MiL learning philosophy of Action Reflection Learning®.

About the MiL Institute: The MiL Institute is an international not-for-profit foundation. We work with value-based business development and business-driven leadership development. Our aim is to help our clients to turn their vision and values into action by designing processes of learning, change, and innovation. We do this through our learning and development philosophy Action Reflection Learning (ARL®). Read more about MiL Institute or contact us at: www.milinstitute.se.

Jim O'Neil

Tools: *Provocative Questions for Encouraging Dialogue; Guidelines and Questions for Engaging Dialogue*

Jim O'Neil has been working for Community Dialogue as their dialogue development worker since April 2009 through funding from the European

Union Special Support Programme for Peace and Reconciliation. Jim states he is privileged to be continuing the vital groundwork and development of the dialogue process in Northern Ireland that was instigated by a number of those who preceded him.

Jim is currently cochair and founder member of Towards Understanding and Healing Project, which deals with key players involved in the Northern Ireland conflict to deal with the past by engaging in a process of storytelling and dialogue. He is also a member of the management committee of the Junction Community Relations Centre in Derry/Londonderry and was a member of the Advisory Committee for the Legacy Project based at the Warrington Peace Centre in England.

Jim's research experience in the area of conflict and peace building has included the following:

- Research into the experiences and needs of former members of the Irish Defence Forces who served on the Irish border during the Northern Ireland Conflict

- Associate researcher on the experiences of the Bloody Sunday victims' families during the course of the Saville Inquiry

- Faith-based community relations initiatives in the Derry City Council area

- Research into how cross border links can contribute to peace building at *Centre for the Study of Conflict, University of Ulster*

About Community Dialogue: Community Dialogue is a charitable organization that empowers people through dialogue and training to address issues of division and exclusion. Our tools, *Guidelines and Questions for Engaging in Dialogue* (includes eleven case studies) and *Provocative Questions for Encouraging Dialogue*, have been used extensively in the Community Dialogue organization. The organization was formed in 1997, some months before the Good Friday/Belfast Agreement, by a group of Unionists, Nationalists, Republicans, Loyalists, and others in Northern Ireland. Contentious issues are addressed in a face-to-face context, dealing with the root causes of division, and people can be "skilled up" to practice dialogue in their own communities. The organization provides a safe context for people who are often diametrically opposed to engage with each other. and offers dialogue experiences through workshops, residential sessions, and training courses. Community Dialogue takes no party-political position on any issue, endeavoring to ensure that it remains impartial during its often challenging and contentious dialogue processes. We also believe that it is much more effective and empowering to raise questions than to answer them. We strive to increase the numbers of Dialogue Practitioners in each community to act as catalysts for positive engagement and transforming of often limited understanding.

Chuck Palus and David Magellan Horth

Tool: *Visual Explorer™*

Charles J. Palus, PhD, is a senior faculty member in Research, Innovation & Product Development at the Center for Creative Leadership. He conducts research on interdependent leadership and creates new knowledge and innovations for the Center's organization leadership development practice. He has been widely published on leadership, including articles and chapters for the *CCL Handbook of Leadership Development,* the *CCL Handbook of Coaching,* the *HBS Handbook for Teaching Leadership,* the *Journal of Applied Behavioral Science,* the *Consulting Psychology Journal,* and the *Change Handbook.* He is coauthor of the award-winning book *The Leader's Edge: Six Creative Competencies for Navigating Complex Challenges,* and coinventor of the *Visual Explorer™* and the *Leadership Metaphor Explorer™,* tools for facilitating creative dialogue. He has designed and facilitated numerous programs, including the *Leading Creatively Program, Facing and Solving Complex Challenges,* and the *Action Learning Leadership Process™.* Prior to coming to CCL he was a research engineer for E. I. du Pont de Nemours & Company, an instructor and designer for the Hurricane Island Outward Bound School, and taught social psychology at Boston College. He received his BS degree in chemical engineering from The Pennsylvania State University and his PhD degree in developmental psychology from Boston College.

David Magellan Horth is a senior fellow at The Center for Creative Leadership. He is an international authority on the confluence of design, innovation, and leadership development. David led the design of many notable CCL programs and is a skilled facilitator of a wide range of them. He coinvented *Visual Explorer, Leadership Metaphor Explorer,* and *Wisdom Explorer.* He and colleague Chuck Palus coauthored *The Leader's Edge: Six Creative Competencies for Navigating Complex Challenges*—honored by the Banff Centre for the Arts for the links it establishes between the arts and business leadership. David is former chairman of the board of trustees of the Creative Education Foundation and recipient of CEF's Distinguished Leader Award for his contributions to the field. He is Visiting Research Fellow at the Center for Entrepreneurship at the University of Greenwich in London.

Prior to CCL, David spent twenty-one years in the IT industry as a design engineer, marketer, and strategist specializing in innovation. He led the work that won the Queens Award for Technological Innovation in 1985. David holds a BSc from England's University of Surrey.

Daniel Rainey

Tool: *Asynchronous Work Spaces*
Daniel Rainey is the chief of staff for the National Mediation Board, and an adjunct faculty member in the graduate dispute resolution programs for Southern Methodist University and Creighton University. He is on the editorial board of *Conflict Resolution Quarterly,* and he is internationally known as a practitioner, advocate, and expert in the field of Online Dispute Resolution. Website: http://danielrainey.us.

Mary Stall

Tool: *Mix and Max*
Mary Stall works in Organizational Effectiveness in the Department of Human Resources at Southern Methodist University. She incorporates visual facilitation and graphic recording as tools in her training and consulting at SMU and with regional, national, and international clients, such as

Dallas Museum of Art; Cox Executive Education; Medical City Hospital; Methodist Health System–Charlton; Boerne RUDAT; San Antonio River Foundation; City of Littleton, New Hampshire; and Mary Kay. Mary may be contacted at mary.stall@gmail.com.

John Sturrock

Tool: *Human Due Diligence Audit*

John Sturrock is founder of Core Solutions Group, Scotland's leading business mediation and training service, and is recognized as Scotland's leading mediator, conducting mediations in a wide range of industries and sectors in the United Kingdom, Europe, and Africa.

John is a visiting professor at the University of Strathclyde and a Distinguished Fellow of the International Academy of Mediators. He acts as facilitator of Scotland's 2020 Climate Change Delivery Group and, in 2010, received the honorary degree of Doctor of Laws from Edinburgh Napier University in recognition of his contribution to mediation.

In a previous role, he established the Scottish Bar's award-winning advocacy skills program and, as a member of the Judicial Studies Committee, designed and delivered the first skills training courses for Scottish judges. He was appointed Queen's Counsel in 1999. John.Sturrock@core-solutions.com.

Introduction

Why Is This Book Important?

BUILDING BETTER TEAMS: *70 Tools and Techniques for Strengthening Performance Within and Across Teams* is intended to fill an important void in the area of team building. This book provides team and group members with the tools they need to work together more effectively and to build a stronger foundation of mutual trust and support. To accomplish this the book eschews the use of role plays, pretend exercises, and vague theories on team building in favor of providing the reader with a set of applied tools and techniques that can make an immediate and direct impact on team performance and relationships. Approached in this way, team building moves beyond a one-time training event to become an ongoing, easily sustainable part of a team's functioning and interactions.

Who Will Benefit from This Book?

Building Better Teams is designed for a wide range of readers. This book will be of value to any professional who is attempting to promote team performance and collaboration within a group context, and can be applied to profit and nonprofit work groups, temporary cross-functional and project teams, community agencies, and volunteer organizations.

Team facilitators will discover that this book can be an important part of their team-building repertoire, while managers and team leaders who have had little prior experience in team building will find the techniques that they encounter here easy to use within their work teams. In addition, organizational development, training, and human resource professionals will find this book a useful and important resource for supporting employee engagement and change management efforts, or for training programs in interpersonal communication, and team development. Finally, if you are a team-building consultant or university instructor you will find that this book can serve as a useful, applied resource for helping your participants gain critical team development skills. As an example, the authors have used this book as a resource in directing team-building consulting activities, as a supplemental resource in graduate courses they conduct on team dynamics and team building, and as an integral part of a graduate-level, international organizational collaboration study abroad course that they coteach each summer.

How Can You Apply This Book?

This book comprises three parts:

Section One, A Systematic Approach to Team Building, explains some of the factors that characterize effective team building, introduces a five-step process for directing a team-building session, and shows you how to select the right team-building tools for your session. If you have never before conducted a team-building session this section provides a good overview of a suggested approach. This section will also be useful when you are getting team members, leaders, and senior sponsors aligned regarding the goals and intended outcomes of team building.

Section Two, Managing Team-Building Challenges, outlines nine critical challenges that teams often encounter and highlights the opportunities within each challenge. This section provides team leaders and members with guidelines for dealing with each challenge and actions they can take leading up to or concurrent with a team-building session to create opportunities within each team challenge. These suggestions also specify some of the tools and techniques included within the Tool Kit.

Section Three, Tools and Techniques for Team Building, introduces Chapter Fourteen, *The Tool Kit,* which offers seventy tools and techniques that you can use when facilitating team-building sessions or managing teams or groups. For each tool, we have provided guidelines and tips for effective application and included a variety of forms and templates.

There are many ways to apply and obtain benefit from this book. If you are planning for a team or group meeting where an important issue is going to be discussed, a decision made, or plan of action developed, then you will find the tools in this book to be very helpful. Chapter Four, *Selecting the Right Team-Building Tools,* will help you choose the appropriate tools for that meeting.

If you are planning a workshop on team building then we advise you to provide each workshop participant a copy of this book. Ask participants to read the first three chapters, as well as the introductions to those selected exercises that you are proposing for the workshop. One useful training technique is to have participants divide into teams of three or four and ask each breakout team to discuss how they might go about applying selected techniques to their own teams or work groups.

Selective tools can also be used to help groups that extend beyond intact teams (such as directing boards or cross-functional teams) to obtain better outcomes from task-focused meetings. Examples would include meetings in which group members are attempting to encourage creative idea generation, establish consensus-based decision making, or see decisions implemented through clear action plans. The *Traffic Light Technique* introduced in this book is an example of such a tool.

If you are planning a major team-building activity then you will want to make use of the *Online Facilitator's Guide.* This guide is available to you free with the purchase of this book. Directions for accessing this guide can be found in the Appendix. The *Facilitator's Guide* provides several resources, including:

- Guidelines for determining when to use team building, and conditions under which team building should not be attempted

- Steps for planning for your team-building session, how to obtain the greatest value from that session, and how to make use of this book in the planning and implementation of that session

- An online version of the *Team Building Assessment Questionnaire©* that you may print and distribute to quickly determine where to direct your team-building efforts

- A PowerPoint template that you are free to download and customize for use in your session

Contact information on the authors is provided should you wish to obtain consulting help in facilitating your team-building event.

Section One

A Systematic Approach to Team Building

THIS FIRST SECTION EXPLAINS the factors that characterize effective team building, introduces a five-step process for directing a team-building session, and shows you how to select the right team-building tools for your session.

Getting Started

Building Better Teams: An Evolution in Thinking

This book had its genesis in a team-building text written by one of the editors (Robert) over ten years ago entitled *The Team Troubleshooter: How to Find and Fix Team Problems*. That said, the authors feel it would be erroneous to refer to *Building Better Teams* as a text revision. Instead, *Building Better Teams* represents a significant shift in the authors' thinking regarding what it takes for teams or groups to build a strong foundation of trust and mutual cooperation, and to forge strong alliances with key organizational partners and stakeholders. In this regard, *Building Better Teams* represents an evolutionary development from its predecessor, in that it incorporates three critical changes in thinking regarding the conditions under which teams learn from their collective experiences. These changes are: (a) rethinking the idea of "teams," (b) a shift from fixing to building, and (c) a shift from conflict management to collaboration.

The First Change: Rethinking the Idea of "Teams"

As organizations continue to evolve, the concept of what is a "team" has also undergone significant change. Not too long ago, the word "team" brought to mind the image of a relatively stable and permanent work unit made up of managers and their direct reports. This concept has quickly morphed to include such diverse groups as temporary project teams, governing boards for nonprofit organizations, teams that operate within government agencies and professional organizations, and large broad-based groups that are attempting to seek common ground on such critical social issues as community sustainability.

In addition, we have seen the proliferation of organizations as global constructs that attempt to bridge national and cultural borders. Many teams mirror these changes in the increasing cultural diversity of their membership. As team-building professionals, it is important that we acknowledge these differences by checking our assumptions regarding the appropriateness and effectiveness of the tools and approaches we bring to the team-building process. Accordingly, this text differs significantly from its predecessor by incorporating the perspectives of consultants from different countries who have implemented team building in a variety of international and organizational settings. These contributors include international mediators, private management consultants, university instructors, and corporate professionals in the fields of leadership and organizational development. We feel that this infusion of talent and diverse perspectives provides a broader foundation for strengthening team performance.

The Second Change: From Fixing to Building

Traditionally, team building has been viewed as a set of interventions that are designed to "fix" a team only after that team has experienced conflict or crisis. The result is that, all too frequently, team building has not been attempted until after team members may have experienced a serious erosion of their performance, interpersonal relationships, and mutual trust. Unfortunately, very often team facilitators and leaders pay insufficient attention to the many ways in which they could take preemptive action to help teams strengthen their performance and relationships—before team members find themselves enmeshed in damaging conflict.

To understand what we are talking about, imagine the flow of organizational communication as a river. Entering the river from upstream we see different parties trying to determine the most effective way to engage in initial dialogues on important opportunities or challenges. If they misstep at this point, differences of opinion may shift to become stronger disagreements, then could escalate into embedded conflicts. Often, farther down the communication stream, a third-party facilitator or mediator will be called in to help the conflicting parties "resolve the problem." *Building Better Teams* offers a team-building approach that can be applied "at the source of the river"; that is, as part of a team development process for newly formed teams or as a set of tools for helping experienced teams engage in initial conversations about important issues or potential opportunities for growth.

The Third Change: From Conflict Management to Collaboration

The original text from which *Building Better Teams* evolved defined *team building* from the traditional, more limited perspective of helping teams identify and fix performance problems. That traditional perspective has given way to an increasing emphasis on techniques that can help teams, work groups, and organizations build a foundation of trust, cooperation, and mutual support.

This change involves more than a perspective shift in how we view team building, for the tools involved in building team collaboration are very different from those used to manage conflicts. Collaboratively based tools vary in their form and function, but have in common the aim of helping to shape dialogue so that different parties enter into their initial discussions in a positive way and develop a constructive view of a shared future. This new perspective and these tools help team members seek common ground as they identify what it is that they can gather their energy around—that is, what supports and strengthens team functioning.

This emerging perspective is supported by research findings from areas such as positive psychology and appreciative inquiry. The rapidly emerging field of positive psychology, as exemplified in the seminal work of psychologist Dr. Martin Seligman, has shed light on the degree to which a team's attention serves to direct its energy. That is, teams perform at their best when they are able to construct a viable and positive image of their desired future, and then work to focus their attention on the strengths and resources that they can bring to bear in actualizing that positive, envisioned state. In other words, we focus our attention on what works, and where possible we seek models of success that we can replicate and build upon. This concept is reflected in what David Cooperrider, a renowned organizational behavior researcher in the field of appreciative inquiry, has termed the *heliotropic principal.* Appreciative inquiry also emphasizes the role that language plays in influencing organizational meaning making and behavior. This book's authors align with this principal to emphasize the importance that language plays in any team-building process, beginning with the way in which a team defines and formulates its needs and desired outcomes. Although an extensive review of positive psychology and appreciative inquiry is outside the scope of this book, at the end of this chapter the authors have listed additional reading on these subjects.

The authors want to stress that we acknowledge the value in helping teams identify and effectively resolve intra- and interteam conflicts; indeed, this book offers a variety of tools for supporting conflict resolution. At the same time, a fundamental premise on which *Building Better Teams* has been developed is that too often facilitators, team leaders, and members rely exclusively on conflict-resolution strategies simply because they have few alternative methods at their disposal. To that end, you will find that *Building Better Teams* emphasizes the application of team building as a set of preemptive interventions that can be used to help teams set the stage for productive and positive dialogues.

Some Underlying Assumptions Regarding Teams

Building Better Teams introduces a team improvement strategy that is based on four underlying assumptions. Understanding these assumptions will help you obtain the greatest benefit from this book.

Individuals Can Affect Team Performance

Regardless of whether you are a new team member, an experienced team leader, an outside facilitator, or one who has been asked to lead a cross-functional team, you can play an important role in helping your team strengthen its performance. This book will show you how. If you are concerned that you lack the influence or authority to make a productive impact on your team, don't be. Throughout *Building Better Teams*, you will be introduced to a variety of tools and techniques that you can use to help make a positive impact on your team. By taking the initiative to share these ideas with others in your team you can help your work group perform at its best.

Team Members Require an Active Voice in the Process

There is a tendency to view team building as a process that is constructed and directed by an outside facilitator. The implication of this view is that a facilitator has the responsibility for defining the team's needs and desired outcomes, selecting the most appropriate team-building approach, and actively leading the team through this preselected process. In short, the facilitator leads and the team blindly follows. In contrast, *Building Better Teams* takes the position that team building is best accomplished when facilitators work with team leaders and members as equal partners in the co-construction and management of the team-building process.

So, if you think that defining the needs and requirements of your team is something that is best left to the "experts," think again. The authors believe that team members and leaders are the ones who are most qualified to understand the types of job demands and challenges that they are encountering. We also believe that people are more likely to take accountability for implementing change when they are fully involved in the change process. What many people lack is a tool kit to help them effectively facilitate team-building sessions. This book is designed to provide those tools, as well as instructions for successfully implementing them.

If you are a team leader you will find that *Building Better Teams* will encourage the members of your team to see themselves as active partners in their team's success. If you are a team-building facilitator you will find that this book provides a method for fully engaging team members and their leaders in the team-building process, by making full use of their combined experience and knowledge of their team's operation.

Up-Front Assessment Is Key to Success in Team Building

Over the years the authors have seen a lot of well-intended team building quickly dissipate into small, ineffectual puffs of smoke, while other teams barely survive the poorly constructed interventions suggested by their facilitators. Many of these negative outcomes could have been avoided if a little more effort had gone into helping teams perform a detailed review of their desired outcomes—that is, how they hope to change as a result of engaging in a team-building event. You can encourage full ownership in the team-building process by providing a mechanism through which team members (particularly those who have difficulty thinking quickly in the moment) have the opportunity to carefully evaluate both their own team requirements and alternative approaches to meeting these options, *before* they engage in a team-building session.

An up-front assessment helps team members focus their time and attention on the most critical topics for review. At the same time, such an assessment helps facilitators flag potential problems, such as lack of trust, which could otherwise derail the team-building process. It also provides a means for facilitators to increase ownership by familiarizing team members with proposed team-building approaches well in advance of the session. This book will introduce you to a simple instrument, the *Team Building Assessment Questionnaire* (see The Tool Kit), which you can use to perform such an assessment.

True Change Comes Through Direct Application

Over the past twenty years, team-building consultants have discovered that there is a lot of money to be made from creating and selling team exercises and training games. These range in form from synthetic role-play scripts and team-building cases that can be commercially purchased, to the many "team survival" simulations that have recently flooded the market. Most of these tools are fun and some may be of value, especially when they are used as a method for introducing professionals to foundational team development skills.

On the other hand, training is never a substitute for a facilitated team-building session. One of the core assumptions on which this book is based is that substantial change occurs when teams or groups are provided with applied tools and techniques that allow them to tackle actual opportunities and challenges. Such an approach makes use of the team's common history and experience and encourages team members to articulate those factors that impede or support their performance.

The authors believe that facilitators who rely heavily on artificial exercises do so because they do not know how to connect, head on, with the team's actual experiences. The good news is that team interventions do not have to be intimidating. If you have a solid plan, you can take the first step toward helping a team maximize its performance and strengthen relationships among team members. Planning your team-building session is introduced next in Chapter Two.

Additional Reading on Appreciative Inquiry

Cooperrider, D., & Whitney, D. (2005). *Appreciative Inquiry: A Positive Revolution in Change*. San Francisco: Berrett-Koehler.

Cooperrider, D., Whitney, D., & Stavros, J. (2008). *Appreciative Inquiry Handbook: For Leaders of Change*. Brunswick, Ohio: Crown Custom Publishing.

Hammond, S. A. (1998). *The Thin Book on Appreciative Inquiry*. Bend, Oregon: Thin Book.

Additional Reading on Positive Psychology

Bakker, A. (Ed.) (in press). *Advances in Positive Organizational Psychology*. Bingley, UK: Emerald Group Publishing Limited.

Donaldson, S. I., Csikszentmihalyi, M., & Nakamura, J. (Eds.). (2011). *Applied Positive Psychology: Improving Everyday Life, Health, Schools, Work, and Society*. New York: Psychology Press.

Lopez, S., & Snyder, C. R. (Eds.) (2009). *Oxford Handbook of Positive Psychology*. New York: Oxford University Press.

Planning the Team-Building Session

The Building Better Teams Model

Although the tools introduced in this book can be used in a variety of team-building applications, the authors recommend that whenever possible the following model be used to guide the approach you craft for your team-building sessions. There are several advantages to working from a structured team-building model.

First, at any one time, every team is confronted with a confusing array of challenges and opportunities, ranging from the addition of new members to the need to overcome difficult performance setbacks. A simple model provides a team with a road map for charting their own course. Instead of feeling that they are being blindly led down an unknown path by a facilitator, the use of an orchestrating model allows participants to obtain a better understand of the logic in the flow of the team-building process and feel that they have an active role in that process.

Second, the use of a structured model also helps reduce the anxiety that some individuals might have regarding participating in a team-building session by showing them that their session will adhere to a logical, well-considered game plan. This is particularly useful when you are working with teams comprising technical professionals, such as engineers, software designers, or finance managers, all of whom typically feel more comfortable when working from a structured plan.

Third, having a structured process raises the comfort level for team members when trust and cohesion are core, underlying issues. A model also provides participants with an element of safety when strong power differentials exist within the team (for example, when you are conducting a team-building session for members who range from directors to administrative assistants). Introducing a clear, easy-to-understand blueprint for the team-building process assures participants that their session won't degenerate into a blame-casting session, or an emotional free-for-all.

Finally, as a facilitator, employing a model helps to ensure that you are operating from a clear, well-constructed blueprint. The *Online Facilitator's Guide* that accompanies this book includes a checklist you can use to ensure that you have the following important guidelines for each of the five steps of the team-building process.

The *Building Better Teams* model is based on five steps that focus on collaboration and trust building, and the importance of helping participants seek common ground. The remainder of this chapter introduces these steps. Additional resources are in the *Online Facilitator's Guide.*

Overview of Five Steps of the Team-Building Process

Figure 2.1 provides an overview of the five steps. The first three steps are introduced in this chapter and may be completed in advance of the actual session. The final two steps of implementation and follow-up are introduced in Chapter Three.

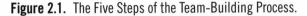

Figure 2.1. The Five Steps of the Team-Building Process.

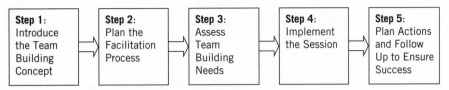

The five steps of the team-building process.

1. *Introduce the team-building concept:* Provide the team with an explanation of what team building is, how a team-building session can strengthen team performance, and the key roles assumed by the facilitator, team leader, and team members.

2. *Plan the facilitation process:* Meet with the team leader and team in advance of the session to plan meeting logistics and obtain agreement for the proposed team-building approach.

3. *Assess team-building needs:* Work with the team to construct a positive and affirming understanding of the topics or issues that will be reviewed during the team-building session.

4. *Implement the session:* Conduct the team-building session using key skills to balance participation, encourage innovative thinking, and evaluate options for change.

5. *Plan actions and follow up to ensure success:* Translate improvement ideas into detailed action plans. Conduct a follow-up meeting to confirm that the team has achieved their desired outcomes and is satisfied with their efforts.

Step 1: Introduce the Team-Building Concept

Confirm the Overall Intent of the Session We recommend that you start out by confirming the overall intent of the program. Below are suggested introductions that you can adapt to three different team-building situations:

- When you are performing team building with a single team: "It is my understanding that everyone here has agreed to use our time today to explore ways of strengthening both your overall performance as a team and your relationships as team members."

- When you are performing team building with two or more teams: "It is my understanding that everyone here has agreed to use our time today to explore more effective ways of strengthening those key work processes and relationships that connect you as teams."

- When you have been asked to help a work group (or groups) use the session to accomplish a particular task: "It is my understanding that everyone here has agreed to use our time today to accomplish . . . [describe the task]. In addition, the team-building techniques that you will be introduced to today can be applied to other team opportunities that you might address in the future."

Clarify the Purpose of Team Building For many people the term "team building" calls to mind certain negative images. Some people may have heard stories of coworkers or associates who entered into team building in good faith, only to have their sessions produce minimal to nothing of value. Others may even have experienced team-building sessions that led to increased conflicts, and the deterioration of communications and relationships among team members. Unfortunately, these situations do occur. When they do the fault lies not so much with the participants as it does the team-building facilitator. Many facilitators have the mistaken notion that the only way to enhance team performance is to use team building as some sort of cathartic release of negative feelings or to encourage "honest confrontation" regarding pent-up resentments. Other facilitators operate from no clear team development model, relying instead on an assorted grab bag of tricks.

The best way to head off these kinds of concerns is to explain the team-building approach that you propose using well in advance of the session. It is equally important that you use this introductory stage not to sell participants on the logic of your proposed process, but rather to actively listen and respond to their questions and concerns. The goal here is to ensure that participants are fully comfortable with and understand your proposed approach. If not, be prepared to adapt the approach to their needs.

Introduce the Guiding Principles of Team Building While it is beyond the scope of this book to provide a detailed review of team-building concepts and theory, we believe that in order for team building to be effective, facilitators need to adhere to the following guiding principles and communicate these principles to their teams in advance of the session.

Search for Common Ground. Team building works when it is focused on those unexplored opportunities, concerns, or issues that members share as a common organizational entity. The process is neither intended to analyze the personalities or behaviors of individual team members nor to function as a disguised attempt at performance management.

Team Members Are Equal Partners. Team building works when members are equal partners in the process and does not work when power inequities exist in the room. The reality of the situation is that you may be working with teams that include members who represent different levels of status and power within their organizations. In such cases, it is important to ensure participants that throughout the team-building process they will have an equal voice in the session.

Team Building Is a Process, Not a One-Time Event. Even though a team-building session might last only a single day, it is important that participants view what happens inside the session as relevant to their ongoing day-to-day experiences. For this reason, participants should have the opportunity to discuss how they can apply what they've learned from the session to future situations. In the same way, team building needs to build upon and support the team's activities outside of the confines of the facilitated session.

Safety Is Important to Success. An important prerequisite for any team-building process is that participants feel safe to voice their honest opinions and explore options for change. A team-building process should never make participants feel vulnerable or defensive. If this occurs it is often a sign that the facilitator does not truly understand the conditions that strengthen team performance.

Clarify Respective Roles Explain that there are several responsibilities that lie outside your role as a team facilitator. Your job is not to do the team's thinking for them, solve their business or relational issues, function as judge and jury on team decisions, or chart a new direction for the team. Individuals who provide such services have shifted away from the role of team facilitator to assume the role of business consultant. In contrast, the facilitator's job is to provide the team with a structured, well-executed methodology for helping participants strengthen their relationships and their performance.

In addition, the team leader's job is to provide key direction and perspective on *task-focused* content. Examples include keeping the team alerted to the perspectives of senior stakeholders or providing direction should the discussion shift to such topics as setting team performance standards or work priorities. At the same time, the team leader needs to enter into the session as an equal partner whenever the team attempts to address *process-focused* issues, such as how team meetings can be designed to ensure creative idea generation or effective decision making. For their part, all team members need to be equally engaged in the process.

Capture Commitment As a facilitator it is important to emphasize that all participants are equally accountable for fully participating in the team-building process and for ensuring the success of its outcomes. When team building does not work it is frequently either because participants are not fully committed to the process or because they lack effective methods for transforming commitments into action. We will discuss the first scenario here and come back to the action point during our introduction to the last two steps of *Implementation* and *Follow Through*. To begin, there are three commitments that are important for you to obtain from participants prior to the start of the session.

Commitment to Stay Through the Entire Session. This commitment is particularly important when you are facilitating a team-building session where some participants may have to fly out immediately after the close of the session. Ask: "We had made a commitment that we would reserve the entire day for this session with a close at five o'clock this afternoon. Are we all still committed to that? Does anyone have any meeting or travel requirements that might require them to leave early?" If they do, consider shortening the session to allow for full participation of the entire team.

Commitment to Work Within the Room. Working within the room means that participants agree to voice any concerns they might have regarding the planning for team building at the time that the process is first proposed. This commitment means that team members will not sit passively by, then engage in after-the-fact critiques after the team-building session is well under way. Working within the room also means that if participants have concerns about how the process is being implemented, they share those concerns openly during the session as opposed to engaging in one-on-one sidebars with other participants.

Commitment to Be Fully Engaged in the Process. This means being willing to fully participate during the process. This also involves sustaining the gains made through the session by working with other participants to transform team goals, decisions, and opportunities developed during the session into plans of action.

Step 2: Plan the Facilitation Process

Once you have introduced the team-building process, the next step is to plan for the team session. You can help the team arrive at decisions regarding the session logistics by posing the following key planning questions to participants:

1. Who within the overall organization will be participating in the session? Are there any key personnel who should attend, but won't be able to attend?

2. Will all participants be attending in person, or will any individuals be attending virtually? If the session will include some virtual members, how will these individuals be communicating with the rest of the group during the session (groupware, Skype software, video- or phone-conference)?

3. How much time has been allocated to the session?

4. Up to this point, what information have participants been given regarding the purpose of the session?

5. What is the most effective way of communicating with all participants so that they understand and agree on the goals of the session,

the respective roles of the facilitator, leader, and team members, and the proposed approach in advance of the session?

6. What steps need to be built into the session to ensure successful follow-up (for example, that any plans developed in the session will actually be carried out and reviewed in the weeks following the session)?

Step 3: Assess Team-Building Needs

Selecting Your Assessment Approach The third step in the team-building process is to help team members self-assess their team-building needs. This involves articulating both what it is that they would like to see changed within their current situation and the desired outcomes that they hope to achieve as a result of participating in a facilitator-led session.

Assessments can either be conducted in advance of the team-building session through individual interviews with the team leader and all members or conducted with the entire team as the first step in the actual session. In the latter case, the assessment discussion can occur as a dialogue with the entire team. A third option is break the team into subgroups, and have each subgroup address the assessment questions separately before reporting back to the entire group. The authors have used all three versions in team-building sessions, and the comparative advantages of each are presented in Figure 2.2.

Framing the Team's Needs Understanding the importance of how the facilitator's use of language can greatly influence the team-building experience. One of the most important discoveries to arise from the fields of positive psychology and appreciative inquiry is the extent to which our use of language shapes how we enter into dialogue with others on important issues. The appreciative inquiry model for group and organizational change emerged from the theory of social constructionism. This theory suggests that the language we use in our social interactions does not just describe what is happening to us, but also plays an influential role in shaping the manner in which we interpret and give meaning to our social experiences.

Figure 2.2. The Comparative Advantages of Three Team Assessment Approaches.

Assess in Advance of the Session	Assess During the Session (Entire Team)	Assess During the Session (Use of Subgroups)
Time Factors		
(+) Saves time during the session	(−) More time required during the session (2–4 hours)	(−) More time required during the session (2–4 hours)
(−) Requires additional time (1 hr. per interview) on the part of the team facilitator	(+) No additional time required in advance of the session	(+) No additional time required in advance of the session
(+) The facilitator has an opportunity to reflect on, and plan for sensitive issues before moving to the next stage of analysis	(−) Assessment is conducted in real time; sensitive issues must be dealt with as they occur	(−) Assessment is conducted in real time; sensitive issues must be dealt with as they occur
Members' Self-Disclosure & Trust		
(+) Provides the highest level of self-disclosure	(−) Provides the greatest challenge to self-disclosure	(=) Provides moderate levels of self-disclosure (the use of subgroups increases safety)
(−) May lower the trust level of team members (who may view the assessment as a "report card" on their own performance); raises the challenge of lack of transparency in how issues are shared, reviewed, and communicated	(+) Discussions of all issues are fully transparent to the entire team	(=) Subgroups share their final conclusions with the entire team (although the team will not have access to the discussions which led them to those conclusions)
Members' Emotions		
(+) May provide a cathartic release for angry or frustrated team members (allows a venting opportunity in advance of the session)	(−) Team members may express some feelings of anger or frustration during the first part of the session	(−) Team members may express some feelings of anger or frustration during the first part of the session (although this typically occurs within each subgroup)

Legend: (+) Offers an advantage   (−) Offers no advantage   (=) Offers some/equal advantage

To illustrate this, let's consider three distinct ways in which the same team-building requirement could be described:

- "We need to rein in those people on our team who tend to dominate discussions and decisions."

- "We need to find ways to stop talking over each other and trying to force decisions on each other."

- "Is there a way for us to more effectively balance participation and encourage consensus-driven decisions?"

The first statement makes the assumption that the team has a problem that resides in certain team members, who are perceived as solely responsible for improving the situation. A team-building event that proceeds from this kind of statement will quickly degenerate into a finger-pointing and blame-casting session, with the team's energy directed toward attempting to "fix" certain team members. The second statement is worded in such a way that accountability for change is shared among all team members. At the same time, this statement continues to direct participants' energy toward what is broken and problematic within their team. In doing so, the statement provides a starting point for discussion that is likely to ensnarl participants in a negative spiral. In contrast, the last question directs the focus of the team's attention toward exploring the steps that members could take to move toward a positive, desired future.

For additional suggestions on how to positively engage a team in their team-building process review the *Reframing Technique* in the Tool Kit.

Looking Beneath the Surface As a facilitator, your goal during the first phase of the team-building discussion is to help participants fully explore all of the factors that contribute to the team's current team-building challenges, as well as the organizational context for change. One symptom of ineffective team building is when participants engage in what we refer to as "surface skimming"; that is, they fail to look beyond the surface of an idea or issue to review it in depth. Effective teams do their homework—they engage in a thorough analysis of all of the relevant factors that can shape and influence their current situation and their desired future.

There are several steps you can take to encourage team members to engage in the careful assessment of opportunities and challenges. First, ask participants to imagine that it is a year in the future and then to consider the following questions:

- If you could create the ideal future for your team—without concerning yourself for the moment with how you get there—what is that future like?

- How do team members work together in this ideal state?
- What does the team still have that we currently have?
- What does the team have that we currently lack?
- What does it feel like to be part of this team?
- How does the team's performance look to an outside observer?

Another important part of a team assessment is to help members understand the interrelationship among three factors: (a) the team's performance results, that is, the most important performance opportunities and challenges facing the team; (b) the team's structure and process, that is, how the team is organized to address its performance opportunities and challenges; and (c) the team dynamics, that is, how team members interact with each other and with outside customers and stakeholders. Quite often team members view these three factors as being completely separate phenomena and fail to "connect the dots" between them. Adding to this potential confusion is that the teams come in a wide range of shapes and sizes, to include permanent manager-led work groups, standing committees, directing boards, and part-time cross-functional project teams, all of which have uniquely distinct characteristics. Given the interrelationship among these three factors, the facilitator's job is to help participants understand how each of these factors directly influences the others. These interactions are shown in Figure 2.3. You may ask why the arrows aim in multiple directions. The answer is that the arrows emphasize the reciprocal interrelationships among these three team factors.

This interrelationship is clearly modeled in a case when the authors conducted a team-building session with a company's online marketing department. The department was charged with producing creative marketing solutions for nonprofit organizations. Initially, the team described their core needs in terms of unrealized performance opportunities. Specifically, the issue was that money was being left on the table because the team could not respond fast enough to customer requests for proposals, and they had difficulty accurately estimating the costs for projects that would generate the required level of profit. During their interviews, team members initially defined this challenge in terms of poor team dynamics.

Figure 2.3. The Interrelationship Among Team Dynamics, Team Structure and Process, and Team Performance Results.

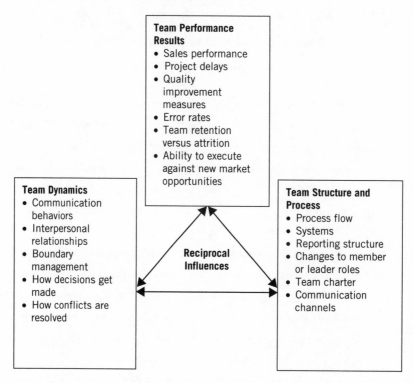

But, let's look at the various members' perspectives more closely. Operations leaders (these were software developers who created products such as e-mail campaigns or websites to support customers' online sales) suggested that the marketing managers were doing an ineffectual job of keeping them informed. Marketing was blamed for making last-minute demands that the Operations team could not complete ("How do they expect us to do a day turnaround on an e-mail blitz when they give it to us at 5 P.M.?!"). Marketing was also blamed for committing to pricing that was too low for projects, based on the number of hours that Operations felt would be required for project completion. For their part, Marketing blamed Operations who, from Marketing's perspective, automatically responded to every request with "No, that can't be done!" or who "sandbagged" cost estimates with unrealistically high time and cost estimates that also provided the Operations team with a high margin of safety.

During this team's session, we asked the team to draw a simple process chart on the board that would illustrate all of the steps that were typically required to turn a customer request into a completed project or service. This provided a good starting point because it revealed areas in which different team members were operating from different assumptions (mental models of how the market-to-product process actually worked). We then used the *Traffic Light Technique*, described in the Tool Kit, to have them identify points in the process that were working quite well and points where potential failure could occur. Finally, we asked team members to identify previous situations in which areas that were typically problematic performed quite well. In other words, we wanted examples of what "we at our best" looked like to the team. We then asked participants to describe what they ideally wanted to see more of in terms of improved team dynamics to make the entire process more effective. The resulting discussions helped the team see how simple changes in team dynamics could lead to significant changes in the team's performance. Examples included bringing operations managers into the initial phone briefings with customers, and having operations personnel stage "early alerts" when they were concerned about meeting schedule or cost commitments.

The importance of the interrelationship, those reciprocal influences, among the three factors seen in Figure 2.3 must be emphasized again. Encouraging members to focus on incremental improvements to the performance factor—to see and create moments of "us at our best"—helps foster positive aspects within team dynamics, such as building the mutual trust and support needed to sustain those positive results. Likewise, teams will benefit from recognizing how team dynamics may need to change to support changes to processes or structure. An example would be rethinking how members need to communicate with each other if certain individuals are about to make the shift from being colocated to working in a virtual capacity. Of course the opposite scenario could occur, that is, if performance begins to change for the worse, those changes may cause stress in members' interactions and have an adverse impact on structure or processes, or both.

One final suggestion: During this initial assessment step it is often useful to solicit input from others outside the team. This may sound like a strange assertion given that we have previously suggested that team-building sessions should be limited to team members. At the same time, this ground rule doesn't preclude a team from seeking out information from others *in advance of* the session. Such input is particularly relevant when it comes from internal customers and senior executive stakeholders. These individuals and groups often have a vested interest in the team's success, and they are able to provide different perspectives on how they view the team's performance, system and process constraints, and ability to communicate across organizational boundaries. Teams are sometimes reluctant to solicit information from other groups or nonmembers because they are concerned that such actions will place them under critical scrutiny or will make them look ineffective. The way to alleviate such concerns is to have team members agree on how and when to ask for outside input. For suggestions on how to manage boundary or interface areas with other work groups and senior stakeholders, review Chapter Ten.

Additional Reading

Ford, Jeffrey D. (1999). Organizational change as shifting conversations. *Journal of Organizational Change Management, 12*(6), pp. 480–500.

3

Implementation, Action Planning, and Follow-Up

Steps Four and Five of the Team-Building Process

Chapter Two introduced the five-step process of team building. The details of steps 1 through 3 were discussed and could be conducted before or during the team-building session. This chapter presents the last two steps of implementation and action planning and follow-up.

Step 4: Implementing the Team-Building Session

With the planning steps completed you are now ready to implement your team-building session. Although the authors have seen team-building sessions take a wide variety of forms, we have found that the most effective sessions tend to share three characteristics, which align with the sequential stages that are presented in Figure 3.1. Let's briefly review the characteristics.

Balanced Participation Teams are typically made up of very different kinds of individuals. Some team members may have dominant personalities, represent positions

Figure 3.1. The Characteristics of Effective Team Building.

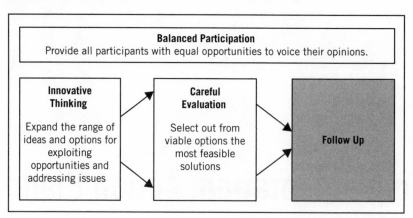

of power, or may be viewed by other team members as being individuals who demonstrate very high levels of technical expertise or knowledge.

Given any of these conditions, such individuals may attempt to force their views on others, or may act in ways that inadvertently discourage others from voicing their opinions. At the same time, other team members may feel they have little to contribute to the discussion and will be reluctant to share their ideas with the rest of the team. Still others may need some encouragement before they feel comfortable participating fully in the team-building process. These differences will be most amplified if your team is made up of people who represent different levels of organizational authority.

Still another factor that you may face in implementing your session is the belief in "team facilitator as hero." By this we mean that team members may rely too heavily on you as the facilitator of the discussion, or the team leader (if that is someone other than you) to make important decisions or develop a suggested course of action. This tendency will be particularly evident if the team members view you as having a strong set of relevant technical skills and experience, or if certain participants are intimidated by your communication style. Given these possibilities, one of your goals as a facilitator should be to create a team experience that encourages full and balanced participation by all team members. There are several steps you can take to support this goal.

First, look for ways to efficiently facilitate the flow of discussion during the session and to elicit the full range of members' opinions and ideas. The *Guide for Balancing Participation*, which can be found in the Tool Kit, provides useful guidelines for when and how to draw out or rein in team members during discussions. As you can see from Figure 3.1, balanced participation is an important factor that can influence the entire course of the team-building process.

A second step is to establish ground rules that foster group participation and stimulate the free sharing of ideas. Representative guidelines might be:

- All ideas are equally valuable.

- Don't censor yourself—even if you are not sure that an idea may be useful, let us hear it anyway!

- Hold back on commenting on any idea until all ideas have been listed.

To encourage full participation, it is particularly important to avoid communicating in ways that may censor others. As the facilitator, if you are not careful it is easy to stifle or dismiss the ideas of group participants. Comments such as "Are you sure that idea would work?" tend to discourage participation. Another tactic that team members might interpret as censorship is the rewording of their suggestions. Consider the following example: a team member suggests creating a team vision statement to help remedy the team's lack of direction. The facilitator responds by saying, "I think I understand what you are trying to say. What you really mean is that we need clearer business objectives, is that right?" Then, without waiting for a response, the facilitator records this edited version of the participant's idea on the flipchart. In this situation, the person who offered the suggestion may feel the team leader is trying to control the flow of ideas, or force-feed solutions onto the team.

There are several steps you can take to prevent this type of situation from occurring. If you are having trouble interpreting the ideas expressed by team members, ask them for clarification instead of assuming that you can find better words to express their comments. If you are balancing the dual roles of team facilitator and leader, hold back on presenting your own suggestions. In an effort to speed up the exploration phase some team leaders begin the discussion by offering a variety of suggestions or ideas. When this occurs, team members may be reluctant to express their own solutions. In addition, the discussion is likely to switch from idea exploration to a comparative review of suggestions proposed by the team leader. Instead, consider soliciting ideas from the rest of your team before offering your own. If you are asked for your ideas early on in the discussion, respond by saying that you would like a few minutes to think through your responses before offering your ideas.

Innovative Thinking In attempting to resolve issues or quickly implement new opportunities some team members may offer the first solutions or ideas that come to mind, or present those they believe will be easiest to implement. Others may seek to appease the team leader and their senior managers by suggesting what they feel are acceptable remedies. Such solutions are safe—they are less likely to provoke conflict among team members—and are probably the same types of recommendations that were proposed in earlier discussions on the same topic. The difficulty is, of course, that such ideas don't necessarily represent the team's best thinking. Ideally, you want to obtain a wide range of ideas, including those that might be considered a little unusual. During the next phase of the team-building process we will discuss suggestions for distilling down the initial list of suggestions by using selection criteria identified by your team. For now, however, we suggest that you encourage your team to generate as many innovative solutions as possible.

To avoid these situations, good facilitators attempt to create a setting in which participants are encouraged to explore alternative perspectives regarding their current situation and desired future. As illustrated in Figure 3.1 this *expansive* phase of the team-building process involves helping the team to "think outside the box" to arrive at the broadest, most innovative array of solutions and ideas. Quite frequently, team building requires members to be willing to completely rethink their traditional approaches to issues and opportunities. When a team-building discussion is going well the results are easy to see. Team members tend to add to and develop one another's ideas, so that their final solution represents a true synthesis of the entire team's thoughts.

There are several facilitation actions you can take to encourage innovative thinking from your team. Teams often assume that their job is to immediately identify the single "best solution." A simple way to get past this barrier is to tell participants that there are probably a number of ways to effectively address the opportunity or issue under review. Based on that assumption, you would like to challenge them to come up with at least five good options for addressing the opportunity or issue under discussion.

You can also lighten the atmosphere by asking for the wackiest idea. No one wants to look stupid. Accordingly, when people are part of a team-building session they tend to be conservative in their thinking and express only safe ideas. To get your team past this obstacle, challenge each person to come up with at least one wild or wacky idea, then encourage team members to take a few risks by offering up your own zany solutions or ideas. Don't worry, initially, about whether these ideas are practical. The point is to shake up everyone's thinking so that the team will find it easier to come up with and add to creative ideas.

Team members sometimes make the mistake of attempting to evaluate ideas immediately as they are presented. If this situation is not checked, your team will move too quickly into the evaluation phase. In addition, some participants may be discouraged from presenting their ideas for fear that they will be under attack as soon as they express their opinions. There are several ways to counter this tendency. One method is to introduce the team-building model shown in Figure 3.1. If team members are aware that they are following a structured team-building approach, they will be more likely to hold off evaluation until the appropriate stage in the process. Also, set ground rules that caution people about making premature judgments. One helpful ground rule is "Allow all ideas to be heard and posted before evaluating any of the ideas."

If participants evaluate each other's ideas as soon as they are expressed, these evaluations may be taken as personal criticisms. Comments such as "Frankly, I just don't think Darrell's idea will work" tend to divide the team. To prevent this from happening, you might add a ground rule that says "Evaluate ideas, not people. Refrain from making comments that could be viewed as personal criticisms." If individuals do prematurely jump into evaluation, redirect their comments. A facilitation comment such as "It sounds as if you are moving into evaluation at this point. In line with our ground rules could we hold off on those comments until the final stage of discussion?"

Careful Evaluation As a team-building session progresses, quite often a number of good ideas are generated. This, in turn, creates the challenge of forcing participants to select among these options on the basis of thoughtful discussion and careful analysis. As illustrated in Figure 3.1, during this *contractive* phase of the team-building process, team members attempt to "funnel down" alternative options to select those that are most viable. There are several steps that you can take to encourage team members to engage in the careful analysis of the ideas that they have collectively generated.

First, team members have a tendency to defend their own ideas. They may also tend to weigh the relative worth of ideas based on who proposed them. To overcome these constraints, detach ideas from their owners. Have your team list all their ideas on a flipchart or whiteboard and number each solution as it is listed. Instead of referring to "Kim's solution" or "Carlos's solution," refer to each idea by its number. This simple action makes all ideas the common property of the entire team. When the ideas are finally evaluated, team members are less likely to take criticisms of a particular idea personally. In addition, as we have previously suggested, if you are the team leader, refrain from weighing in on the ideas listed until others on your team have spoken. Similarly, if one member of your team tends to sway the others, call on this person last during the discussion. In addition, the *Multivoting Technique* and *Traffic Light Technique* introduced in your Tool Kit can be used to discourage team members from becoming too attached to their own ideas, by forcing them to cast "votes" across different ideas. A different version of this idea is behind the *Gallery Technique.*

Before team members begin the analysis phase get them to agree on the approach that they will use for comparing and evaluating alternative ideas and suggestions. You might start off by saying something like:

> Before we try to evaluate the ideas that we have in front of us and determine those we want to implement, it would probably be helpful to take some time to carefully review all of the potential ideas we

have listed to make sure we really understand what is involved in implementing each solution. We could, for example use the *Plus/Delta Technique* to list the pros and cons associated with each idea. As an alternative we could create a formal *Decision Matrix* for comparing ideas against preset criteria. There are probably several other possible approaches. What approach would you like to pursue?

- When faced with complex problems, some teams are so inundated with data that they begin to suffer a kind of "analysis paralysis" that can bog down the discussion of ideas. To remedy this situation set a fixed time limit, such as ninety minutes, for team analysis and review. Tell team members that you will perform a check-in at the end of this time to see if they feel that they have made enough progress in their analysis to move on to evaluation. At this point in the discussion it is sometimes helpful to pose three questions to your team:

  - "Given everything we know about this situation, what are the one or two primary factors that should influence our decision?"

  - "What facts do we absolutely have to know before we can move forward in decision making?"

  - "Which aspects of this issue or opportunity can we tackle with incomplete information?"

At the conclusion of this phase of the discussion remind participants that implementation does not have to be on an "all or nothing basis." They could decide to place each idea into one of the following four categories:

1. Ideas that can be immediately implemented

2. Ideas that have merit: we know we want to implement them but need additional time beyond the session to think through the best implementation method

3. Ideas that require additional study: we simply don't have the information needed to evaluate their worth or feasibility

4. Ideas that we choose to discard

Once again, the *Traffic Light Technique* introduced in the Tool Kit is one method that can be used to help participants quickly evaluate ideas based on these categories, while the *One-to-Ten Technique* and *Team Commitment Audit* are two tools that can be used to confirm that participants are committed to moving forward in implementing selected changes.

STEP 5: ACTION PLANNING AND FOLLOW-UP

This last step is about ensuring success. It is about taking the steps needed to translate good intentions into detailed action plans, and evaluating progress against those plans. To better understand this, consider that in some ways a team-building session is analogous to a surgical procedure. We wouldn't think much of a surgeon who performed whatever surgical adjustment was required, then handed the patient a needle and surgical thread saying, "Unfortunately, this is all of the time I have. You will need to finish up here." If that sounds bizarre, we would suggest that quite often times this is what happens in team building. Many well-intended team-building facilitators invest so much time in the preliminary stages that they never move to action planning. At the end of the team-building session the walls are covered with colorful flipcharts filled with many formulated ideas—all of which lack detailed action plans. The last words that participants hear from the facilitator are something like, "Well, that's all the time that we have today. I know that we didn't get into the details of implementation but I'm sure that you can do that on your own." And, of course, nothing ever happens. To ensure that your session is a success we would ask that you follow one simple guideline based on the surgical metaphor: *Never cut into an area unless you have set aside sufficient time to also suture and close.* For an all-day session this might mean setting aside the last two hours to complete the last two stages of Action Planning and Follow-Up.

How to Facilitate Action Planning A solid action planning process is essential for evaluating the results of a team-building session. Without a disciplined action planning process in place, it becomes difficult to determine, in the weeks following the session, why the session may have failed. Was the lack of success due to applying the wrong team-building techniques, incorrectly defining the team's performance requirements, selecting relatively weak change actions, or translating team decisions into actions? When action planning is poorly structured it becomes impossible to determine. A concise, unambiguous action plan that is fully supported by your team will help you avoid such disappointing outcomes. A good action plan should cover the following topics:

- What is doable? How much improvement activity can we successfully implement and manage over the next few weeks?

- What is fair? How can we ensure that everyone on our team is an equal partner in our improvement plan and is committed to its success?

- Where do we need help? What areas of the project require the help or support of other work groups or individuals? How will we go about securing this help?

- What could go wrong with our plan, and how can we plan around potential obstacles and act now to mitigate potential risks?

The five steps for constructing a team action plan are summarized below.

Step 1: Identify Required Actions. The first products of team improvement discussions are good intentions that have not yet been crafted into concrete improvement actions. That is, team members often start off by talking in general about desired results, but fail to pinpoint the precise actions they will take to achieve those results. Your challenge as a facilitator is to convert these good intentions into a list of required actions. Table 3.1 highlights the differences between intentions and actions for four team improvement areas.

Step 2: Agree on Desired Outcomes. It is important to help team members reach agreement on the results they expect to obtain from each action. If they feel that a meeting with an internal customer service group will help raise customer satisfaction levels by 20 percent over the next two months, then they need to say so. If they expect a change in the team's internal communication process to completely eliminate rework and errors caused by poor communication, they need to be explicit about the desired outcomes.

Table 3.1. Differences Between Intention and Action

Team Improvement Area	Intention	Action
We want to. . . strengthen our forecasting and troubleshooting on projects.	We want to develop the ability to anticipate potential obstacles and barriers that could derail projects, keep each other informed on such changes, and collectively plan to address them.	During the next two weeks, each project leader will create a troubleshooting checklist detailing potential risks and proposed risk mitigation actions for their respective projects. These will be posted on our shareware site so that we can recommend suggested changes. We will conduct monthly team reviews to determine those areas in which project status is "green, yellow, or red."
We want to. . . improve team communications.	We will schedule more meetings.	During the next three weeks, Teresa will schedule two videoconferences. The meetings will take place from 1 to 3 P.M. Eastern time to accommodate participants from different time zones.
We want to. . . obtain greater clarity on our future direction as a team.	During the next few weeks we will discuss our team vision.	By the 15th of this month our team will meet to draft a vision statement. Prior to the meeting each team member agrees to compile a list of anticipated changes in customer base, service features, and organizational structure that are likely to occur over the next two years, and which could influence the direction that we need to take as a team.
We want to. . . improve the perceived quality of our service to our internal customers.	We will ask our internal customers for feedback on our performance.	On the 23rd of this month, Jim and Lisa will conduct separate focus groups with representatives from our engineering, finance, and IT departments to obtain suggestions for how we can improve our service to these internal customers.

Clear definitions of anticipated success criteria will help the team reach alignment on its improvement process. Without obtaining this alignment during the session, it is possible that a team could successfully implement its improvement plan yet disagree completely on whether the plan was a success. It is especially important to articulate those "soft outcomes" that are difficult to articulate. If, for example, a team hopes that its members will become more "mutually supportive" as a result of the team-building experience, what exactly do they mean by this? Do they want team members to be more willing to pitch in and help one another during peak work periods, or are they hoping that more experienced team members will exhibit a greater willingness to coach and mentor some of the newer members?

Step 3: Clarify Accountability for Specific Areas. Quite often, several team members will volunteer to work together to complete a given task. Whenever this occurs, suggest that one team member take the lead in coordinating these efforts. Even when participants will be depending on others outside their team to complete certain action items, a team member should be assigned to initiate and follow up on the actions by these outside contributors.

Step 4: Construct an Action-Planning Chart. An action chart provides team members with a clear breakdown of accountabilities, and a means of visualizing the flow and timing of project steps. If posted for review during the session it also helps members to anticipate potential obstacles or roadblocks. This book contains several tools, such as the *Action Planning Chart* and *Real-Time Implementation Planning* that can help you complete this step of action planning. A key point here is to encourage the team to designate one individual who will be responsible for tracking the team's progress on key activities. It is important to remember that the team leader or facilitator is not supposed to assume full responsibility for policing the actions of the team. A good option is to suggest that team members rotate this responsibility among themselves. There are a number of good groupware tools on the market that can make this a less onerous task.

Step 5: Troubleshoot the Action Plan. One of the most effective ways to encourage full accountability for the success of the team-building process is for team members to collectively troubleshoot the plan. This means that participants are able to anticipate, *before* they commit to action, the types of roadblocks they are likely to encounter during implementation and the steps they should take to eliminate or overcome these problems. A troubleshooting discussion encourages team accountability by increasing individual empowerment. Team members are much more likely to take the initiative in responding to crises if they agree in advance on how to handle such crises. One final aspect of troubleshooting involves auditing the team action plan for balance and fairness. If a quick look at the plan reveals that one team member has been burdened with almost half the action items and other team members are not carrying their weight, some actions should be reassigned.

During the troubleshooting process, you should address the following questions:

- What could go wrong with our plan?
- What trigger events might alert us to the onset of these problems?
- What is the most effective way to keep each other informed regarding the onset of these problems?
- What steps can we take now to prevent these problems?
- What steps do we plan to take to correct these problems, should they occur?
- What is our agreement regarding the degree to which each of us can feel free to take immediate action to prevent or address any obstacles that could potentially derail our action plan, without first requiring approval from our team leader or team review?
- Outside our team, on whom can we depend for support?

How to Facilitate a Follow-Up Meeting We recommend that as the facilitator you schedule a follow-up meeting with the team approximately eight to twelve weeks after the team-building session. It is highly recommended that you schedule this meeting during the last few minutes of the team-building session, so that all participants have reserved time on their calendars and publicly voice their commitments to the plans that they made during the session. The timing of this meeting is important, as you need to allow participants sufficient time to make progress on their action plan, yet provide follow-up quickly enough to encourage participants to continue to make progress on their improvement efforts.

The follow-up meeting is intended to accomplish two things. First, it requires the team to evaluate their progress against identified improvement actions. Second, it encourages participants to reflect on whether the team-building session has proven to be a positive experience that has helped to strengthen team dynamics and relationships. The following questions can be sent out to participants in advance of the follow-up meeting and be useful in fostering personal reflection on the team-building process:

Questions Related to the Action Planning Process

1. Are we clear about the commitments that we made during our team-building session?

2. Have we made sufficient progress in completing each of our action items? Are we maintaining momentum on our plan?

3. Have we kept each other alerted to difficulties or challenges we've experienced in completing our plan?

4. Are we satisfied with our results?

5. Have we effectively managed the implementation of our actions with key organizational stakeholders and work groups?

Questions Related to Team Dynamics and Relationships

1. How has our experience in this team-building process affected the way in which we communicate and interact with each other?

2. What have we learned from this process about how we function as a team? What surprises have we encountered?

3. What worked well for us in this process that we would like to see replicated in other aspects of our day-to-day work?

4. What team issues, concerns, and opportunities still remain to be addressed?

General Guidelines for Conducting the Follow-up Session

1. With sufficient planning and the above questions as a guide, a lot can be accomplished in a relatively brief (90–120 minute) follow-up meeting.

2. Strive to involve all participants in team building in the follow-up session as well.

3. Perform a check-in call with the team leader a week in advance to gauge the team's motivation coming into the session, and to identify any changes that have occurred in the team's structure, charter, or priorities that could affect the follow-up session.

4. Open the follow-up session by thanking all participants for keeping their commitment to implement and follow up on their action plans, and for putting full effort into the team-building process.

5. Begin by projecting onto the screen (or re-creating on a flipchart) the action plan that the team had created during the last session. Ask those members who were responsible for taking the lead on each item to discuss the progress that the team has made in each area. During this step, stop periodically to gauge responses from other members.

6. Systematically walk through the questions regarding the action-planning process and team dynamics above, asking team members to discuss their thoughts on each question.

7. At the end of the discussion conduct a brief go-round in which you ask each participant to briefly share what participating in the team-building process has meant to him or her.

4

Selecting the Right Team-Building Tools

Guidelines for Selecting Tools

Once the team's core requirements have been identified and prioritized, the next step is to select, from all of the techniques and tools provided in this book, those few that are most appropriate for a given team-building session. The following three guidelines can help you identify those team tools and techniques that will be most applicable for your session. Having said that, one of the lessons that we have learned through the years is that good facilitators are flexible. They are willing to adapt their initial team-building tools to any new information obtained during the team-building assessment or preliminary planning session that might indicate the need for a different approach.

Guideline 1: Match Tools to Team-Building Scenarios

As we have previously mentioned, teams take a variety of forms. At one end of the spectrum are those large groups whose members meet over a short period of time to accomplish a specific goal or reach a critical decision. At the other end are those permanent work groups that might meet over several sessions, with the goal of strengthening relationships among team members.

The first guideline that we propose is for you to select facilitation tools and techniques that support the type of team-building situation that you are facing. Table 4.1 shows how facilitation approaches and related team-building tools can be adapted to meet the needs of four different team-building scenarios.

Guideline 2: Select Tools by Stages in the Facilitation Process

In the previous two chapters we introduced a structured model for guiding the team-building facilitation process. Regardless of the team-building challenges that you are likely to face, there are certain team-building tools and techniques that we have found to be particularly useful at certain steps of the facilitation process. In Table 4.2 we suggest how to match tools to the steps of team building.

Guideline 3: Match Tools to Team-Building Requirements

During your team-building assessment and planning process you will sometimes encounter issues that are unique to a particular team. At the same time, we have found that a large percentage of team requirements are related to one of the following nine team-building challenges:

1. *Clarifying Future Direction:* Helping the team to clarify its long-term direction and focus, and ensure that it is directing its time, energy, and resources to pursue that direction.

2. *Fostering Team Innovation:* Helping the team to develop innovative thinking and innovation.

3. *Establishing Mutual Trust and Collaboration:* Helping the team to establish a work climate and communication processes that support mutual trust and collaboration among members.

4. *Managing Change:* Helping the team more effectively anticipate and plan for significant changes, and encouraging team members to be more open to change and innovation.

Table 4.1. Matching Team Characteristics and Challenges to Facilitation Guidelines and Tools.

Team Type and Characteristics	Team-Building Challenges	Team-Building Facilitation Guidelines and Tools
Intact Teams Permanent teams comprised of a single leader and direct reports. The leader is responsible for setting the team's direction and performance standards, and administers performance consequences (merit increases, promotions, and so on).	Because the team leader holds a high degree of power, other team members may have trust and safety issues that make it difficult for them to openly discuss issues.	In advance of the session, discuss with the team leader to use discussion guidelines that can encourage open communication. Use the *Nominal Group Technique* and other similar tools that support anonymous idea generation and issue exploration.
Temporary Teams Cross-functional teams or task forces that are formed to complete certain objectives (gathering and evaluating data, making improvements to work processes, and so on) and then disbanded.	Team leaders seldom have power to direct the actions of members. The temporary nature of such teams means that they have less time for incremental improvements	Employ tools, such as the *Action Planning Chart*, that can help clarify task and project accountabilities. Use the *Needs Checklists for Team Members and Team Leaders* to clarify role expectations.
Inter-Team Building Team building that extends across two or more functional or departmental groups, or outside the organization to include certain customer, vendor, or external stakeholder groups. By definition these groups depend on each other to coordinate work efforts and achieve common goals.	Team building across teams focuses less on interpersonal relationships and more on ways in which teams can work together in such areas as team charters, work processes, and service expectations. Because different teams report to different managers it can be difficult to ensure effective follow-up after the session.	Use the *Customer Assessment Matrix* and *Group Interaction Matrix* to gain alignment on such issues as customer requirements and areas of interdependency. Employ tools such as the *Action Planning Chart* to ensure follow-up to the session.
Large Groups Groups of more than thirty individuals who seek to accomplish goals, reach decisions, or address issues within one or more facilitated group meetings. Examples would be directing boards, homeowners' associations, and community action groups.	When working with large groups, it may be difficult to provide all participants with opportunities to voice their views and weigh in on team decisions. Large groups tend to incorporate widely divergent agendas, values, and issue perspectives.	Tools such as the *Traffic Light Technique* can be used to consolidate group input, and to provide participants with a visual model of team alignment. Tools such as the *Team Alignment Pyramid* can help large groups of participants to identify areas of common ground.

Table 4.2. Matching the Team-Building Step to Facilitation Challenges and Representative Tools.

Team-Building Step	Facilitation Challenges	Tools
Assessment	Framing the Team's Needs	*Reframing Technique* *Human Due Diligence Audit* *Team Building Assessment Questionnaire* *Visual Explorer™*
	Looking Beneath the Surface	*Needs Checklists for Team Members and Team Leaders* *Turnaround Feedback* *Team Leader Feedback Questionnaire* *Opportunities/Threats Matrix*
Implementation	Balanced Participation	*Gallery Technique* *Guide Sheet for Balancing Team Participation* *Nominal Group Technique*
	Innovative Thinking	*Gallery Technique* *Group Brainwriting and Electronic Brainstorming* *Quiet the Critic Exercise* *Microanalysis Technique* *Nominal Group Technique*
	Careful Evaluation	*Decision Matrix* *Traffic Light Technique* *Multivoting Technique* *Plus/Delta Technique* *Baby and Bathwater Technique*
Action Planning and Follow-Up	Action Planning	*Action Planning Chart* *Real-Time Implementation Planning*
	Commitment to Action	*One-to-Ten Technique* *Team Commitment Audit* *Goals/Action Matrix*
	Follow-Up Meeting	*After Action Review* *Follow-Up Team Building Questionnaire*

5. *Building Commitment:* Helping the team to capture member accountability and commitment to the team's success.

6. *Managing Organizational Boundaries:* Helping the team establish guidelines and processes for coordinating their actions with other work groups, external customers, and senior sponsors.

7. *Working Virtually:* Helping the team adapt communications to support virtual, distributed membership.

8. *Overcoming Setbacks:* Helping the team "recharge" after encountering performance setbacks.

9. *Managing Across Cultures:* Helping the team that is attempting to manage members who represent a diverse cross-section of national cultures.

In Section Two of the book we discuss these nine team-building challenges in depth. The *Team Building Assessment Questionnaire*, in the Tool Kit, is a simple method you can use for identifying significant team strengths and improvement opportunities in advance of a session. Once you have done this, review Sections Two and Three to discover those tools that are particularly useful when helping a team address a particular challenge.

Guideline 4: Match Tools to the Demands of Your Session

In preparing for your team-building session, consider adapting tools and techniques to the unique demands of the team and their session.

Plan Around Time Constraints Some teams only have a few hours to work together, whereas others can afford to invest several days in a team-building session. At the same time, some of the tools introduced in this book, such as the *One-to-Ten Technique*, require only a few minutes to complete; others, such as the *Decision Matrix*, may require several hours. Other tools, such as the *Team Scoping Document*, are best completed in advance of the workshop for use by participants during the session. For this reason it is important to select team-building tools that match your team's time constraints.

Address Power Inequities In some teams all members wield equal power; other teams are characterized by wide disparities in the power and status levels of members. An example of the former situation would be a cross-functional team comprised of professionals from across different departments in an organization, who do not report to each other. An example of the latter would be a team comprised of a second-level manager, a few first-level managerial direct reports, and several nonmanagerial associates. In this situation, lower-ranking members are more likely to be hesitant to voice their concerns, or may be reluctant to take issue with positions that are presented by their managers.

To counter these types of constraints, make use of tools and techniques that are designed to provide team members with a higher degree of safety. As examples, the *Nominal Group Technique, Group Brainwriting and Electronic Brainstorming*, and the *Gallery Technique* all accomplish this by making use of anonymous idea generation and by encouraging team members to silently reflect on each other's suggestions.

Prepare for Virtual Participation At times you may be conducting a team-building session that will include some virtual participants. Unfortunately, even with the use of such technology as groupware, video-conferencing, and Skype, virtual teams (or individual members who are participating remotely) are at a disadvantage if they are presented with exercises, such as the *Gallery Technique* or the use of *Mix and Max*, which require real-time face-to-face participation; but with some pre-planning certain team-building techniques can be adapted to virtual applications. As an example, consider how you could adapt the *Decision Matrix* to virtual team building. In this situation, you could send out an initial e-mail query to all participants well in advance of the session explaining the use of the tool, and asking them to select decision criteria and options. You could then use this collected input to identify the most important criteria and options. A second e-mail could then be distributed asking participants to rate the relative importance of each criterion.

With this data in hand, a third e-mail could be distributed asking participants to provide ratings for each decision cell (see *Decision Matrix* in your Tool Kit for additional details). The completed decision matrix could then be distributed shortly before the team session, and reviewed via a conference call or groupware format. In summary, with a little forethought you can identify certain tools and techniques that can be adapted for use by virtual teams or participants.

Be Sensitive to Cultural Diversity At times you may be conducting team-building sessions with diverse groups of individuals who represent different cultural perspectives. To support you in such situations we have provided tools, such as the *Visual Explorer*™, that have proven to be readily adaptable across cultural settings. Note that other techniques, such as *Team Leader Feedback Questionnaire* and *Turnaround Feedback,* require that members feel comfortable providing their leaders or other team members with critical feedback—a precondition that might vary widely across national cultures.

As a general caveat, when working with culturally diverse groups, take additional time in advance of the session to (1) introduce the team to alternative tools or techniques that could support the same team-building requirement, and (2) ask team members the degree of relative comfort they have in working with these different options. Select only those options that allow participants to experience a high degree of safety in the session. Chapter Thirteen will provide suggestions and unique tools for facilitating cross-cultural teams.

Section Two

Managing Team-Building Challenges

THIS SECTION OUTLINES NINE critical challenges that teams often encounter and highlights the opportunities that exist within each. This section provides team leaders and members with guidelines for dealing with each challenge, and actions they can take leading up to or concurrent with a team-building session to create opportunities within each team challenge. These suggestions also specify some of the tools and techniques included within the Tool Kit.

5

Clarifying Future Direction

The Importance of Establishing Future Direction

Take a team, shake up its reporting structure, and change its membership. Next, give that team a hefty load of projects and accountabilities and assume that team members will intuitively understand the most pressing priorities. To make things more interesting, make organizational changes that dramatically alter the team's charter. Now place all of these events within the context of a fast-paced organization, one that is rapidly changing its markets, services, and structure. In today's volatile work environment, scenarios like this are increasingly common. What happens next, however, depends a lot on whether the team has developed a clear sense of its long-term direction.

For teams that have developed well-constructed vision statements, targeted long-term goals, and clearly delineated priorities, these challenges may be frustrating but they are not overwhelming. Like small but sturdy boats knocked about by a turbulent storm, such teams manage to stay on track because they have developed very effective radar systems for checking their current positions in relation to their long-term goals. As a result, they are able to make quick adjustments whenever they discover that they are veering off course. More important, their team members are motivated because they believe their day-to-day activities are closely linked to the overall goals of their organizations.

How to Tell When This Is a Challenge

When teams try to function without a sense of long-term direction, however, the future can appear murky and uncertain. Under such conditions they may begin to feel that their actions lack purpose and meaning. They have greater difficulty sifting through competing priorities, and determining what is really important and where they should focus their attention. The signs of a lack of direction are easy to see.

Failure to See the Big Picture

When team members are unclear about their future direction they may have only a vague sense of what they are attempting to accomplish together over time. This may show up in an inability to explain the team's priorities or key objectives to other work groups or organizational stakeholders, or through a lack of understanding of the details of your team's strategic goals. In addition, professionals who lack clear direction have difficulty understanding how their efforts link to higher-level organizational goals and initiatives. Here is a test: Ask the other members of your team what they think about a significant organizational event such as a recent web address of your company's quarterly earnings review or a new product rollout. If you get back only blank stares, chances are that "lack of clear direction" may be an issue for your team.

Organizational Uncertainty

Under conditions of great uncertainty it becomes more difficult to discern the overall direction of the organization, and the potential impact of large-scale changes on your team. Does the recent merger mean that a layoff is coming? Will our rapidly expanding product portfolio mean that we will have to jettison our current sales training process? Does our company's loss on a major patent infringement suit mean that we will be conceding one of our key markets to our largest competitor?

When changes take place at the highest levels of your organization, team members begin to ask themselves these types of questions. In doing so they are trying to determine how the ripple effects of these changes are likely to show up in the team's objectives, success measures, and priorities. Without some clarity on future direction, team members will make decisions that are based on faulty information and unfounded assumptions.

Change Resistance

When team members lack clarity on the team's future direction they are much more likely to actively resist change. After all, most of us are willing to put up with the stress and aggravation that typically accompanies changes to systems, processes, procedures, and priorities—if we clearly understand how our teams hope to benefit from those changes in the long run. Consequently, change resistance is frequently a signal that team members either regard these types of changes as arbitrary and unnecessary, or as counterproductive to the team's long-term goals. Additional suggestions and tools for addressing the issue of managing of change can be found in Chapter Eight.

Diffused Efforts

Every year many teams complete a formal annual planning process, only to find that, as the year progresses, they must continue to revise their goals and performance. Unfortunately, team members may not take the time to periodically meet together to discuss shifting priorities, resource constraints, and success measures. The result is that performance issues and conflicts may occur because some members are working from an outdated playbook.

Even when team members manage to stay abreast of changing priorities they may not know how to translate these new priorities into day-to-day actions. The members of a service team may know that one of their objectives is to support the company's sales efforts. They might also understand that to do this they will be expected to use their service calls to uncover new opportunities for securing product sales or service contracts. Beyond this, however, they may have never discussed what these changes actually mean in terms of how they are expected to approach their jobs differently on a day-to-day basis, or how they will be expected to reallocate their time to support these new goals.

These areas of confusion can cause some team members to invest large amounts of energy on activities that appear to their coworkers to be of little or no value, and may give rise to conflicts regarding the most effective way to allocate scarce resources.

Passivity

Another sign of lack of direction is when team members become overly dependent on their team leaders to guide their efforts. When professionals are confused about their team's intended direction and priorities they become more passive. When faced with critical problems they may wait for instructions before acting. In the same way, they will be less likely to seek out or respond to opportunities for strengthening their team's performance.

The Opportunities Embedded in This Challenge

From the preceding paragraphs it may seem easy to assume that when a team lacks direction it is due to weak leadership. However, even strong, effective leaders face this challenge when they are working in an organizational environment that forces them to deal with accelerated change and a high level of uncertainly. In addition, many teams are under such intense time pressure that it is difficult for them to periodically detach themselves long enough from short-term firefighting to refocus on their long-term direction.

The good news is that there is a lot that a team can gain by making long-term direction the centerpiece of a team-building session.

Stronger Engagement

Such a session can help team members feel that they are taking an active part in setting the direction for their team, rather than following passively in the direction laid out by their team leaders. This shift in perspective usually results in members assuming a higher level of personal accountability for their team's success. It also keeps team members focused on what they can change, rather than full of angst about factors that are beyond their control. In a team-building session they may find that those large-scale factors that cannot be directly controlled can at least be better understood. Work in this area also reminds participants that they are part of something larger than themselves, which takes shape in their overarching vision, mission, and long-term goals.

Increased Resilience

For a team that finds itself stuck in a performance rut (more on this in Chapter Twelve), a discussion on future direction can be energizing and motivating. At the same time it can increase a team's resilience—enabling them to thrive when faced with difficult performance setbacks. The reason for this is that obtaining clarity on vision, mission, goals, and priorities enables team members to place their individual efforts within a larger, more meaningful framework and helps them understand how their separate efforts come together to form the whole. It also helps them to place short-term setbacks within the broader perspective of long-term gains.

Developing "Next-level Thinking"

Articulating a long-term vision, mission, and supporting goals requires that team members gain a bigger, more expansive picture of those external organizational and environmental factors that need to be considered in determining the team's future direction. For a nonprofit organization, such external changes might take the form of declining foundation support from key organizational sponsors. For a corporation, these changes may involve alterations in the organization's marketing strategy, or unexpected moves by competitors.

Helping team members gain this big-picture vision does more than just increase their knowledge of their organization and the external work environment. Through the process of collectively engaging in this action, team members begin to "think at the next level." By this we mean that team members are encouraged to step back and look at the full scope of their team's collective future efforts through the eyes of their team leader and organization. We believe that this is one action that organizations can take to accelerate leadership development, as it encourages members to look at potential opportunities, threats, and constraints from a broader and more complex perspective.

Stakeholder Alignment

For a recently formed team, exploring the issue of future direction provides a great starting point to gain alignment with the team's organizational stakeholders. As team members engage in in-depth discussions concerning their vision and strategic priorities, they are in a better position to articulate the team's long-term focus. They are able to explain to stakeholders the potential impact of emerging challenges and opportunities, and how the team plans to organize itself to effectively address these challenges and opportunities. Work in this area also provides team members with the tools they need to help internal customers and key stakeholders better understand the criteria the team has developed for allocating its time, energy, and resources among competing priorities. It also places the team in a better position to successfully negotiate for additional resources, or to gain the sponsorship it needs to move projects higher up the executive agenda.

Timely Midcourse Corrections

Meeting periodically to clarify long-term direction enables teams to perform midcourse corrections as new conditions arise. The fact is that teams are dynamic entities that must continually change and adapt to new circumstances. Although vision statements and strategic plans serve a valuable direction-setting function, they only work if teams periodically review these documents to reassess their relevancy. Many times such a review will show that a team has drifted off course. Members can then discuss how they need to alter their current direction if they hope to achieve their long-term direction. At other times, such a discussion might reveal that external circumstances have changed so dramatically that the team needs to reevaluate its existing vision, mission, and supporting goals in light of those changes.

How to Initiate a Team-Building Session on This Topic

There are two different paths that teams can take to envision their future—the future is about problems or opportunities. With an effective facilitator's guidance on this topic, teams can discover and coconstruct a future of potentiality.

Introducing the Team-Building Topic

If team members are unsure as to whether they should begin team building by exploring this topic, refer them back to the comparative scores found for each of the nine team-building challenges shown on the *Team Building Assessment Questionnaire.* If participants did not complete the questionnaire, an alternative approach would be to make use of the *Team Alignment Pyramid* in your Tool Kit. Using this pyramid as your starting point, have participants weigh in on how important it is for them to discuss their mission and vision, compared to the other team development factors shown on the Pyramid, such as "member roles and accountabilities."

We have suggested that team building has been traditionally viewed as a problem-based intervention intended to (1) help members identify what is dysfunctional or problematic within their team and, (2) generate solutions for addressing those problems. We also suggested that this problem-focused approach tends to be reactive; it keeps members focused on what isn't working well within the team, and leads them to assign blame (usually to other team members) as the "underlying cause" of those problems. An inevitable by-product of this problem-based approach is that it causes participants to engage in blame casting and fault-finding, and to spend more time justifying the past than in creating an envisioned future. An alternative to this ineffectual process is when participants decide to direct their energy in coconstructing a positive, desired future, and in determining the actions they can jointly take to make this desired future a reality.

Facilitators play a major role in determining which of these two very different approaches are taken by guiding the team along what we have termed the "entry path" into a team discussion. A facilitator who wants to establish a positive entry-path into a discussion might suggest to participants that they frame the issue of "future focus" in terms of one of the following initial questions. Consider using these questions as a starting point for discussion. At the same time, give participants the leeway to construct their own framing question that fully addresses their unique concerns.

- "During today's session would you like to work toward painting a clear picture of what you want your team to look like and function five years down the road? When you think of what it would be like to experience being a part this future team, what images come to mind?"

- "Would it be helpful for you to spend your time today jointly identifying the key challenges and opportunities that are currently confronting you, and developing a clearer picture of how you would like to address these challenges and opportunities?"

Team-Building Activities That Support Future Vision

If team members have completed the *Team Building Assessment Questionnaire* prior to the start of the session, ask them to compare their scores for questions 1 through 3, which deal with the issue of clarifying team direction. Use these scores to determine which of these questions represents the most important topic for discussion. If participants did not complete the questionnaire, ask them to use the *Multivoting Technique* to determine which of the following issues they wish to pursue during the session. If the team wishes to discuss all of these areas, we recommend proceeding with them in the order presented.

Please note that the Tool Kit provides details for addressing most of these topics. In addition, we have suggested tools for certain pre-workshop activities that could be completed in advance of the team-building session to accelerate work within the session.

Suggested Session Topics for Future Direction

- Identifying large-scale organizational changes and environmental trends that could significantly impact the team's future direction

- Constructing a *Team Vision Summary*

- Reviewing long-term goals, success measures
- Clarifying team priorities

How to Take Supportive Actions

There are several steps you can help your team take to establish clearer direction. Careful considerations will help you determine which action steps are most applicable to the challenges faced by your team.

Scan the Horizon

One step a team can take to more clearly chart its own future is by mapping out organizational change factors that are likely to have a serious effect on the team's future direction. This might include some of the following approaches:

- Team members could volunteer to sit in on the staff meetings of affiliated work groups
- Invite senior managers (all of them, not just those directly above you in the reporting chain) to meet with the team at different times and share their views on the company's future direction
- Ask team members to rotate in tracking the latest media coverage on your company that is posted on both your company intranet and the external Internet, and share this information with the rest of the team
- Invite key corporate customers and suppliers to share their views on your organization's future direction
- Review customer surveys (sales surveys, customer service data, employee engagement surveys) that can shed light on any important changes in your customers' requirements
- Distribute pertinent materials to your team, such as copies of your company's annual report, marketing plan, strategic plan, manpower forecast, and product developmental plan—all of which provide valuable information on corporate direction

Given that this area is tightly related to that of change management, you might suggest that team members review Chapter Eight prior to exploring this topic. Many of the scanning tools discussed in Chapter Eight, such as the *Customer Assessment Matrix*, the *Change Events Technique*, and the *Change Management Grid,* can be used to obtain in-depth information on emerging large-scale changes before your team begins discussion on this topic.

Identify Industry-Wide Trends and Changes

While you are looking *inside* your company to detect future changes that are likely to affect your performance, you should also look *outside* your company to identify industry-wide changes that are shaping the future of your field.

Consider sending your team on a scavenger hunt for significant industry trends. For example, one team member could be asked to scan current issues of leading business and trade journals for articles that might provide clues to industry trends. Another member could be your team's liaison to professional organizations, which perform annual surveys to track key trends. A third could be asked to utilize trade and professional networks and news groups on the Internet. A fourth could make use of contacts with customers, vendors, or external consultants—all of whom would be able to fill in different parts of the puzzle regarding emerging industry trends.

In addition, teams have several other options for keeping abreast of changes in their industry or sector:

- Attending professional and trade seminars that focus on key trends in your industry

- Having team members join professional Internet chat rooms where they can track emerging trends

- Sponsoring a future forum, composed of yourself and the team leaders of other comparable functions within leading local organizations, for the purpose of exchanging views on emerging trends within your industry

At some point, call your team together for a meeting that focuses on consolidating these trends into a composite picture of the changes that are taking place in your professional field or industry. Next ask your team to assess the relative importance of these trends. As the third step, use the *Scenario Forecast* to develop alternative scenarios that take into consideration the potential interactions of these trends. The *Running the Gauntlet Technique* can then be used to determine the extent to which different team goals would be achievable, should any of these scenarios take place.

Help Your Team Construct a Vision Summary

During the last few years, much has been written on the "vision statement"—perhaps too much, for we feel the term has been vastly overused and has lost a lot of its utility. In fact, the concept of constructing a team vision has become a favorite target for Dilbert™ and other cartoons that enjoy poking fun at the latest in the corporate fads. Part of the problem is that the term "vision statement" is an oxymoron. A vision statement is supposed to be a succinct statement that captures a group's future direction; yet, we have never encountered an organization or team that has been able to compress a description of its future direction into a single sentence.

In addition, the concept of "direction" implies a choice among competing options. For a company, this means determining where to focus its markets within different customer segments and where to advance in the area of technology and services. For a team, it means formulating a clear picture of how to develop its strength as an organizational contributor. Unfortunately, many organizations and teams are too afraid of foreclosing on options. As a result, instead of writing a sharply focused description of their desired futures they end up creating vague and meaningless tag lines such as "To be number one in our field" or "To be the product innovator within our industry." Teams also encounter problems if they don't do their homework and instead attempt to pull a vision statement out of thin air, with the result that the statement is totally disconnected from future trends.

Finally, it goes without saying that a vision summary should be future-focused. Although this sounds rather self-evident, it is amazing how many teams view their vision statements as simple extrapolations of the past. When this occurs a team merely looks back over the last three to five years of its history and asks, "How can we do better at this?" In actuality, a vision summary may direct a team along a completely different line of thinking, as it challenges team members to explore new ways of applying their strengths and capabilities.

A good vision statement should cover three areas:

1. Clarify any changes to the team's customer base; the composition of its customers, emerging sectors, or changing requirements. This point also applies to those support groups, such as Audit, HR, IT, or Finance, that support their organization's internal customers

2. Specify those changes or improvements that the team intends to make to support the shifting requirements of its customers and to capitalize on emerging opportunities

3. Explain how the team intends to work more effectively to address significant constraints, such as changes to the team's charter, or the loss of organizational power or resources

The *Team Vision Summary* in your Tool Kit provides more information on how to construct a vision summary. One final comment is that if your team is a temporary project team, it faces unique constraints and opportunities with regard to establishing future direction. One tool that can be very useful in setting the stage for a discussion on this topic is the *Team Scoping Document* that is also in your Tool Kit. Additional instructions for applying this tool can be found in Chapter Eleven.

Set Clear Priorities for Action

One of the worst managers I (Robert) ever had sat down with me during my first week on the job and handed me a list of what she expected me to accomplish during my first ninety days on the job. This new list was three pages long and included over one hundred different projects, any of which could have easily consumed half of my time. Needless to say, I did not stay with that organization very long, nor did my manager or several of my coworkers. The fact is that many teams and team leaders simply don't know how to focus their efforts and set priorities for action. As a result, much is done ineffectually while key projects languish for lack of time, resources, and commitment.

On the other end of the spectrum, we have heard that one of the things that Steve Jobs, Apple's former CEO, attributed to his incredible success, was his ability to say no to many attractive opportunities in order to focus full organizational effort on those few opportunities that provide the greatest gain. We could not agree more. In fact, as executive coaches and consultants we have found that one of the fastest growing areas in the field of leadership coaching is in how to help leaders achieve greater "executive focus."

This issue becomes even more urgent in the current business climate, in which many organizations are frantically scrambling to stay solvent and successful. During times like these, teams come under pressure to spread their energy among a variety of competing projects and priorities, making the issue of setting clear priorities even more of a survival issue. When you stop to consider it, there are two components to this issue. The first is getting your team to use available data to set clear priorities. Second, we have to acknowledge that no team is fully autonomous. In order to set priorities teams need to convince their stakeholders of their rationale for setting priorities, and to keep from being sidetracked from those priorities with the emergence of every new project idea or proposed initiative.

Three tools are particularly relevant to this challenge of setting priorities. Team members can use the *Goals-Values Matrix* to see where they are aligned on both work values and organizational goals. The *Customer Satisfaction/ Importance Matrix* can be used to learn more about the relative priority that external or internal customers place on different team deliverables. Finally, the *Team Decision Matrix* can be used to develop for evaluating the relative importance of competing team projects.

Additional Reading

Barner, Robert (2010). *Accelerating Your Development as a Leader.* San Francisco: Pfeiffer/Wiley.

6

Fostering Team Innovation

The Importance of Sustaining Team Innovation

As paradoxical as this may sound, a team's continued success can eventually pose a serious challenge to its ability to remain agile and innovative. A team that experiences a long period of success uninterrupted by difficult challenges or setbacks is likely to find that members are firmly nestled within their collective comfort zone. Under these conditions team members may grow complacent and make only marginal efforts toward improving their performance. After all, why mess with success? Should the team encounter new and demanding challenges, team members may respond with routine or safe solutions. In short, their capacity for innovative thinking will be blunted, leaving them less able to tackle difficult challenges or exploit new opportunities that may suddenly arise.

Complacency can be particularly damaging to teams that function within such areas as marketing, sales, and design—areas where creative thought is crucial to exceptional performance. Its efforts are subtle and insidious, for unlike many other team challenges, the lack of innovation shows up not so much in errors, rework, or damage to interpersonal relationships but in ideas and action plans that are mediocre and unimaginative. If left unchecked, this problem will restrict the scope of a team's activities, and the team may never realize its full performance potential.

Teams may also find that their ability to innovate can be constrained when short-term, immediate pressures loom large in front of them. As we write this section millions of professionals in the United States and other developed countries are out of work. Those who are employed worry about their job security. When teams operate under organizational conditions where job loss and restructuring are likely occurrences, the tendency is to focus all efforts on short-term survival. The scenario begins to resemble one of an old *Star Trek* episode in which the Enterprise is under attack and the captain feels constrained to shut down everything but the essential life-support systems.

Complacency isn't the only reason for a lack of innovation. Other conditions may give rise to this challenge, such as those outlined below.

Insular Views

Exposure to cutting-edge ideas and best practices within their industries allows teams to explore their limits and test new work approaches. Unfortunately, some teams suffer from a type of organizational inbreeding that provides little access to ideas and individuals outside their organizations. The most isolated teams are usually the ones with the greatest deficits in creative thinking. Not only are they cut off from the flow of new ideas, but they also don't have access to informational networks that can keep them apprised of evolving ideas within a given area. When such teams finally do try to innovate, they end up reinventing the wheel because they don't realize that their new ideas and solutions have already been applied, tested, and improved by peers in other organizations.

A related cause is what I call the "not invented here" syndrome. The team may be operating within a work culture that emphasizes applied experience over creative thinking. In this type of work culture, ideas are often killed before they receive a fair hearing, and team members may be criticized for suggestions or solutions that represent departures from the status quo.

Consequences That Discourage Risk Taking

In some work environments, team members feel that innovation is seldom rewarded and failure is consistently punished. With consequences of this sort in place, team members quickly learn that they're likely to suffer criticism for proposing new ideas and untested solutions to problems. On the other hand, if they adopt or support solutions proposed by senior-level team members or their team leader, they avoid the risk of failure. As a result, such teams tend to wait passively for direction from their leaders and managers.

Censorship

Newer and less-experienced team members tend to be strongly influenced by the opinions of their experienced and senior counterparts. Within some teams, the team leader or selected team members exert subtle but powerful control over the team's innovative thinking process. There are many ways in which these dominant team members censor and restrict the innovative ideas of the others. These behaviors include:

- Sarcastic or critical responses to the ideas of other team members

- Aggressive, inappropriately timed challenges to team members to come up with complete solutions when they are just beginning to formulate new ideas

- Arguing that because the team has already partially explored a given line of thinking, it doesn't merit additional effort

- Implying that the presenter of an idea lacks the experience or skills to be taken seriously by the team

- Taking a team problem-solving discussion off-line with subsequent, clandestine discussion with selected team members

Whatever form the censorship takes, the result is usually the same—new or junior-level team members are reluctant to express new ideas and have great difficulty obtaining a fair hearing for their ideas.

Lack of Challenge

Innovation requires a work climate that compels team members to leap beyond barriers to problem solving so that they explore totally new approaches to their work. There are many reasons why teams do not feel challenged. They may simply be underutilized. It could also be that the organization has very low expectations for the team, which discourages team members from testing and strengthening their abilities. Another reason may be that the team has never felt pressured to change because it's been insulated from the performance of its competitors. (Nothing is better at creating a burning platform for change than the knowledge that competitors have gained a strategic performance advantage.) Another common cause is over-staffing, which allows team members to focus their attention on a relatively restricted set of routine tasks and assignments.

Isolation

Innovation is a synergic process that thrives within work environments where team members learn from and build on one another's ideas. This type of symbiotic learning may take many forms—from team members who exchange ideas on a particular project, to the team leader who shares an exciting new Internet research site with her group. Whatever its form, innovation is severely handicapped when team members lack ready access to one another, or if team norms and practices discourage them from freely discussing their ideas.

Isolation also takes the form of allowing yourself to be cut off from key emerging trends that shape your organizational success. We recently read a news story in which a CEO of one of the first PC manufacturers smugly dismissed tablet and notebook computers as "just a fad"—interestingly, this company has lost huge market share over the past few years. Clearly this type of thinking is very misguided and runs counter to prevailing market trends. Given that professionals tend to emulate the behavior and thinking of their executives, obviously when this kind of regressive thinking is taking place at higher leadership levels in an organization it produces a "runoff effect" that limits the kinds of innovative thinking that occurs at lower levels in the organization.

How to Tell When This Is a Challenge

The signs of complacency and lack of innovation are quite varied and may be rather subtle. As you review the following team behaviors, give some thought to which of these behaviors you have observed in your own team.

Lack of Confidence in Ability to Meet New Challenges

Quite often, a vicious cycle develops as a team's complacency leads to a lack of innovative thinking, which in turn leaves team members even less prepared to deal with new situations. Teams that have lost their ingenuity rely heavily on tried-and-true approaches when attempting to solve work problems and are easily thrown for a loop when confronted with a problem that can't be solved by their usual methods. Their automatic, by-the-numbers remedies may prove totally inadequate for unique and unusual challenges, such as entry into a totally new product or service area.

If this cycle continues for a prolonged period of time, team members may begin to doubt their ability to tackle difficult challenges. Each new task will be seen as a potential threat rather than an opportunity for strengthening overall performance. As a result, team members may hesitate to take on challenges or explore emerging possibilities.

Ignorance of Cutting-Edge Technology and Work Methods

Teams that lack innovation not only fail to continuously refine and strengthen their technical skills, but are often unaware of cutting-edge developments in their particular professions.

We recall a discussion that took place a few years ago with a senior-level HR executive regarding the subject of Internet-based recruiting and résumé-screening systems. The executive conceded that such systems might be appropriate for entry-level workers. At the same time, he asserted that seasoned managers and executives would never utilize the Internet as a serious job search avenue. We hastened to point out the number of major international executive-recruiting firms that had opened up Internet gateways with the intention of attracting such audiences. This news came as a shock to our colleague, which gave us a keener insight into how far behind he had fallen in terms of keeping up with new developments in his field. More recently, we have seen a similar situation play out in the emerging field of social networking. Quite simply, there is a wide disparity in the ability of executive recruiters to keep pace with the increased impact that social recruiting systems such as LinkedIn, Facebook, and Google are having on corporate recruiting and employment branding efforts.

Mundane Solutions and Missed Opportunities

It is easy to spot teams that have lost their ability to innovate by looking at the minimal level of creativity they display in their inventive and problem-solving activities. Such a team, three years in the future, will be offering the same service features to its customers, applying the same solutions to problems, and performing its functions with the same work methods.

Similarly, complacent teams often fail to anticipate and make the most of new opportunities. We know of a conference planning group that lost a major contract when one of its competitors approached an important corporate client with an innovative idea for completely revamping the format and presentation style of the company's annual corporate convention. The meeting team that lost the contract proposed the same tired and hackneyed format they had been providing for the past several years.

If you have observed a steady, relentless stream of customer defections, it may be because they have begun to seek out more innovative suppliers for their needs. The same situation applies to internal support groups such as IT support, finance, or human resources. We have witnessed a number of situations in which internal customers, seeking more cost-effective and innovative solutions to their needs, have circumvented their internal suppliers in favor of outside consultants or vendors. Once this scenario occurs it becomes very difficult to rebuild your internal brand as an innovative business partner.

Defections in the Ranks

Sharp, creative professionals are attracted to work environments that inspire innovation. If the best and brightest members of a team begin to jump ship, either through transfers or voluntary terminations, perhaps these individuals believe that their fellow team members and leader don't place a very high premium on innovative thinking.

Case in Point: The Marketing Team

A marketing team responsible for managing the campaigns of a large medical equipment manufacturer underestimated the potential impact of the Internet within its specialized field and actively resisted suggestions from members of the senior team that it explore this new arena. Satisfied with its established set of marketing skills, the team didn't bother to keep pace with new developments in this area.

When the company CEO realized how far behind his company had fallen in Internet-based sales and marketing, he replaced the vice president of marketing with an outside candidate who was capable of moving the marketing group in this new direction. At this point, team members finally woke up to the seriousness of their situation. They realized that, despite their proven skills in reaching out to customers through television, radio, and print advertising, they would soon be left far behind by their competitors unless they began making substantial progress in Internet-based advertising.

The Opportunities Embedded in This Challenge

The great irony is that teams who harness innovation are able to do more than drive team performance; as members generate and implement creative ideas they also boost their confidence in their ability to tackle and overcome future work challenges. Teams that practice a high level of innovation naturally assume they must and can continually improve their performance. With each innovative idea team members raise their joint expectations about what is possible and achievable for them as a work unit. More important, they do this not just by working more diligently but also by remaining open to a variety of options for increasing innovation.

These groups tend to be early adapters; that is, they are the first in their organizations to experiment with new work methods and processes. They constantly scan the horizon to track new opportunities in their fields. They look for ways to seed their teams with outsiders who can provide a fresh, creative perspective on their job functions. These are the groups that are so frequently called on by their organizations to take the lead in exploring the potential of new markets or tackling extremely complicated assignments. Truly innovative teams don't see these situations as trying or threatening; rather, they view them as opportunities to stretch their abilities and explore stimulating and novel work challenges. For that reason, there tends to be a strong link between a team's ability to innovate and its capability in dealing with another challenge discussed in Chapter Eight.

How to Initiate a Team-Building Session on This Topic

We usually avoid props or gimmicks when we are conducting team-building programs. However, when dealing with the challenge of innovation we some-times make an exception to this rule and try to produce a creative environment for the meeting. This could involve such things as making sure that the team-building session is far removed from the typical workplace and takes place in a conference center that lends itself to an informal setting. We also try to avoid the use of rectangular tables (which remind participants too much of their office desks) in favor of small, round tables that provide a more relaxed setting. Walking into the room you would find the tables covered with colorful tablecloths, with small items, such as toys, scattered across each one to engage members. Yes, we know this may sound a bit unusual, but the fact is that innovation is synonymous with play, and a somber environment runs counter to the type of creative energy that you are attempting to generate in the room.

With the team assembled, it is time to kick off the session. It is not uncommon for facilitators to start off this type of session by framing it as a problem-solving discussion. Accordingly, the first words that participants will hear will be something such as: "Let's talk about the things that are preventing us from being more innovative." Unfortunately, if the team is having difficulty because it sees itself as struggling to stay afloat in a sea of organizational turbulence and volatility, then leading into the discussion with a negative query will only serve to put participants on the defensive. Here are some alternative options:

First, try starting the session by asking participants to recall situations in which they have, as a team, previously worked together to come up with innovative ideas. List these situations for discussion, then ask what they have in common. In other words, what was unique about how the team performed under these conditions? Responses might include any of the following:

- Team members spent several days together off-site to work on the topic in a concentrated way

- The team was able to bring in outside resources to support them in the process

- Team members felt that in all of the situations they had been provided with full, in-depth information on the area in which innovation was required

The next step is to engage in a team discussion regarding what it would take to replicate these innovative conditions in future situations.

A second option is to divide team members into subgroups, then ask each subgroup to identify one broadscale, high-impact change that is now occurring in their organization that will require them to shift away from "business as usual" to take creative action. For example, one of our corporate clients, an organizational development team, encountered severe resource constraints after a major layoff. This prompted the team to take a close look at the true "value-added" obtained through each of their activities, to identify those that should be reduced or eliminated. It also eventually forced the team to look for alternative options, such as the use of graduate interns, to help address their staffing shortfalls. The *Scenario Forecast, Opportunities Assessment,* and *Change Events Technique* are three tools that can be very useful in helping you explore potential change areas that could spur the need for innovation.

A final option is to use the *Team Vision Summary* to engage participants in developing a clear and detailed picture of how they would like their team to function, and what they would like to have achieved, three to five years in the future.

While these options are not intended to serve as solutions for building innovation, they do at least provide a platform for kick-starting a discussion on this topic.

How to Take Supportive Actions

There are a variety of steps that you, or the other members of your team, can take to foster a spirit of team innovation. Consider some of the following suggestions.

Set the Stage for Creative Thinking

If your team is stuck in a pattern of noninnovative thinking, perhaps team members do not believe that their ideas and suggestions are fully encouraged and supported. If you are the team leader, one way through this impasse is to sit down with your team and describe a work function or project that requires their full creative efforts. Set the stage for creative thinking by letting your team members know that you encourage and welcome their ideas. Here are some actions you can take to communicate your receptiveness to others' ideas:

- When team members voice tentative ideas, draw them out by telling them you would like to hear more.

- Show that you intend to give careful consideration to team members' suggestions by recording all ideas on a board for latter review.

- Refrain from offering your own ideas until everyone else has had an opportunity to speak.

- Play the role of traffic director by gently reining in dominant team members and giving others an opportunity to voice their thoughts.

- If a team member has trouble expressing an idea, paraphrase his or her comments and then invite the rest of the team to build on these ideas, or invite the individual to come back after the team meeting to speak to you about any additional thoughts.

Conduct a Structured Brainstorming Session

While the phrase "structured brainstorming" may seem like an oxymoron, it's not. The problem with brainstorming as it's traditionally envisioned is that team members are asked to throw out for review any and all ideas, in any order, thus allowing verbally dominant individuals to monopolize the discussion.

As an alternative, conduct a "go-round" and ask your team members to present only one idea at a time; members may pass temporarily if they can't come up with an idea. Continue around the circle until you've gathered all ideas from your team. Next, ask your team if there's any way to combine or modify certain ideas to create new ideas. Take a few additional minutes to identify these consolidated ideas, and then make your final selection from this expanded list.

Two tools that you can use for encouraging idea generation from team members are the *Gallery Technique* and *Group Brainwriting and Electronic Brainstorming*. These techniques are also useful if some participants are hesitant to offer up their ideas, or others tend to dominate the conversation. In addition, electronic brainstorming is an effective means of initiating brainstorming with a distributed team prior to the start of the session. The *Kill the Critic Exercise* is one playful approach for preventing members from criticizing ideas as soon as they are presented. Finally, the *Idea Rotation* technique can be useful when you are attempting to encourage a team to simultaneously brainstorm ideas for addressing several different issues, team opportunities, or challenges. This technique can be particularly useful when your team comprises subgroups who hold very different perspectives on the topics under discussion.

Suspend Limitations

Ask team members to temporarily suspend any limitations they believe stand in the way of the team's innovation. If needed, you can ask members to list the constraints—time, money, staff, lack of information—that stand in the way of solving a given problem. List these constraints on a flipchart and explain that you'll come back to them eventually, but for the next thirty minutes, you want your team to pretend they don't exist.

For example, if "lack of funds" was previously identified as a principal constraint, you might say to your team, "If money were *not* an issue, what would be the ideal solutions to our effort?" After you've identified all potential ideal solutions, go back and ask how they might be modified to meet the constraints.

Develop Graphic Solutions

Encourage team members to use pictures or graphics to illustrate the problem in question. This may sound a bit silly, but we frequently find that when team members are encouraged to model or represent problems through the use of cartoons, drawings, or icons, it liberates their thinking and enables them to address subtleties they may otherwise have overlooked. Two tools that we have included to support the creation of visual models for innovation are *Mind Maps* and *Visual Explorer*™. In addition, the *Microanalysis Technique* can help team members deconstruct a problem into its component parts and then reassemble those parts in new and creative ways. Detailed instructions for applying these tools can be found in your Tool Kit.

Make Use of Creative Software

Several software programs have been designed for Mac and PC systems that support designing creative solutions. A good example tool is *ThoughtOffice*™ that contains templates loaded with questions from over 200 functional experts and business leaders that provide questions designed to encourage the carefully formulation and exploration of problems and opportunities. Another useful idea generation tool included in your Tool Kit is the *Creative Whack Pack*®, available both as a card deck and as an application for the iPad and iPhone.

Import a Fresh Pair of Eyes

A sure way to charge your team's creative battery is to bring in an outsider—someone who has not been influenced by the team's thinking process. These visitors do not have to be technical experts. Their job is not to provide expert advice but to ask questions that nudge team members beyond their assumptions. When using these outside observers, we recommend the following approach.

Begin by asking a team member to provide your observer with a basic overview of the opportunity or challenge facing your team. This explanation should be stripped to its essence, devoid of jargon or technical terminology. Sometimes this first step will help your team see the opportunity or challenge in a new light. Proceed by asking your visitor to observe as your team explores the topic under review. For the first thirty minutes or so of the team's review discussion, the observer should take notes and prepare to ask questions. Once the team has had ample time to engage in their own discussion, the visitor should feel free to join in the conversation at any time to ask questions for clarification. Your visitor should then share his or her observations and ask any probing questions that might guide your team to uncover additional information.

Another version of this approach is to suggest that different members of your team ask to sit in on part of the department meetings held by your internal customers or support functions. Quite often a chance engagement at one of these meetings can reveal upcoming changes to business processes, customer requirements, or operational systems that pose incredible opportunities for your team. For example, our sitting in on meetings of our respective company's North American and international sales and operations teams resulted in developing a service delivery proposal that resulted in a greatly expanded support role for our human development and training departments.

Conduct Best Practice Reviews

If your team is too complacent, several weeks prior to your team-building session ask team members to volunteer to conduct a best practice review. Best practice reviews provide a more formal opportunity for examining processes through a fresh pair of eyes. A best practice review compares the best work processes, methods, and procedures of world-class organizations to uncover those that can be imported into your organization. It is an excellent technique for selecting good ideas from other companies.

A best practice review could be with a world-class organization or (if time or money are restrictions) a local organization that has established a great reputation in your team's field of expertise. We have found that a good starting point for recognizing these organizations is to note those that are listed as one of the most innovative organizations in business journals such as *Fortune* or *Forbes*. A second way to identify them is to look for innovation award winners that are recognized in annual professional conferences. Still another option is to contact professional associates through the use of a professional social network, such as LinkedIn, and ask for their recommendations.

When conducting best practice reviews (an Internet search will reveal several books in this topic) there are two caveats to keep in mind. First, to produce a useful study, narrow the focus of your best practice questions. For example, a training department that asks, "What organizations out there are doing really innovative work in the field of leadership development?" will not know where to focus its best practice efforts. A better question might be, "What organizations out there have found innovative ways to perform valid outcome studies demonstrating the ROI of leadership development programs?" Second, before your team sends people out to conduct a best practice study, agree in advance on the questions that should be asked. This helps to ensure that the best practice interviewer doesn't waste the interviewee's time. Also, if you plan to conduct best practice reviews at more than one organization, taking this step helps you make certain that the same questions are being asked of different organizations. This enables you to look for common themes across responses.

An interesting opener for the discussion is to have those teams who conducted the best practice studies discuss their findings. Then ask your team the following four questions:

1. "What is it about the performance of these other organizations that enables them to retain an innovative edge in our field?"

2. "How does this innovative performance show up in their products or services?"

3. "How is this exceptional performance supported in their processes, systems, and procedures?"

4. "What have we learned from these organizations that could be applied to our own team?"

If your team is strapped for resources, a creative option is to make use of undergraduate or graduate interns at local universities. Quite often interns are searching for a "showcase project" that helps them exhibit their skills to an organization. One such showcase project is to make an intern (or small group of interns) responsible for a best practice review on a specific topic, including a final presentation to your team (and perhaps, higher-level managers). One advantage of taking this approach is that the interns are able to focus 100 percent of their work time on this dedicated project. In addition, they come into your organization without the kinds of "we did that before and it didn't work" objections that are sometimes raised by work associates.

Extend Your Reach Through Social Networking

Teams are beginning to realize that they can dramatically improve their collective performance by leveraging the knowledge, contacts, and expertise that are available through social networks. Chapter Eleven provides an in-depth discussion on extending the team's reach using social networking. In addition, the *Organizational Social Networking* tool in your Tool Kit provides additional information on the possible applications of enterprise social networking, as well as a summary of several social networking services that are can be obtained by organizations.

On the Internet, Facebook and LinkedIn provide two of the most common examples of social network systems that have attracted a great following in the past few years. Facebook pages are leveraged by companies not only to keep customers and associates updated on products and services, but also to build relationships and provide thought leadership through weblogs. LinkedIn provides an excellent means for extending your circle of contacts and for keeping those contacts updated on your professional activities. Moreover, the numerous LinkedIn special interest discussion groups will enable your team members to take part in communities of learning. For example, we follow and sometimes contribute to discussion threads within subgroups, such as those focusing on international leadership development and organizational development. Reviewing topics gives us the opportunity to track trends in thinking within different professional groups; posting questions is one of the fastest ways of gaining diverse perspectives on a topic of interest.

Organizations have already discovered that they can use social networks to accelerate learning and knowledge creation. Being open to using social networks provides an excellent means of staying connected with customers or in developing lead generation for those potential customers who might be interested in the team's products or services.

7

Establishing Mutual Trust and Collaboration

The Importance of Building Trust and Collaboration

Building trust and collaboration within any team is a critical part of success. Quite often, team leaders and members focus so much on the day-to-day tasks of meeting objectives, negotiating with other work groups, and solving technical problems that team relationships are left out of the equation. Work life would certainly be a lot easier if we could treat a team as if they were nothing more than some sort of logical, predictable machine. Then we could simply program the team with its objectives, place it on automatic, and wait for it to achieve its stated goals.

On Conflict and Collaboration

As we know, this "automatic team" is not the way things work. Teams are composed of people who are sometimes unpredictable, uncooperative, and contradictory. In addition, all teams face pressures that make it difficult for their members to work together in harmony. A team can find itself under pressure to meet stringent deadlines or conform to exacting productivity or quality standards. Members may experience the stress caused by long hours or severe working conditions, or the tension induced by the need to continually negotiate the best approach for meeting goals and managing team resources. Sometimes, team members may disagree on how to pursue objectives or manage the team's customers or suppliers. When we consider the larger picture, teams can also find themselves caught up in the stress and uncertainty of the kinds of broader organizational changes—mergers, restructuring, redefining of corporate charters—that can rock teams to their foundations.

Faced with these pressures, even members of the most exceptional teams will occasionally find it difficult to establish an atmosphere of trust and collaboration. When we come down to it, the question is not whether the members of your team sometimes find themselves enmeshed in conflict; at times, all teams experience internal conflicts. The true question is, are these conflicts so pervasive and damaging that they could pose a serious obstacle to your team's long-term success?

It is also important to keep in mind that just as peak health is more than the absence of illness, true collaboration involves more than conflict management. Both health and collaboration call for *preemptive* actions for positive future outcomes. For teams, one way to visualize this is in terms of three levels of positive team interaction. The minimal goal is that teams should strive for effective *conflict management.* At this level, team members are willing to address conflicts and work quickly to resolve them, before they create deep divisions within the team and escalate to create additional problems. Next, teams who have progressed beyond conflict management are able to develop a work environment characterized by intrateam *cooperation.* At this level, team members are willing to provide each other with support and assistance when requested, and to also share resources, time, and information to accomplish team goals.

Finally, some teams are able to progress beyond simple cooperation to achieve full *collaboration.* At this level, these team members continually look for ways to provide each other with support and assistance and frequently volunteer such assistance before it is requested. They can withstand the stress of disruptive change because at the end of the day they are confident that they can rely on other team members for help. During idea-generating sessions team members often build on and strengthen each other's ideas, with the result that together they are able to find creative solutions that could not have been reached.

One of the most common myths that we have encountered in the field of organizational development is the assumption that teams have to progressively work through these stages. We have heard many well-intentioned consultants say that teams who have not participated in painful conflict resolution sessions are somehow denying or minimizing conflicts, and will therefore never become strong teams. We have even seen some team-building facilitators go so far as to challenge teams who contend that conflict does not represent a core team development issue.

To draw an analogy, the belief that a team needs to move through a stage of deep conflict before it can move to collaboration is a bit like saying that someone who wants to obtain a level of optimal health cannot do so until she has first taken the time to make herself ill. The fact is that all teams experience some level of conflict. The real question is where the team chooses to focus its limited time, energy, and resources.

The Team Leader's Role in Supporting Collaboration

If you are the team leader, it may be that you believe that the burden for establishing a trusting and collaborative work environment rests entirely on your shoulders. Not only is this inaccurate, but there are many reasons why this false belief can be detrimental to both you and your team. The fact is that team leaders who appoint themselves sole arbitrators and harmonizers for their teams are headed for disaster. Assuming such a role makes drastic demands on your limited time and energy, and it places you in a patronizing, parental position by encouraging your team members to abdicate personal responsibility for preventing and solving conflicts with their coworkers. In addition, by attempting to resolve every issue for team members, you deny them the chance to develop skills that will be of use in managing a variety of conflicts, such as those involving other teams, customers, or suppliers. Inevitably, intervention-type "rescues" for team members backfire. No matter how impartial you try to be, some team members may view your actions as unfair and arbitrary. Alternatively, you may be hoping to rely completely on a professional third-party facilitator for assistance. Although facilitators may be able to teach important relationship skills and guide team members through conflicts, they can't help you manage your team's day-to-day operations. Instead, a team must learn to discover new ways of interacting that support sustainable collaboration.

How to Tell When This Is a Challenge

When teams have difficulty working collaboratively they tend to exhibit a number of consistent signs and symptoms.

Missed Opportunities

When team collaboration is missing, members forfeit their chances to leverage their collective intelligence, knowledge, and skills against tough work challenges or unique opportunities. Missed opportunities sometimes occur, not because team members are intentionally working against each other, but simply because they fail to look for synergies in their common efforts. Two examples come to mind for us.

We know of a biotech company that had set a goal of increasing the sales of its products to physicians, clinics, and hospitals. At the same time, due to budget tightening the company had asked each sales director, whose teams specialized in different product clusters, to set sales priorities on the basis of potential revenues. Several months later the sales team finally got together to compare their lists. It was then that they realized the extent to which sales accounts overlapped. In fact, one chain of health clinics, which had actually been listed as a low priority by all sales directors, rose to the top of the list when all of the potential revenue figures were added up! It was at this time the company realized that they needed to abandon their piecemeal approach to sales and start collaborating.

The second example comprises two identical cases in separate organizations. The first involved groups of managers within an engineering department that, unknown to each other, had separately secured contracts with the same consulting firm. The second involved siloed leaders who had secured separate contracts with the same firm for e-learning development for their respective business units. Once both discovered this, umbrella contracts were arranged at a substantial discount for their organizations. More important, this situation made them realize how much money they had been throwing away by working in isolation. In both cases, once collaboration was put in place, not only did operating budgets improve, but best practices for services were enhanced through proactive sharing of ideas.

Self-Imposed Isolation and Communication Breakdowns

If teams relationships are tense and stressful some team members may choose to deal with the situation by isolating themselves from the others. Although this may prevent arguments, it also slows down work efforts and creates information bottlenecks. Team members who seal themselves off in their offices or cubicles and simply stop communicating with the other members of their team are just digging in for a long siege. Isolation often leads to territorial behavior among team members. Signs include establishing firm boundary lines around work areas, PCs, responsibilities, and even support personnel. When team members attack coworkers for infringing on their turf, the results are turf wars that can demoralize the entire team.

When team members are isolated they fail to keep each other informed of significant events, changing circumstances, or emerging problems or opportunities. In the same way, information that a manager shares with certain team members is not passed along to other coworkers. This lack of communication interferes with the smooth flow of work processes. In addition to being reluctant to maintain physical and verbal contact within the team, team members may also hesitate to offer help to coworkers. When people who formerly worked well together begin to look out only for themselves, it is a sure sign that a team is caught up in an ongoing cycle of conflict.

Formation of Cliques

Another sign of lack of collaboration is when team members form into allied camps. Sometimes this involves soliciting support from individuals who hold strategic positions in other teams or pressuring their own team leader to take sides on issues. When certain members consistently oppose other members, regardless of the issue under discussion, their behavior relates not only to the matter at hand but also to long-standing grievances between the factions. Team members may seek help in outmaneuvering or overpowering their opponents, or may try to isolate them from the rest of the team. This behavior leads to the formation of mutually hostile cliques. Cliques ostracize other team members and target them for retribution, which may involve excluding them from meetings or e-mail distribution lists or pointedly ignoring them in social situations.

Limited Accessibility

Team members sometimes have difficulty developing strong relationships because they lack ready access to the others. They may be separated by geography, work shifts, or heavy travel schedules that make face-to-face meetings impossible. For their part, team leaders may be spread too thin, expected to exert overwhelming amounts of control, or so busy addressing problems at higher levels in the organization that they have very little time to spare for their team members. Under these conditions it is difficult for members to develop a cohesive common ground for pursuing team objectives and strengthening relationships among members.

Lack of Alignment on Goals and Priorities

A key ingredient to collaboration is that team members are aligned regarding the value or feasibility of business objectives, the relative priorities that should be placed on competing projects, and the performance expectations that are set for projects. When such alignment is lacking, teams can quickly slide from collaboration into conflict.

We know of one international sales and marketing firm that demonstrated a very good customer growth rate for several years. Unfortunately, to secure their contracts, sales representatives often committed the company to service agreements that were extremely unprofitable and difficult to implement. A new manager was brought on board to redirect the team's activities. This leader tried to convince her team to make dramatic changes to the terms and conditions in the customer agreements. At each stage of the process, this leader met with an enormous amount of resistance from her staff. Eventually, she won over her team, but not before she was forced to terminate two team members who had steadfastly dug in their heels and refused to change their sales approach.

Ambiguous Roles and Responsibilities

Closely related to the issue of lack of alignment on goals and priorities is lack of clarity on team roles and responsibilities. A common source of irritation for team members is when they experience uncertainty about their respective roles in managing customers or suppliers, providing project direction, or representing their team to key stakeholders. Without some clarity on these issues, team members are prone to erecting protective barriers around their job responsibilities or engaging in petty bickering over accountabilities. Problems in this area also quickly become visible to people outside the team and, if left unaddressed, can damage the team's reputation with other departments and groups.

Lack of Collaboration and Conflict Management Skills

From time to time, every team needs to resolve some tough work issues. If team members don't have the skills to obtain consensus, these situations quickly degenerate into extended conflicts. Teams do not necessarily have to reach complete agreement on all issues, but the very act of striving for consensus makes team members feel that their needs and concerns have been given a fair hearing. When team members lack a forum for airing their concerns or seeking resolution on issues, or if they don't know how to manage the process of consensus building, they may feel that their only options are force and intimidation.

Many people reach adulthood armed with only few ineffectual communication tools, such as verbal domination, intimidation, or sarcasm. Such individuals may lack the skills needed to build collaboration or tactfully resolve conflicts. These basic (though maladaptive) tools, along with a high degree of technical proficiency, may enable a person to perform well in the first few years on the job. Eventually, however, such an individual will encounter increasingly complex and subtle business and organizational issues. At this point, the absence of relationship skills becomes evident to the organization at large. If left uncorrected, these deficiencies may eventually result in career derailment with the person reaching a career plateau or being terminated.

The fact is that team conflicts seldom appear without warning. It is easy for the astute observer to spot the nonverbal clues of imminent conflict— tenseness in the voice and face, growing physical agitation, sudden flare-ups or silence in team meetings, covert meetings behind closed doors, formation of cliques that exclude other team members who may not have interpersonal skills to perceive that coworkers are irritated or frustrated by their behavior. If these warning signs remain unnoticed or unaddressed, the result can be a major altercation; small conflicts can quickly escalate quickly until they're out of control. This is one of the most common symptoms of a team that is trapped in conflict. If relatively small one-on-one disagreements swiftly expand to engulf other team members, the team leader, or (even worse) senior managers, your team has a serious problem that demands prompt attention.

Different Communication Styles

We all have very different communication styles. Mine (Robert) tends to be fairly task focused and directive: I think on my feet, get to the point very quickly, avoid small talk, and remain focused on my tasks at work. Mine (Charlotte) tends to be very focused on gaining understanding in more thoughtful and accommodating ways; I like to ask exploratory questions and understand what is working and what are perceived challenges before I discuss them with others. Though the two of us have very different communication styles, each day we manage to collaborate on projects such as this book, while working with a variety of professionals who represent every conceivable communication style. For example, one of our associates has a communication style that is characterized by the following features:

- She is more likely to warm up to a topic slowly with a lot of small talk.

- She tends to shift quickly among many topics.

- Instead of analyzing and itemizing key points before participating in a discussion, she prefers to walk in with a blank notepad and work through her ideas in the moment as she presents them.

You can see that having different communication styles could make communication between us very difficult. Fortunately, recognizing our differences makes it a lot easier to work together effectively. In the same way, if the members of your team don't understand how communication styles affect their relationships with their coworkers, they are less likely to make allowances for their differences and more prone to experience those differences as irritations.

Use of Intimidation and Manipulation

In the worse-case scenario, some team members may try to gain power and influence by engaging in arguments, veiled threats, or other forms of intimidation. A common tactic is to attempt to verbally dominate other members during team meetings. Although this tactic might create the appearance of agreement within a specific situation, team members who feel they are bullied may fight back later in less obvious ways, such as manipulation and withdrawal of support.

Closely related to intimidation is the element of interpersonal manipulation. If team members lack mutual trust they will tend to increase their own personal sense of safety by trying to outmaneuver one another on the organizational chessboard. Some of the most common tactics used in manipulation are false rumors, denial of support, inciting coworkers to actions that interfere with the work of targeted team members, and blatant character assassination. Over time, this process could very well lead to an escalating game of one-upmanship involving all parties. Another form of manipulation is the well-known corporate game of trying to make a coworker look bad in the eyes of a team leader and senior managers. For example, a team member might wait for an opportunity to expose a coworker's mistakes in public instead of discussing the matter in private, or, at the first sign of a performance problem, team members may immediately implicate other individuals as the source of these problems.

The Opportunities Embedded in This Challenge

For some leaders the words "team trust and collaboration" conjure up images of teams that are too far removed from the hard-edged realities of the business world. After all, doesn't an emphasis on collaboration result in teams that become too bogged down by consensus-driven decision making? Isn't a certain amount of win-lose competition absolutely essential for meeting tough performance standards? We believe the answer is that collaboration and results-driven performance are not mutually exclusive; in fact, the second builds from the first.

First, any team or group has only so much time and energy available to it at any one time. Team members either dissipate that energy internally, by becoming preoccupied with conflicts and manipulative game playing, or they direct it outward to accomplish organizational goals and objectives. An example which is familiar to all of us is the team member who responds to a coworker's e-mail request for assistance, not with a simple phone call requesting additional information, but with an angry e-mail response that is also copied to the team leader, other team members, or senior leaders. We have all seen how such an event can set into motion a series of escalating conflicts that can eventually cost the team needless stress, territorial rifts, and time delays, while dividing team members along battle lines. When we look back on such conflicts we are often amazed at the time, effort, and energy that have been wasted on them. The opposite is also true, in that when team members collaborate they discover that they are able to jointly identify solutions to problems that they would never have discovered for themselves.

Collaboration also extends a team's "central nervous system." By this we mean that it supports the fast and efficient exchange of information among team members. It enables those members to quickly track changes in organizational and business conditions that might easily be missed by any one person, and supports synergy through the tradeoff of skills and expertise. Collaborative interactions strengthen team decision making by exposing team members to diverse perspectives on business and organizational issues.

For large-scale groups, such as community action organizations or professional groups, stronger collaboration allows otherwise disenfranchised members to feel that they have a voice in decision making. Innovative group collaboration techniques, such as the World Café and Open Space Technology, provide members with safe environments for building dialogue on critical issues and can provide a simple platform for consolidating input from hundreds of individuals in a relative short period of time. If you are interested in finding out more about these techniques, we recommend the following two books. *The Change Handbook: The Definitive Resource on Today's Best Methods for Engaging Whole Systems* (2nd Edition) by Peggy Holman, Tom Devane, and Steven Cady (Berrett-Koehler, 2007) provides brief but clearly presented summaries of dozens of group collaboration techniques, such as the World Café (also see http://www.theworldcafe.com). *The Handbook of Large Group Methods: Creating Systemic Change in Organizations and Communities,* edited by Barbara Benedict Bunker and Billie T. Alban (Jossey-Bass, 2006), provides over twenty detailed cases showing how different group collaboration techniques have been applied in corporate and nonprofit agencies in settings around the world. We think highly of these resources, having used both of these books as texts for the graduate-level, one-week course on *International Organizational Collaboration* that we conduct each summer through Southern Methodist University (for additional information on this course, e-mail disputeresolution@smu.edu).

Finally, it is important to consider that team members tend to replicate the types of communication styles and relationships that they have formed within their teams when they form relationships with external work groups. By this we mean that a team that is experiencing a high degree of internal conflict will likely find this conflict flowing over the boundaries to other teams. In the same way, when team members are armed with the skills needed to build mutual trust and cooperation they quickly find ways to transfer these skills to building stronger relationships with internal support groups and customers.

How to Initiate a Team-Building Session on This Topic

Quite often it helps to provide teams with a bit of "sink-in time" before starting in on a team-building session. By this we mean giving them an opportunity to think privately about some of the issues that will be discussed in team building before engaging in the actual session. This is particularly true when the team will be addressing issues that might be difficult to discuss, such as in the case of the topic of team collaboration. One way to get teams thinking about issues before they come into the session is to provide them a few questions in writing that encourage them to think about the topic. The technique *Provocative Questions for Encouraging Dialogue* in the Tool Kit provides additional guidelines and suggestions for framing these types of questions.

Now let's turn our attention to the team-building session. As mentioned earlier, as team-building facilitators we operate from the belief that it is important to encourage teams to view team building as an opportunity to build on existing strengths, rather than as an audit of everything that is "broken" in the team. These two different views of team building are reflected in the different approaches that facilitators take in leading into the topic of building team trust and collaboration. We believe that starting off a team-building session by asking, "What do you think is causing the conflicts that we are experiencing in our team?" will tend to cause participants to become mired in the past, and to engage in mutual attacks and defensive posturing.

An alternative approach is to ask team members to help you map out on the flipchart or whiteboard a lot of the organizational and environmental change factors that are currently affecting team performance (the *Mind Maps* tool can be very useful here). Include in this discussion those emerging challenges and constraints (lack of time, resources, conflicting organizational priorities, and so on) and opportunities (for the growth or strengthening of the team's product and service outputs, for example) that are likely to consume the team time and energy. At this point in the discussion many of the tools and techniques that we discussed in Chapter Five can prove quite helpful, including such related tools as the *Opportunities Assessment, Scenario Forecast,* and *Change Events Technique.*

This lead-in usually directs participants' attention to the efforts they face in marshaling limited resources against those challenges and opportunities. A second step could be to have participants use the *Traffic Light Technique* tool to rate potential challenges and opportunities as high (green), moderate (yellow), or low (red) in terms of potential impact on organizational performance. With this step completed the facilitator could then ask, "Given what you see here, where are our most significant opportunities for collaboration?" The *Reframing Technique* can help you think of alternative ways of wording the initial team-building question to provide a positive entryway into the team discussion on this topic.

Another variation of the *Reframing Technique* is to create a two-by-two matrix, with the vertical line representing the degree of potential impact that each challenge or opportunity could have on the team. The horizontal line represents the degree to which each challenge or opportunity could be successfully pursued independently by the team leader or selected members. Items that are rated low in interdependence could be pursued by someone without the involvement of the entire team. Items that are rated high in interdependence require a level of orchestrated effort in order to succeed. Following this step, have participants write down each challenge or opportunity on a sticky note. They then negotiate among themselves where they should place each sticky note on the matrix, with the intent of focusing on those items that score high on both impact and interdependence. Either of these approaches can be used to identify areas for collaboration, and both provide good segues into the continued review of this topic.

Finally, as you give some thought to the steps you could take to encourage open discussion during the session, you might find it helpful to review the *Guidelines and Questions for Engaging Dialogue* and *Provocative Questions for Encouraging Dialogue* tools.

How to Take Supportive Actions

There are several steps that teams can take to build stronger, more collaborative relationships. Following are supportive team-based guidelines, as well as suggested actions for strengthening one-on-one relationships between team members.

Gain Alignment on Goals and Expectations

Quite often, team relationships begin to degrade because team members lack a common understanding of their goals and priorities, and the performance expectations that have been set for them by their organizations. There are several reasons why such situations occur.

Your team may never have had the opportunity to sit down and openly discuss these expectations. To compound the problem, leaders sometimes assume they have supplied their teams with complete information on projects or responsibilities because there are no questions from team members. "No questions" translates mistakenly into "no problems." Alternatively, team members may communicate their understandings in language that is vague or misleading. For example, an individual who requests that a project be completed "as soon as possible" gives others team members no idea of what they need in terms of a firm completion date. At the same time team members may use fuzzy language when confirming their understanding of others' expectations. And finally, if you are the team leader your expectations may have changed significantly over time as you attempt to meet the changing requirements of your customers or senior managers. If this is the case, you need to consider whether you have taken the time to pass this crucial information on to your team.

If any of these situations exist in your own team, it is important to find ways of helping your team better understand each others' expectations. As a starting point for team discussion, team members should pinpoint the types of performance expectations on which they need additional clarification. They also need a vehicle for keeping each other posted on those large-scale projects in which they are engaged that could have implications for others on the team, and for posting alerts on organizational changes or environmental trends they are tracking that could potentially have an impact on the team's performance.

The most effective vehicle for doing this is the staff meeting. Too often team staff meetings are "report outs" on each member's list of project activities, causing meetings to bog down in detail, and preventing participants from spending their limited time discussing critical issues. It is often useful to set aside one team meeting to negotiate project areas for team review. A simple way to do this is to create a "split-sheet" breakdown of (in column one) those activities that can be effectively managed through one-on-one discussions with team members and the team leader, versus (in column two) those high-impact project milestones that need to be shared with the entire team.

Two tools that are useful in helping teams gain alignment are the *Goals-Values Matrix* and the *Team Alignment Pyramid.* The *Goals-Values Matrix* can be used to help team members discover the degree to which they are aligned on their goals and values, or where they hold separate views. The *Team Alignment Pyramid* can be used to help a team identify those team factors (vision, mission, goals, roles, norms, and so forth) on which they lack alignment and require additional discussion.

For geographically distributed teams, an effective option is to consider creating a team website that could include updates as well as shared document folders so that team members can have immediate access to project plans and changes in project schedules. For additional information on this idea review the *Asynchronous Work Spaces* tool.

Discuss the Need for Support and Assistance

This action involves specifying the types of support and assistance you and your team members require from each other. For example, suppose your team depends heavily on a certain software program, but only one team member has been trained in its use. Now assume that this person conveys that she is having more and more difficulty in keeping up with the team's needs for the use of this software. In this case, your team might identify "training in the XYZ software system" as an area in which they could use additional support from you, their team leader. If your team is pressed for time and budget it certainly would not make sense to have everyone attend a formal training class. In this case, a brainstorming session by our hypothetical team could yield the following alternative solutions:

- Select only one team member to attend an off-site training class
- Find out if inexpensive training classes are available through local community colleges or trade schools
- See if additional funds are available through the company's tuition reimbursement program
- Ask for one-on-one or small-group coaching assistance from the IT department or from employees in other departments who have already been trained on this software

- Explore the possibility of having the skilled team member informally train or coach a few other individuals while working with the software package

- See if the team can purchase a self-directed web-based training package that can be used by employees on their own time

As you have been reading, you may have identified very different options that would enable this team to meet its training needs. With careful consideration, it is quite possible to come up with creative ways of providing support while working within your team's scheduling and cost limitations.

During your team discussion, take the time to fully explore options for eliminating obstacles to mutual support. Once you do this, it is important to go beyond generating a simple list of possible actions for providing requested support and assistance. Without some solid planning, these actions may never be implemented. The *Needs Checklists for Team Members and Team Leaders* in the Tool Kit can help your team establish an effective, open dialogue on this issue. In addition, the *Team Support Chart* can help expedite this planning process.

Ask Participants to Reflect on Each Others' Strengths

One way to build on the previous suggestion is to ask team members to each take a few minutes to reflect on the following question: "Who else on our team has skills and experience that could be of use to you on selected projects? Be prepared to tell them what they bring to the table that you find valuable as a team member." Next conduct a go-round in which you ask each person to share what they have written. Ask listeners to hold off all of their comments until everyone has had a chance to speak. This type of activity accomplishes two things: (1) it provides each participant with a solid affirmation as their contribution as team members and, (2) it provides a constructive way for each person to solicit help and assistance from their peers. Following the go-round ask if anyone is willing to make a public commitment to provide other teams with requested help and assistance, and write all commitments on the board for later discussion.

Recall Collaborative Successes

Sometimes it is beneficial to ask team members to help you identify previous situations that participants view as examples of successful team collaboration. This step is more than just a "feel good" technique; it also helps to encourage participants to ask themselves, "What is it that we do differently when we are performing at our collective best?" and then look for ways to replicate that kind of behavior in the future.

Related to this, it is important that teams take the time to pause occasionally and celebrate small common wins as they occur. This celebration could be something as simple as ordering in pizzas for a working lunch. The important thing is to bring everyone's attention to what is working in the area of team collaboration.

Build Trust by Increasing Transparency

When the members of a team have a low level of trust in each other or their team leader, it is sometimes because they feel that information is not being fully shared with them or the entire team. This is particularly likely to be the case when the team is operating in an organization that has been experiencing layoffs and severe cost reductions. Under these conditions, people tend to become more distrustful of being excluded from closed-door meetings, or being cut out of information loops.

If you think that there is a need for greater informational transparency within your team, ask other team members to help you identify: (a) recent projects or change events on which they would have liked to have more information, and (b) any future projects or events in which information sharing will be critical.

The next step is to agree on effective strategies for sharing information, taking into consideration limited time and staff availability. For example, when presenting this topic it is not uncommon to hear that many team members would like to attend a variety of meetings so that they feel that they are keeping up with what is going on in their organization, yet it makes little sense to force a team to suffer from meeting overload. A reasonable alternative might be for attending members to agree to post on the team's shared document site the most important decisions and conclusions that were generated in a meeting.

If you are the team leader you may be hesitant to pass on to the members of your team information that you obtain from senior-level staff meetings. For many leaders, this hesitation is based on the concern that some of this information is restricted to senior-level leadership. In our experience, leaders tend to err too much on the side of caution in sharing information with their teams. If you are encountering this situation, the next time that you are attending senior-level briefings ask for a clear way of distinguishing between which information points can and should be passed down to direct reports, and which points should not be distributed. A number of organizations have gone to "meeting in a box" formats, which include briefing points that should be distributed on key subjects as well as suggestions for handling anticipated questions.

Identify Communication Hot Spots

Every team has a few communication areas of special concern that, if left unaddressed, can severely damage team relationships. Examples include:

- How choice assignments are assigned to team members
- How work is allocated among team members
- How team budgets and resources are distributed
- How members represent your team to other work groups or customers
- How commitments are made to senior managers

If you are the team leader, invite your team to help you identify communication hot spots that require special attention. Similarly, it is wise to map out the locations of what we call "organizational quicksand." This means generating a list of key objectives and upcoming projects, and then scanning this list for issues that could, if not carefully managed, result in team conflict.

Examples include deciding which team members will be assigned to choice projects and who will take the lead on those projects, and how to allocate scarce resources among competing projects. After listing areas of potential conflict move on to discuss ways of addressing them.

Experience has shown that the more time you spend discussing emerging conflicts, the more damaging such discussions will be. Most people find it easier to think dispassionately about solutions to potential problems than to regain their objectivity once they are deeply submerged in them. The *Threats Analysis* tool is one method your team can use to systematically identify potential problem areas, evaluate their potential impact, and determine appropriate preventive and corrective actions.

Encourage Members to Understand Each Other's Perspectives

It is helpful to encourage team members to stop and take the time to understand each other's perspectives before assuming that they fully understand the other party's concerns and priorities. The Tool Kit contains several techniques that can be used to encourage a team to step back and listen to the views other members. Among these are the *Gallery Technique, Mix and Max*, and the *Idea Rotation* method. The latter two techniques are also very useful when you are addressing differences or conflicts that are represented by opposing subgroups within your team.

Create Opportunities for Sharing Feedback

We all like to think we're relatively objective and have a realistic idea of how we appear to others. In truth, there are several reasons why it may be very difficult for any of us to get an accurate read on our communication styles.

First, we are often so engrossed in resolving technical and business problems that it's difficult to detach ourselves from the situation and clinically observe our behavior. In addition, we humans are not so much rational creatures as we are rationalizing creatures; in other words, we can always be counted upon to come with a good excuse for our own behavior. If we're creating problems for other people on our teams, we may find it difficult to honestly admit our role in initiating the conflict. You should also keep in mind that most of the feedback you receive on your leadership style probably comes from a few dominant, vocal members of your team who may not truly represent the views of your entire team.

Finally, there is a phenomenon we refer to as "image lag." Speaking simply, this means that once we form a self-image, it is fairly impervious to change. Quite often, a person's self-image lags several months or years behind actual changes in appearance or behavior. When you look in the mirror, the person you see may not be the person you are today but the person you were a few months ago. A good friend of ours recently completed an intense work-out and diet program that lasted six months. Still, when she stands in front of the mirror, she sees the same "overweight" person who's been looking back at her for the past several years. It will take a while for her new self-image to register. For all of these reasons, you may want to try some of the following approaches to develop an accurate assessment of your leadership style.

The easiest way to obtain the desired information is to let team members know you welcome their feedback. If this represents an unusual action on your part, don't be surprised when the first couple of invitations are either ignored or rejected. Team members may also respond by "throwing you a bone"—in other words, they may start off by providing you with innocuous and guarded feedback in order to test your reaction to their input. If you feel that team members are reluctant to provide critical feedback on your leader-ship style, consider asking a peer in another work team (someone who has closely observed your interactions with your team) to give you feedback on how you might come across to your team.

To encourage all members of your team to openly share feedback we sug-gest that you make use of the *Turnaround Feedback* tool.

Use Maps and Metaphors

Most conflicts involve a battle of words in which opposing sides sit across a table, lobbing insults and accusations at each other. During this kind of "face-off" the other person is viewed as the "source" of the conflict.

Now change the scenario. Have the conflicting parties turn their chairs to a whiteboard. Then ask one person to draw out the situation that they are struggling with, in the way that she understands it. Give her leeway to create process flows, diagrams, or cartoons—whatever works. Ask a second person to remain silent, listen, and take notes. Now ask the second person to create his own graphic model of the situation, or give him the option of building on the first person's model. As both parties return to their seats and try to interpret what they are seeing, a strange thing happens. They engage in what psychologists refer to as "externalizing" the problem; in other words, the "problem" is no longer the other person, it is this situation that they have jointly diagrammed and which each of them is struggling with.

Consider the following example. A few years ago, we were facilitating a process improvement team when it hit a brick wall at one of its meetings. More specifically, team members were firmly divided into two camps over the best way to design a customer-complaint management system for the company. Instead of forcing the team toward agreement, we asked participants to divide into their respective subgroups. We then asked each subgroup to use a portion of the flipchart to write down their particular version of the process section on which they disagreed. Participants were not allowed to continue the discussion until all other elements of the process flow had been mapped. We then posted the two versions for joint review. By the time were ready to move back to our sticking point, the team could see clearly which of the two versions would most effectively meet their needs.

Another technique is to ask individuals to use images, icons, or drawings as a visual metaphor for describing the team issue they are working with from their perspective. There is something about this technique that enables people to listen to the perspectives of others in a nondefensive way. It enables team members to look past discrete data points to really LISTEN to the other parties. One of the authors (Robert) published a detailed case study, *The Dark Tower* (see Additional Reading), describing how this technique was used to get an operations team to share their experience regarding the massive, traumatic changes that were taking place in their organization. If you would like to explore these options we recommend the *Visual Explorer*™ and *Mix and Match* tools, as well as World Café, discussed earlier.

Establish Ground Rules for Managing Conflicts

Everything that we have suggested up to this point is focused on helping team members search for common ground and options for collaboration. At the same time, we readily admit that at some point every group encounters intrateam conflicts. Accordingly, it is often helpful to spend some time within the team-building process developing team ground rules for working through difficult team issues. Some of the most useful general guidelines include:

Avoid Personal Attacks The minimal requirement here is that in expressing concerns team members avoid getting personal. Stick with the facts about how another team member's behavior is affecting you and the rest of the team.

- For example, a statement such as: "You're irresponsible and only think about your own priorities" is a personal attack.

- A step forward is, "During the past month, you made commitments to attend two project meetings and then backed out at the last minute because it was inconvenient for you. We really had to scramble to find someone to take your place, and that's not fair to me or the rest of the team."

- Still better is a statement that gets at the underlying need or concern without implying a criticism. An example would be: "During the past month, you made commitments to attend two project meetings and then backed out at the last minute because it was inconvenient for you. We really had to scramble to find someone to take your place. Because your input and expertise are really important to me and the other people on our team we need hear that you are willing to fully meet these types of commitments."

Work to Prevent Heated Outbursts Some team-building facilitators contend that engaging in such emotional venting during team discussions helps to clear the air and provides some kind of cathartic release. In reality such angry outbursts just drive conflict underground and put others on the defensive. Suggest to team members that if they feel they are starting to lose control of their emotions, they should ask for a five-minute cool-down period before continuing the discussion.

Approach the Other Parties Directly Team members should agree that if they have issues with each other they will approach each other directly to discuss those issues, rather than gossip with others on the team. It also means that when they are about to discuss difficult issues that might elicit anger or defensiveness from another party, whenever possible they will try to conduct a face-to-face meeting with that person. If this isn't feasible they will engage in a phone discussion. Only as a last result should team members attempt to address emotional issues through e-mail.

Never Assume Hostile Intent Team conflicts are most often caused by such factors as communication breakdowns, unclear roles, and conflicting agendas, not by a desire to do harm to others. If you don't understand the reasons for another person's behavior, ask about it and reevaluate your assumptions.

After the team has agreed on their ground rules it is useful to periodically set aside time during team meetings to discuss whether team members feel that everyone is adhering to those ground rules.

Act Immediately to Control Conflict

If you are the team leader, when conflicts arise make an effort to contain them. As we have already cautioned, team conflicts have a way of quickly spreading beyond control. Some of the following actions may be helpful for you:

- Remind team members about guidelines they developed for managing conflicts.

- When you hear of a conflict between team members, meet with them individually and perform a brief check-in to determine if they're trying to address the issue. Ask them to take responsibility for the situation and get back to you as soon as they have a resolution.

- If you see team members arguing in a team meeting or a public forum, tell them their conduct is hurting the team. Suggest they should strive to find a resolution and perhaps work privately with a neutral party to do so.

- Caution team members against inflammatory e-mail (flaming) or voice mail. Suggest allowing twenty-four hours to think through a message before sending or leaving it.

- Meet briefly with team members who are trying to pull coworkers, or individuals outside your team, into their conflict. Explain firmly that they have a lot of freedom in deciding how to resolve their disagreement, but when they begin to affect the team's reputation, it becomes *your* problem, and one that you won't tolerate. Warn them about behaving in ways that could permanently damage their team.

Take Steps to Manage and Contain Conflicts

There are several steps that may be taken preemptively and in the moment with team members to help manage conflicts.

Avoid the "Kitchen Sink" Syndrome We use the phrase "kitchen sinking" to describe the common practice of beginning with one point of disagreement and then throwing in a variety of unrelated topics. In other words, people toss everything into the discussion, including the kitchen sink, and the next thing you know, the argument has grown to cover additional and possibly unrelated topics and is suddenly even further from resolution.

Team-related arguments are subject to the same laws of exponential expansion. To keep conflicts from widening in scope, it's important to intervene promptly during the first few minutes of a discussion by saying something like, "Before we go further, let's see if we can at least agree on how to define the issue we're facing. The way I see it . . ." and then offer a brief, objective description of the issue at hand. As soon as one party throws an unrelated issue onto the table, note the shift in agenda and ask if digressing to a second topic is desirable at this time.

Pursue Alignment on an Incremental Basis If you are trying to resolve several issues at once, suggest tackling them in ascending order of difficulty, from the most minor to the most complicated. Start with situations that you feel can be easily resolved and gather positive momentum as you continue your discussion. By the time you get to the hardest ones, you'll already have found a few areas of agreement, and the tension level should be somewhat lower.

Place Disagreements in Context When communication begins to break down people tend to focus on those points on which they strongly disagree. These will be the first points mentioned during the conversation and tend to set a very negative tone for the rest of the discussion. Counter this reaction by reminding team members of all the agreements they have been able to reach up to this point. For example, you might say something like the following:

> I think it is important to stop and place this disagreement in perspective. We all know we have been experiencing an increase in customer service problems, and we all agree we need to correct this problem. In addition, over the last hour, I have heard a lot of agreement on our need for a customer survey that includes representation from our four key market areas. We also agree that we need to create this survey in time for our next customer service forum. It seems the only issue left to resolve is whether this survey should be designed internally or farmed out to a consulting service. Is that about it?

This kind of statement reminds team members of the overall progress they have made toward resolving key issues.

Break Down Issues into Their Component Parts A related approach involves encouraging opposing parties to first break down issues into their component parts so that team members can separate out those aspects of the issue that are acceptable from the unacceptable. Quite often, once this type of breakdown is performed, what initially appears as a huge area of disagreement suddenly appears a lot more manageable. The *Baby & Bathwater Technique, Microanalysis Technique,* and *Plus/Delta Technique* are three methods for breaking down potential problems or solution sets into their component parts. If the conflict in question centers around strong disagreements regarding the desirability of moving forward on a proposed course of action, the *One-to-Ten Technique* can be used to gauge member commitment levels to the proposed decision, while the *Team Commitment Audit* can be used to pinpoint the sources of disagreement regarding members' willingness to commit to the proposed course of action.

Identify Underlying Concerns Another related approach involves helping conflicting parties articulate the underlying needs and concerns that fuel the strong positions they're defending. Each time your team reaches agreement on a point, summarize it verbally. Then, if team members concur with your summary, record the statement on a flipchart. This suggestion may sound trite, but in fact it's easy for team members to forget those points on which they've already reached agreement when they're caught up in the heat of a discussion. Conversely, we have witnessed many conflict-resolution sessions in which apparent agreements don't hold up once they're set down in writing.

Temporarily Table Sensitive Issues for Later Review If team members are working through a series of topics and come to a log jam on a certain issue, write it down on a flipchart and then go back to it at a later time. This allows you to gather positive momentum from areas of agreement while you consider the best way to approach the area of deadlock. At the same time, team members with strong feelings about the conflict will have a chance to cool down and evaluate their reviews.

Perform Periodic Check-Ins with the Conflicting Parties If you are facilitating the resolution of a conflict between two or more team members, stop the action occasionally and ask three questions:

- "How do you think we are doing?"
- "Are we making progress on this issue?"
- "Do you feel your views are being heard?"

This type of check-in provides a temporary time-out for individuals who feel they are locked in conflict. One method for performing a check-in is to "freeze" the action and ask team members to provide anonymous feedback on how effectively they feel they are working together on an issue.

Provide Coaching for Conflict-Prone Individuals

If you find that some team members have a hard time working with others, consider sending them to an outside seminar or workshop that specializes in interpersonal relationship skills. There are a variety of such seminars available. As your first sources of contact you might consider contacting the American Management Association (AMA) or the Center for Creative Leadership (CCL) in Greensboro, North Carolina. The AMA and CCL run a variety of good leadership workshops. In addition, CCL conducts several public workshops that make use of a combination of communication simulations, training, and feedback from other program participants. CCL also offers 360-degree surveys that provide consolidated, anonymous feedback on participants' behavior from coworkers, managers, and direct reports. For additional suggestions on how to conduct managerial feedback we refer you to Robert's book *Accelerating Your Development as a Leader* (Pfeiffer/Wiley, 2011).

Additional Reading

Barner, Robert. (2008). The dark tower: Using visual metaphors to facilitate emotional expression during organizational change. *Journal of Organizational Change Management, 21*(1), 120–137.

8

Managing Change

The Importance of Becoming a Competent Change Manager

Rapid, highly unpredictable change is a consistent feature of today's corporate landscape. Whether we are talking about the large-scale changes inherent in corporate restructuring or mergers, or the thousands of micro changes that accompany such actions as redefining team charters or replacing team leaders, all change tests the adaptive capacity of professional teams. We would argue that the ability to creatively adapt to change is a mega-skill that supplies underlying support for team performance. At this point in the discussion, we are sure a few skeptical readers are thinking, "The whole idea of change management is unrealistic. The changes that *my team* is currently experiencing are simply too large to control." Our response to this statement is that while effective teams know they may not be able to control change, they also acknowledge that they can certainly prepare for it and manage its impact on their work functions.

Depending upon their approach to managing change, teams can be placed into one of the following categories: entrenched, reactive, proactive, and preemptive.

- *Entrenched* teams live in denial. When faced with major change, they either ignore it or convince themselves that it is just a temporary aberration. They believe that, sooner or later, things will get back to normal. It goes without saying that entrenched teams are extremely brittle. Once they chart out a course, they proceed in a lockstep manner, regardless of any new and contrary information that may suggest the need for midcourse corrections.

- *Reactive* teams are slow to respond to change and usually take action only after the situation is obvious. They demonstrate a minimal amount of flexibility in that they attempt to make some small adjustments to their plans. With these teams, preventive planning is virtually nonexistent.

- *Proactive* teams try to get out ahead of change and consider the possible implications of events that are just starting to take place. However, they are hampered by a kind of "team myopia"—they look ahead only to events that are just coming into view on the horizon. In addition they seldom consider the business implications of large-scale changes, and instead notice only those that directly affect their own operations.

- *Preemptive* teams have long-term vision. Regardless of their day-to-day work pressures, they continually scan the horizon to track trends and changes that can affect not only their own operations, but also the overall performance of their companies. They invest a considerable amount of effort in thinking through and preparing for all contingencies, and whenever possible, they attempt to influence the course of business events. They anticipate and try to shape change instead of just waiting to react to it. To do this, such teams develop the ability to:

  - *Anticipate change*, by accurately assessing the potential impact of a change event and identifying those specific change factors that are most likely to seriously affect their team's performance

- *Respond flexibly and creatively* to unfamiliar situations that may require new types of creative solutions

- *Maintain their focus*, by using their business strategy and objectives as organizational lodestones to navigate disruptive change

- *Cope with the stress* that often accompanies rapid change, which often involves factors beyond their control

- Take a *proactive approach* to change, such as acquiring new competencies and business information to avoid technical obsolescence

In summary, we view change management is an essential mega-skill for teams and work professionals, a skill that can substantially influence a team's effectiveness and organizational reputation.

How to Tell When This Is a Challenge

Within every team, the inability to adapt to change reveals itself in many different ways. As you read through the following symptoms, try to determine which of these behaviors apply to your team.

Anxiety About the Unknown Future

Stress is an increasingly common factor for all teams. Much of this is due to the vague anxiety that accompanies having to plan for an uncertain and possibly threatening future. Before we go further, let us stop for a moment to distinguish between what we mean by fear and anxiety. *Fear* is attached to a known and tangible set of events. *Anxiety* is that vague sense of apprehension arising from a set of events that have not yet taken distinct form. For many people, coping with anxiety is a bit like trying to cut through fog with a butter knife.

When teams focus on vague worries, you will observe members fretting over possible scenarios by making comments such as "But what if the restructuring results in downsizing for our department?" rather than directing their energy toward dealing with the manageable aspects of change. It is reasonable to assume that every team will encounter at least one large-scale change that produces a lot of anxiety. For entrenched teams, however, anxiety becomes the prevailing, habitual response to any new and demanding situation.

Lack of Foresight and Denial

A team's ability to adapt to change depends to a large extent on its ability to (a) anticipate changes in its work environment, and (b) make the distinction between changes that are merely innocuous events and those that represent significant threats or opportunities. Some people don't display a great deal of foresight. They usually fail to see a change until they come face-to-face with it. Even then they have difficulty identifying, out of a variety of change events, those that can significantly affect their performance.

A related response is the tendency to meet impending change with blanket denial. Despite abundant information to the contrary, team members will staunchly insist that a large-scale change will never take place, or that somehow something will happen to alter the course of events. To outside observers, it will appear that team members have their heads buried in the sand.

Once change does occur, brittle teams respond to the resulting stress by trying to ignore the process and cutting themselves off from the organization flow of information. In my (Robert's) second book, *Crossing the Minefield* (AMACOM Press, 1994), I referred to these individuals as "entrenched bunkers," for, like soldiers trapped in a devastated war zone, they bury themselves in concrete bunkers to wait until "the whole thing blows over." They try to convince themselves that a major, permanent change is only a temporary aberration—a fad or a freak event that should be ignored and allowed to correct itself over time.

Information Vacuums

Self-imposed isolation can be both a symptom and underlying cause of ineffective change management. Take, for example, a team that is stranded in the organizational boondocks, located so far out of the mainstream of the company's informal, internal networks that it is the last to hear of impending changes. Another version of this problem involves teams that cut themselves off from their professional and technical fields and are simply unaware of new developments. A different issue is faced by teams that keep abreast of internal organizational changes but fail to maintain their networks with customers, suppliers, outsource providers, and consultants. External groups offer invaluable and uniquely objective views of a team's organization that could enhance its ability to anticipate and respond more effectively to change.

Sometimes, team leaders themselves help create information vacuums by failing to keep their teams apprised of significant upcoming events. Team leaders play a critical role in guiding their teams through disruptive change. They are the primary connecting link between teams and senior managers and are frequently in a better position to interpret the impact of impending change. When team leaders don't accept this responsibility, their teams will be less prepared to adapt to change.

Slow or Poorly Coordinated Responses to Change

Visualize an organization as a train running down the track of change. Within this train some teams take the role of organizational engine and others are freight cars, with entrenched teams bringing up the rear as the caboose. The latter teams are very slow to respond to change, and when they do their responses are weak and ineffective. The members of entrenched teams fail to take the time to analyze a change and determine the factors behind it, and identify those aspects that could be modified or to which the team might successfully adapt. In addition, the high degree of stress experienced by such teams makes it difficult for them to visualize adaptive options. Instead, for entrenched team members, the change event is likely to be perceived as a complex, convoluted, and potentially overwhelming experience.

The members of an entrenched team have a difficult time distinguishing between changes that are just beginning to surface (and, hence, are still somewhat controllable) and those that are well under way. This problem is compounded by the team's lack of foresight. Inevitably, the team fails to note an emerging change event (or intentionally ignores it) until it is bearing down on them. At this point, they leap into action and try to resist it—an approach that's about as effective as jumping in front of a speeding truck with a stop sign in your hand.

Defensive Attachment to the Past

We have a favorite saying that "You can't drive forward while looking in the rearview mirror." Teams that are having difficulty adjusting to change try to defend themselves by hanging on to the past. When faced with change, they cling fanatically to the technical competencies, solutions, and beliefs that worked for them in the past. You can hear this perspective echoed in the team's comments:

- "It worked in '05, so why can't we do it again?"
- "This marketing research is a bunch of garbage! What makes them think our customers' service expectations are changing?"

The entrenched team's answer to a unique and challenging situation is to apply the tried-and-true approach, even if it is not remotely applicable to the impending change event.

A few years ago we observed this situation firsthand, in the form of a corporate IT director who continued to resist the transition from an out-dated operating platform to a new and innovative software system. The problem was that because the IT director had been instrumental in selecting the original system he clung to his belief in its superiority. He held on to his belief, despite the common knowledge that it was increasingly inadequate for his company's needs. The problem became more apparent by the fact that the new system was being promoted by every member of his senior staff, including the new CEO. The deadlock ended with the replacement of the IT director and part of his team. Unfortunately, although this individual was a brilliant technical specialist he lacked a basic understanding of the company's business strategy and requirements.

Ignorance of the Mechanics of Change

Recently, we had a discussion with a good friend who is a team leader at a large financial services company. He told us about a management presenta-tion he had attended a few weeks earlier, in which the company's IT director outlined her plans for major revisions to the organization's server network. Our friend had several concerns regarding the feasibility of the proposed project time line but confided to us that he didn't feel comfortable expressing these concerns at the meeting because he wasn't an IT expert and didn't want to sound foolish. We have seen this type of scenario played out time and time again in many organizations. Team members hear about plans for a large-scale change that is about to occur in their company, but they are reluctant to venture out and confidently gather the information they need to make informed decisions. Not wishing to look ignorant, they remain uninformed and lose out on opportunities to effectively manage change.

Failure to Understand the Ripple Effects of Change

So far, for the sake of simplicity, we have approached the subject of change as if it were a series of isolated events. In reality, of course, things are usually a little more complicated. Consider the following chain of events. A change in market strategy leads a company to rethink its organizational structure. Proposed revisions to that structure reveal huge competency gaps in the company's senior management. A review of these gaps suggests that the company lacks the talent it needs to pursue its business objectives. The company responds by initiating an aggressive search for outside talent, while it roots through the lower strata of the organization in search of buried leadership talent. As these new leaders come on board, they put in place a number of their own changes, forcing their departments and business sections to reevaluate their current objectives, budgets, and staffing locations.

Many of these changes occur close together in time, with the result that a team may face a confusing array of overlapping changes. For some, the prospect is so overwhelming that they simply give up, hide in their bunkers, and wait for the danger to pass. In short, they fail to unravel the complexity of organizational change.

Other teams focus their attention almost exclusively on changes that originate *outside* their work areas, while failing to consider the effect of the many changes they initiate *within* their areas of control that directly affect other work groups. Thus, an HR team might propose changes to job posting or performance appraisal systems without first gathering input from key stakeholders about the effect these changes may have on the performance of these line operations.

Such managers are poor change stewards because they don't understand that an important part of their leadership role involves analyzing the more subtle, long-term effects of proposed changes to organizational and business systems. In the end, the resistance and hostility they encounter from poorly considered changes place them in a weaker negotiating position in their organizations. The widespread reaction among management is likely to be that team leaders who can't direct changes in their own backyards are not qualified to offer advice on proposed changes to other work functions.

No External Sensing Array

When teams have difficulty managing change, it is often because they have neglected to establish the types of networks (or, "sensing array") that can alert them to important changes in their work environments. The fact is that every team faces problems that must be resolved immediately. However, when a team diverts all its attention and resources to tackling the problem of the day, its members tend to lose sight of the bigger picture. No matter how pressured a team is feeling, it needs to continually channel at least part of its energy into scanning ahead to understand the overall business environment within which it is operating.

Teams that thrive on change have done so, in part, because they have developed an extended sensing array. They are heavily networked within their industries and professional groups, and they keep current on emerging trends within their fields. They are also internally networked, and make an effort to stay in contact with others in their companies who can keep them current on organizational changes that might affect their groups.

Victim Mentality

The victim mentality is both a symptom and an underlying cause of poor change management. A reactive team is easy to spot because its members talk as if they are passive victims of forces beyond their control. They spend hours discussing the unfair actions of their senior managers or the negative repercussions of a business change that "came out of the blue." In all cases, they view these events as something that happened without warning and over which they have no control.

Once in place, the victim mentality feeds on itself. Team members who think of themselves as victims tend to attract like-minded people to the team. They socialize with others who support their perceptions of their own helplessness and the unfairness of others. A victim mentality fuels a self-fulfilling prophecy, because assuming they are helpless victims discourages team members from trying to anticipate and manage change (after all, what good would it do?). These actions, in turn, make the team less prepared to deal with future events—a situation that further solidifies its victim position.

Resistance to New Information

Teams are sometimes resistant to new information that contradicts their current belief systems. This is especially true for teams whose members experience a high degree of team loyalty and take an elitist and insular "us versus them" position with respect to others in the organization. Not wanting to appear disloyal, the members of such teams sometimes hesitate to share information that might be contrary to the team's set objectives, positions, and norms. Groupthink like this can lead even the best-performing teams to filter out potentially dangerous problems, which may leave them vulnerable to changes that are already developing.

Static Planning

Another sign of poor change management is when teams formulate plans that take into consideration only a very narrow set of contingencies. Such teams are analogous to campers who assume there will be consistently sunny weather. They put a lot of work into designing Plan A but completely neglect to come up with a backup plan. Teams like this tend to follow their plans in a rigid, inflexible manner. They don't understand that a plan is a living document that should be continually reexamined in light of changing business conditions.

The Opportunities Embedded in This Challenge

While organizational and business changes automatically call to mind potential threats and challenges, they can also present the prepared team with exciting and unique opportunities. First, when teams learn to tackle changes head on they develop a higher feeling of personal control. This is important for psychological health and team performance, given that a number of research studies have suggested that a major factor that determines a person's level of personal resilience is directly related to the degree to which that individual feels that he or she has at least some control over the final outcome of disruptive change. A team that strengthens its ability to manage change will become a more *resilient* team, one that is able to quickly adapt to, and even thrive, under conditions of turbulent change. High levels of personal resilience are, in turn, directly related to greater optimism and the ability to effectively manage stress, an ability that is particularly important within today's volatile work climate.

Teams that learn how to manage stress are also able to identify and address organizational and business changes in their early stages, while these changes still can be effectively managed. In the same way, such teams are in the best possible position to uncover and exploit changes that represent emerging opportunities. Examples include changes to customer requirements or process improvement opportunities, or industry and technology trends that could provide a strong boost to an organization's performance.

Another important consideration is that stronger, more effective change management leads to greater personal accountability among team members. People can't be held accountable for managing changes when they don't know about those changes. For this reason the mantra "but I didn't know. . ." tends to be associated with excuse making and substandard performance.

As team members become more competent change managers they tend to do a better job in looking beyond their boundaries to consider how changes in their own projects, priorities, and processes are likely to affect adjacent work groups and customers. At the same time they create vehicles for staying alert to organizational changes that will have an impact on them. As a team improves its "sensing array" it becomes adept at gauging how it needs to integrate its performance into that of the larger organization in which it is embedded.

Finally, teams that become adept in change management are more likely to be brought into senior-level decision making at the early stages of a major organizational change—a scenario that can increase a team's organizational reputation and clout.

How to Initiate a Team-Building Session on This Topic

Several days prior to beginning this session, challenge your team to identify those team-based changes and broader organizational and industry changes that are likely to exert a significant impact on your team over the next twelve months. Examples of the former would be changes in the team's reporting structure, resource availability, or work priorities. Examples of broader organizational and industry changes would include changing customer demographics or buying patterns, trends in market intrusions by competitors, evolving technology trends in your field, or proposed governmental legislation that could dramatically affect how your organization operates.

First, before starting the session review the *Guidelines and Questions for Engaging Dialogue* found in your Tool Kit, which can help you examine actions you can take to encourage an open discussion of this issue. Consider starting off the discussion by guiding the team in describing the organizational change landscape in which they are operating, before you move into a discussion of how team members would like to strengthen their effectiveness in change management. The point here is to help the team sort out, from all the changes that are erupting, those that demand their attention. Effective tools for use at this stage are the *Customer Assessment Matrix*, the *Change Events Technique*, or the *Change Management Grid.* These tools help participants obtain in-depth information on emerging large-scale changes.

A second option for evaluating the change landscape is the *Mind Maps* tool, which can help participants map out the most important change challenges and opportunities they are currently facing, as well as those emerging changes looming on the horizon. Together, these tools provide an encompassing framework for examining individual change events.

Another step you can take early in the team-building session is to ask the team to identify two change events that have happened over the past few months. Select one change event that didn't turn out as planned, as shown by the occurrence of unanticipated shortfalls, excessive risks, or the failure to identify mitigation actions for those risks, performance problems, or communication difficulties with external work groups or organizational leaders. Select a different change event that your team felt they had effectively managed. Without focusing on the personalities of the team members who managed those two projects, see if your team can identify some of the key factors that accounted for the different outcomes within these two situations. For example, when compared with the poorly managed event the effective change management situation was probably one in which:

- Good communication channels were established, and information was quickly passed on to key personnel

- The team accurately gauged the risks and payoffs embedded in the change event

- The team aggressively worked to identify options for managing change early in the change scenario

- A detailed change management plan was developed and closely monitored

- The team sought the advice of outside experts

Your team's list of factors may be very different, but the important point is that they work to identify those factors that made the difference to success, and which could be replicated to support future change events. The *After Action Review* tool provides a more structured approach for analyzing change events (or significant team performance events) in a way that shifts the focus from blame-casting to process analysis.

Based on this discussion, you could ask your team in which of the following aspects of change management they would like to improve their skills. One option here is to use the *Multivoting Technique* to help participants quickly rank the relative importance of these challenges:

1. Managing the stress of change

2. Making the unknown knowable (identifying potential threats and opportunities associated with changes, and taking steps to fill in information gaps)

3. Learning from others who have been there (establishing processes to benchmark more effective approaches to managing specified changes)

4. Learning to identify the signs of organizational change (setting up early warning systems for tracking emerging changes)

5. Consider the potential long-term effects of change (understanding the potential ripple effects of changes initiated by the team)

6. Lowering resistance to change (learning how to manage "blockers" and overcome organizational resistance to change initiatives)

How to Take Supportive Actions

The strategies you employ to help your team anticipate and manage stress depend, in part, on such factors as your team's experience level, degree of cohesion, and overall adaptability. Keep these factors in mind as you attempt to determine which of the following improvement actions are appropriate for your team.

Create an Early Warning System

Early warning systems enable teams to prepare for large-scale changes and possible problems, and help members to shift the focus from problem management to problem prevention. Problems and changes tend to gather momentum and become harder to control as they develop, much like a snowball gains mass and speed as it travels downhill. As their influence spreads, what may start out as small process or system issues can soon affect other areas outside the team. With time such problematic changes can grow unchecked—until they eventually extend beyond the team's influence. For example, if a manufacturing team fails to identify product defects that occur in its production processes, these defects will eventually come to the attention of customers, resulting in increased warranty costs and lost sales. Early warning systems enable teams to tackle problems before they become too big to manage. As a final thought, it is impossible for individual team members to keep track of all potential problems and changes that could affect their teams. When team members keep each other updated on critical developments they are able to close information gaps, and to develop a more complete picture of the change situation they are confronting.

There are several steps you can take to set up a formal process for tracking emerging trends that could affect your team's performance.

Start by asking, "What are the major business drivers that shape and influence our team's performance?" Then ask, "For each of these factors, what are the most important trends that can shape our performance?" For an HR recruiting team, such a trend might involve the application of mobile technology and social networking to professional recruiting.

Next, determine the best vehicles for tracking these trends. These could be professional or trade chat rooms on the Internet, industry seminars, or planning meetings with key organizational leaders, external consultants, or university researchers who are taking the lead within certain critical change areas. Finally, determine how to allocate accountability for trend tracking among your team members, such as having a member volunteer to represent your team on important cross-functional project review meetings, or having a Google keyword alert set up to automatically notify your team of new articles on a particular subject.

There are two tools in the Tool Kit that you can use for creating an early warning system. The *Early Warning Chart* can be used to help your team identify key change areas for monitoring, as well as those "red flag" indicators that could signal that the change area in question is taking a dangerous trend. The *Listening Post Chart* can be used to stay in touch with the changing needs of your customers.

If part of your early warning system involves anticipating the concerns and expectations of your key internal stakeholders, your Tool Kit has several tools that can be useful. Among these are the *Stakeholder Analysis Chart* and *Team Sponsor Evaluation Form*. In addition, the *Stakeholder Hats* technique is a useful exercise for helping your team identify the pros and cons that different stakeholders are likely to perceive concerning proposed changes.

Expose Your Team to Other Points of View

Create situations that compel team members to question their assumptions about the future—especially those that, if wrong, could end up being disastrous for them. If team members attend meetings conducted by other departments, they may be able to better understand the broader changes that are taking place within your organization.

Consider bringing your team into contact with departmental or outside experts who could help troubleshoot your planning processes. For example, before your team advances too far in planning an IT-related solution ask a member from your IT group to join you to offer input and advice. You might also call upon senior managers, peers in related corporate functions, recognized leaders in your industry, and new hires who have recently been imported from your competitors. Outside consultants can also play a valuable troubleshooting role and often have the advantage of their past experience with a variety of organizations that have already progressed through the same change scenarios. Additional suggestions for exposing your team to new perspectives can be found in Chapter Six.

Implement a Thorough Troubleshooting Process

This means identifying the preventive and corrective actions your teams should take to plan for the future. Preventive actions allow you to shape the outcome or affect the likelihood of an event, whereas corrective actions help you manage changes once they are under way.

Aside from assisting your team with assessing potential threads and opportunities, the troubleshooting process provides a number of other benefits. First, it represents a vehicle for developing user-friendly, graphic overviews of the potential obstacles and opportunities associated with your project. This kind of review process makes it easy for your team to tackle the assessment of a project or decisions in incremental stages as well as to look back and analyze the success of past decisions. In addition, these exercises can be used to supply your stakeholders with a quick outline of your team's thought processes while also gaining their input. And finally, the simple act of mapping out obstacles and opportunities can help teams view challenges as more manageable because they have been examined and understood. For related tools review the *Threats Analysis, Opportunities Assessment,* and *Preventive and Corrective Action Plans* found in your Tool Kit.

One way to sort out potential obstacles and opportunities is to engage your team in rigorous scenario planning. The *Scenario Forecast* technique shows how to help your team generate detailed scenarios that are based on critical broadscale change factors. In addition, the *Running the Gauntlet Technique* provides a systematic method for testing proposed projects or initiatives against different scenarios.

Avoid Creating Unnecessary Stress

During times of rapid change, your team is likely to experience at least a moderate degree of stress. Although you may not be able to eliminate this change-related stress entirely, if you are the team leader you can make small adjustments to your management style to ensure that you don't needlessly add to your team's stress level. If you are a type-A person—driven, intense, and aggressive—work on tempering your style. Cut back on the amount of coffee you drink and track your stress buildup over the course of a typical day. Try to schedule meetings with team members for times when your stress level is still fairly low. For many managers, this may mean conducting sessions early in the morning, before they've been boxed in by e-mail and voice mail messages. Try to remember that your team members take their cues from you.

If you appear highly stressed and out of control, your team may begin to doubt its ability to handle this situation. Now is the time to slow down and appear calm and organized before you attempt to give direction. Be wary of reacting with loud and abusive behavior when you run into work problems. Instead of jumping right to the attack, try to get some answers first. In addition, avoid such actions as pitting team members against one another in win-lose competitions. Other leadership behaviors that can create unnecessary team stress include vacillating on decisions, procrastinating on action, withholding information, and failing to confront wild rumors.

Finally, periodically check in with your team to gauge each member's stress level. If certain team members appear to be burning out, ask the entire team to help you develop a plan for balancing the workload more fairly. For additional suggestions on how to manage work-related stress, refer to my (Robert's) book *Lifeboat Strategies: How to Keep Your Career Above Water During Tough Times . . . or Any Time*, available via the Internet through iUniverse.com.

Make the Unknown Manageable

One way to reduce the stress associated with a complex event is to chop it up into bite-size pieces that are easier to examine and understand. The more ill-defined and nebulous a change, the more we tend to fill in the details with our imaginations, sometimes by envisioning the worst possible course of events. The *Change Management Grid* found in your Tool Kit provides detailed instructions for how to identify critical information gaps about emerging change events, and steps for addressing these gaps. This tool also includes an illustrative case. In addition, the *Change Events Technique* provides a method for reviewing the potential impact on your team of large-scale change events that are occurring (or may be about to occur) within or outside of your organization. Finally, the *Threats Analysis* and the *Opportunities Assessment* tools provide instructions for identifying the relative impact and likelihood of different threats and opportunities that are associated with a given change area.

Learn from Others Who Have Been There

When you think about it for a moment, almost any change event you can envision has already been weathered by some other organization. Instead of convincing ourselves that our change event is unique and unprecedented, why not make use of the collective experience of other organizations? To better understand how it works, consider the following example. A few years ago, I (Robert) was given the task of preparing an organization for the introduction of an ISO 9000 program. I soon realized that few people in the company really understood the tremendous amount of money and coordinated effort involved in the introduction of this program. To address the problem, I brought in a senior line director from a noncompetitive company, who gave senior managers a very candid presentation outlining his company's procedures for ISO 9000 certification and the initial difficulties he and other executive-level managers had faced in trying to grasp the true scope of this effort.

Similarly, if you are about to guide your team through a difficult change, why attempt to reinvent the wheel? Instead, contact people who have already been through similar change events and who are known to have managed them effectively. They may be your counterparts in other companies, or they may be hidden within your organization. They may even be outside consultants who have guided many companies through a similar type of change. This course of action offers several advantages:

- An opportunity to learn from the mistakes and best practices of others

- Access to excellent troubleshooters who can help you identify the weaknesses in your change-management plans

- Fresh pairs of eyes with no personal agenda who can provide calm, detached points of view

In addition, these external experts may provide support and enhanced credibility as you attempt to convince senior management of the merits of your change-management proposal. Remember the old adage: "A prophet is never respected in his own country." Sometimes senior managers are more willing to listen to advice when it comes from the outside.

Learn to Identify the Signs of Organizational Change

Years ago, we moved from our long-term home in the South to the New England area. During our first winter, an older neighbor (a long-time native of the area) asked us if we had purchased a snow shovel. We told him that we didn't think there was any hurry. After all, the latest local weather report indicated we still had a few weeks until heavy snow would be upon us. Our neighbor just laughed and proceeded to tell us about several nature signs that suggested we were in for heavy snowfall. He was right. To the eyes of this experienced native, the warning signs were plain to see.

In the same way, large-scale organizational change events don't just appear overnight. They usually follow a number of precursors—subtle but significant warning signs that suggest your organization is about to experience a change in direction. The *Early Warning Chart* found in your Tool Kit provides both a capture form and detailed instructions for how a team can create its own early warning system for tracking emerging changes. In addition, the *Change Analysis Chart* provides a breakdown of nine key broadscale change areas for monitoring.

Consider the Potential Long-Term Effects of Change

As we explained earlier in this chapter, when you initiate a major change event you must think through its implications and how it might affect others in your organization. Never make the mistake of underestimating the degree of resistance you will meet when trying to initiate change. Part of your planning process should include identifying those concerns that are likely to be raised by resistant individuals in your organization, and the steps you can take to overcome these concerns. If you develop a reputation for being an effective change catalyst, others are more apt to follow your recommendations when change-related issues are up for negotiation.

The *Forecast Grid* in your Tool Kit provides a method for systematically assessing the potential impact of any large-scale business initiative that your team may be initiating, while the *Team Adaptation Diagram* can help your team systematically analyze the alterations to team processes, resources, customers, and so forth that may need to be adapted to adjust to changing conditions.

Lower Resistance to Change

When your team is attempting to implement a change there are several steps you can take to overcome resistance to change by others in your organization.

Build Ownership and Support One effective method for eliminating resistance is to look for ways to foster a sense of ownership among your detractors. You can do this by:

- Involving them in the design of your project
- Integrating their input into your project plan

- Capturing agreement by increments, by convincing blockers to support the first few steps of your plan while agreeing that any additional support will be contingent on the success of your initial project results

Lower the Risk Level for Change Look for ways to make the changes generated by your project less threatening to others in your organization. Suggest that you try out your business initiative on a limited basis with a small pilot group. Another option would be to incorporate a test-and-review period into your project plan. If the question of who controls the project appears to be an important issue, invite potential blockers to take part in the project review process, or even consider enlisting their support as cosponsors. If they claim they don't have the time to participate in these activities, ask them for the names of people who they feel would be good project advisers or reviewers. You could also develop a formal control system that incorporates such elements as approval gates, sign-off documentation, or risk-mitigation actions that help your project appear less formidable and more manageable.

Identify a Surrogate Consider whether part of the resistance you are experiencing is a direct response to *you* as the project leader. (Yes, we know you are a likable person and everyone should be grateful that you're leading your team, but perhaps, just perhaps, you have made some rivals along the way.) If this is the case, you may be better off having a team member or sponsor pitch your project to your detractors.

Do Your Homework Be prepared to provide evidence that your project is well designed and your recommended changes are well considered. For instance, make sure you've considered questions such as the following:

- Do you have data from surveys or interviews indicating how the business initiative will be received by customers and employees?

- Do you have access to financial data that justifies the cost of your project?

- Which team members or project sponsors are viewed as knowledge experts on the business initiative you are attempting to put into place?

- Has your project team followed the recommendations of these experts?

- Have you considered performing a best-practices study to demonstrate that certain world-class organizations have already undertaken the changes proposed by your team and that these organizations have met with exceptional results?

Choose the Time and Place for Your Battles Many project leaders make the mistake of viewing their projects as strictly task-focused events. They are confident that if they are armed with sufficient facts and solid logic, they will be able to sway even the most adamant blocker. Unfortunately, blockers are not completely logical and objective; they are human beings and tend to display all the usual human insecurities and emotions. You are apt to find blockers entering into their first discussion of your project predisposed toward anger, frustration, or anxiety. If you are talking to a person who tends to spout off without first getting the facts it is especially important to consider your approach. As uncomfortable as it might be, we always recommend that your best choice is to set up a series of private one-on-one meetings before facing your opponents in a public forum. Private meetings enable you to address at least some of their concerns, while defusing their emotions. Taking this step also shows others that you are making an effort to gain their support, and gives you time to identify and prepare for any objections that might surface later during public review. Finally, if your blocker is very influential, a private discussion provides an opportunity for initiating damage control before this person attempts to sway the opinions of others in your organization.

Begin Your Change Discussion on a Positive Note Once you have selected the best time and place for your meeting, your next task is to determine your approach. We recommend that you open the meeting with a brief statement that sets the stage for productive, amiable discussion. For example, "Jeff, thanks for meeting with me today to discuss the change in personnel policy that our team is considering. I wanted to hear your views on this project and see if we can incorporate your ideas and concerns into our project planning process."

Identify the Concerns Behind the Objection After you have set the stage for discussion, be prepared to sit back and listen. Try to hear your blocker out completely before coming back with any arguments or rebuttals. Remember, you are not involved in a debating contest. You only win if you leave this person's office with more support than you had when you entered. Another step you can take to ensure the success of this meeting is to probe patiently for the true concerns and needs that lie behind your blocker's initial objections. There are four questions you can ask to uncover these concerns:

- "At this point in the project, what are some of your main concerns?"
- "What do you feel we need to do to make this initiative a success?"
- "What do you want to see happening in this situation? From your perspective, what are the desired outcomes of this project?"
- "What can I do to gain your support?"

Build a Base for Negotiations Through a Progressive Review of Project Issues Engage your blockers in dialogue to find out how to secure their support. A suggested technique for creating this dialogue is the progressive review of project issues. Begin by describing the opportunity, challenge, or problem that led to your project. Before you can move forward with negotiations, your blockers must be able to agree with you on the validity and significance of the business requirements that have created the need for your project. Once you have gained this initial agreement, move on to a discussion of the validity, feasibility, and necessity of your project objectives. Your next step is to reach agreement regarding your project success criteria. Do your blockers agree with you that your success criteria constitute a reasonable method for evaluating the success of your project? If they do, try to secure support for your project plan. It stands to reason that if they agree with you on the above points, then the only remaining area of concern would be the approach you plan to take to achieve your objectives.

Trade Minor Concessions for Support Occasionally, you will find that you are able to secure support from potential blockers if you're willing to make minor adjustments to your project plan. Although your first response might be to resist such concessions, ask yourself whether these adjustments would significantly interfere with your project outcomes. Examples of reasonable accommodations might include:

- Adjusting your project timetable
- Building additional safeguards into your project, such as review sessions or sign-off points
- Revising your project so that it also supports your blockers' personal performance objectives
- Adding to your team a few individuals whom your blocker considers highly credible, or enlisting them as resource experts
- Selecting a different location or population for initial test of your project

Avoid the mistake of immediately refusing these kinds of minor requests if you can trade your cooperation for much-needed support. Successful project leaders know the value of winning over potential blockers and make substantial efforts to do so.

Additional Reading

For more information on the relationship between perceived personal control and resilience:

Peterson, C., Maier, S. F., & Seligman, M.E.P. (1995). *Learned Helplessness: A Theory for the Age of Personal Control.* New York: Oxford University Press.

Seligman, Martin E. P. (2006). *Learned Optimism: How to Change Your Mind and Your Life.* New York: Vintage Press.

Southwick, Steven, Vythilingam, Meena, & Charney, Dennis S. (2005). The psychobiology of depression and resilience to stress: Implications for prevention and treatment. *Annual Reviews of Clinical Psychology,* Vol. 1, 255–291.

9

Building Commitment

The Challenge of Building Commitment

In Chapter Two, we discussed the three commitments that team members need to make before they can proceed with team building. These involve being committed to staying through the entire session, working within the room, and fully engaging in the team building process. We refer to these commitments as "initial antes," because just as a poker player is required to ante up a certain amount of money to stay in the game, unless these three commitments are in place a team-building session cannot move forward. At the same time, the ability of team members to make and keep commitments to each other and their customers may surface as an ongoing performance issue that requires review.

Whenever you ask people to change, you are asking them to step out of the comfort zone defined by their current behavior and routines and try things that may be new and unsettling. It is understandable that team members may feel some anxiety about making firm commitments to achieve agreed-upon goals or make requested improvements to performance.

This is particularly likely to be the case when team commitments will require members to ramp up their performance to meet tough work challenges or master disruptive change. Some people may believe that they don't have the time to take on additional projects, or they may think that the issue or opportunity under review is too large or complicated to successfully tackle. To others, the change area they are addressing may appear too sensitive to be resolved through team discussion. Still others may place the responsibility for improving their situation solely on the shoulders of their team leaders or facilitators.

Capturing team commitment means getting team members to acknowledge that they are all responsible for making their team a success. They must understand that although leaders and facilitators may provide necessary guidance and direction, each member must be firmly committed to the team's success. In the end, in order for team members to offer their personal commitment, they must feel that the value that they can potentially gain from change outweighs the discomfort of stepping out into the unknown.

How to Tell When This Is a Challenge

Building commitment within teams does not happen overnight, but can be created over time once warning signs are identified and addressed. As you read through the following signs, consider which of these behaviors apply to your team.

A Focus on Activities, Not Results

When teams lack effective methods for locking in commitment, their members are forced to develop rough guesstimates about their performance, based on the amount of time and attention that they invest in different activities. Unfortunately, such activity-based evaluations can easily fool teams into believing that they are making valuable organizational contributions when their employees are actually deriving little from their activities.

Thus, a corporate training team may brag about the numbers of hours of training they have provided, yet be unable to demonstrate whether this training improves organizational performance. In the same way the members of a sales team may convince themselves that they are doing better in new account penetration, based on their number of sales calls rather than top-line revenue.

Moving Targets and Slipped Commitments

Another indication that commitment may be a team challenge is when targets appear to be continually receding into the distance. Deadlines slip and then arguments are presented after the fact about what had been originally promised. In the same way, there are frequently disconnects between what team members promise and what is actually delivered.

On a day-to-day basis these symptoms reveal themselves in a number of subtle but important ways. E-mails aren't returned and information or reports are not delivered as promised. Small, incremental slips in schedule continue to add up until major milestones are completely missed.

Dissatisfied Customers

An important warning sign is when the products and services generated by a team are not well received by its customers. A more critical issue is that a team lacks the information needed to identify the underlying root causes of such satisfaction. Is it because the team did a poor job in delivering what was promised, or that what was promised was not really what the customer needed? A related issue is when a team appears unable to keep pace with their customers' changing needs and requirements.

In contrast, when teams make the effort to understand and respond to changing customer requirements they quickly strengthen their performance. Effective teams ensure that they meet customer commitments by creating unique avenues toward a better understanding of how their products and services are currently viewed by their customers:

- Retail stores regularly employ "mystery shoppers" to evaluate such factors as responsiveness to customer inquiries or effectiveness in dealing with customer complaints.

- Some organizational teams establish intranet web pages where their internal customers can post comments or questions regarding the team's services. Others make use of survey tools such as SurveyMonkey to embed simple online surveys into their company websites. They use these surveys to obtain real-time feedback from their internal customers on proposed changes to work processes or procedures.

- Many hotel owners and general managers periodically spend a night in one of their own hotels to evaluate service from the guest's point of view. These visits can uncover small service problems that need to be addressed, or best practices that can be exported to other hotel locations.

- One computer company observed its nontechnical employees as they attempted to read, interpret, and apply instructions for connecting and installing the company's hardware components. Only then could team members understand the difficulty that many external customers had been experiencing in assembling and installing the company's products. By watching fellow employees struggle through this process, team members became aware of significant improvements they could make to their "no hassle" assembly instruction booklet.

Vague Accountabilities

Still another warning sign that commitment may be an issue is when team members have difficulty determining the respective roles they play in managing projects or accountabilities. This shows up in a number of ways. Members may have difficulty explaining where their responsibilities end and those of other team members begin. Customers are likely to be jerked back and forth when they make requests for assistance. (How many times have you called a company for service, and found yourself shuttled back and forth between different employees because the company didn't know who was accountable for a particular function?) Team responsibilities may "fall between the cracks" because each team member assumes that another member is managing a particular team accountability. In any team the poorest performers will often take advantage of these areas of ambiguity to make excuses for shirking responsibilities.

Safe Bets

Team commitment issues frequently reveal themselves in team members who set low performance targets. Members may frequently "sandbag" their objectives by padding them with surplus time, resources, and money. In addition, few team members are willing to raise their hands when their leaders solicit volunteers to take on tough projects. When team members set the safest possible targets and shun stretch goals, it is a sure sign that commitment is an important team issue.

Nasty Surprises

The final warning sign is when the team keeps encountering "nasty surprises" in the form of commitments by team members that were not fully honored. The problem here goes beyond not meeting commitments to include actually hiding, or minimizing information about, problems that could present roadblocks to the team's ability to accomplish its objectives. Why does this happen? Because some team members understand that once problem areas or difficulties are exposed, they will be held accountable for correcting them.

The Opportunities Embedded in This Challenge

Several powerful, positive things happen when team members are willing to make firm commitments to their team's success. The most obvious benefit is that a team begins to realize its full potential. They accomplish far more than they ever knew they could, and they develop a collective confidence about their ability to take on tougher goals. A part of this confidence comes from the fact that team members are more willing to raise their performance standards because they know that they can count on their coworkers to meet agreed-upon deadlines, quality standards, and resource commitments.

Examples of this can be found in every organization. Not too long ago the authors worked with an online marketing group that had been suffering from declining performance. This work unit was responsible for helping its clients, who were nonprofit organizations, to develop creative online marketing solutions to support fundraising. Such solutions might range from

the creation of unique websites designed to capture the attention of potential sponsors, to e-mail blitz campaigns aimed at broadbased fundraising.
During our team-building session it became apparent that commitment was
a critical issue for this team. The group's marketing managers would frequently create artificial deadlines for the operations team (a group that was
responsible for web design and software support) under the assumption that
the operations team couldn't be relied upon to meet agreed-upon deadlines.
Given this assumption, the marketing managers believed that the only way
to create a safety net was to establish artificial deadlines (that is, saying "We
need it by Wednesday" when they actually needed it by Friday).

For their part, the operations team knew what their marketing counterparts were doing. They expressed their concern that that the marketing team
not only presented "fake" deadlines, but would also give them projects at the
last minute (making a 5 P.M. request for an e-mail blitz that needed to be
completed the next day). In addition, the operations managers felt that the
marketing team often made design commitments that were totally unreasonable. Unfortunately, since the operations managers were not included in
the initial marketing discussions with customers, they usually heard about
these unrealistic promises to customers after the fact.

In response, the operations team would either engage in extensive hag-
gling with the marketing team over project deliverables or they would engage
in "sandbagging"; that is, building in a safety buffer by artificially inflat-
ing their projected delivery dates. As a result of these issues, quite often the
team's efforts to meet customer commitments would either result in project
delays or excessive costs caused by needless employee overtime and outside
contract support.

During the team-building session both parties began to see how their
inability to set and keep valid commitments was costing the entire team
revenue and customer satisfaction. When both parties created a process for
making improvements in this area, the results showed up in bottom-line
improvements that surprised the entire team.

The point here is that when people agree on and consistently keep team
commitments they soon discover that they are able to streamline their team's
operations and significantly improve their overall performance. Such a team

also develops a reputation as being a work group that can be counted on to deliver as promised. In today's difficult work environment that kind of organizational reputation is worth a lot in job security and work satisfaction.

How to Initiate a Team-Building Session on This Topic

An effective approach for kicking off this session is to challenge the team to first look outside itself to determine the degree to which it is, or is not, consistently meeting its commitments to its internal and external customers, senior stakeholders, and internal support groups. This approach helps team members understand how the ability to meet individual commitments is tightly linked to the team's organizational reputation as a reliable work unit.

The challenge encountered here is it is difficult for any team to perform an objective self-appraisal on its ability to meet commitments. To overcome this problem, prior to launching the team-building session it is helpful to have team members conduct a few interviews to find out how their team is viewed by key organizational leaders and work groups. (For detailed information on useful tools for gathering this information you may want to skip ahead to Chapter Ten.) Armed with this information, during the team-building session you can work with the team to develop a split-sheet *Team Commitment Audit.* In one column list those areas where your team is viewed by others as keeping commitments. Use the other column to list areas where your team could improve its ability to act on commitments. After giving team members a few minutes to privately review this information, lead out with the following opening three questions:

1. "What actions are we taking to demonstrate our commitment to good performance?"

2. "What could we be doing better?"

3. "How could strengthening our overall ability to meet commitments to others in our organization improve our overall reputation as a team?"

Posing these questions encourages participants to stop and reflect on how much their professional reputations and their team success are tied to their ability to consistently meet commitments.

An alternative lead-in for the session (we sometimes combine both options) is to divide participants into subteams. Next, ask each team to identify another work group within your organization, or an external supplier, that has developed a good reputation for meeting its commitments to your team. Ask each subteam three questions:

1. "How does it feel to work with the team?"

2. "What does this team do that makes it stand out from other work groups in our organization?"

3. "Which of these characteristics would you like to see replicated by our own team?"

When the subgroups reconvene ask them to compare their notes, then look for common themes that extend across all subgroups.

Having established this broad context for discussion you can now segue into a discussion of how team members can improve on making and keeping their commitments to each other. When teams venture into this topic their natural tendency is to start off by sharing their frustrations with the failure of certain team members to keep their commitments. As with the other team issues that we have discussed in this book, such a lead-in creates just the opposite of its intention, as team members engage in defensive posturing and deny personal accountability for the team's problems. To tell another person that they don't keep commitments is to make a personal attack on their integrity, and people will go far in defending their egos.

As an option, consider reminding participants that they have to be careful of assuming bad intentions on the part of other team members. There are several reasons why team commitments may not be consistently met, including lack of clarity on commitments, lack of agreement on commitments, the failure to pinpoint project accountability, and the failure to renegotiate commitments when faced with changing conditions. These and other factors can be listed on the flipchart, with participants determining which factors are most relevant to their own situation.

How to Take Supportive Actions

As facilitator, you play an important role in guiding members on the path to commitment. The seven actions below are methods you can use for this journey.

Help the Team Visualize Their Desired Future

For team members to make a substantial commitment to success they have to feel that they are working toward a joint outcome that is meaningful and exciting. The starting point is a vision statement that team members can use to create a crystal-clear picture of future possibilities. In addition, teams have to see the natural linkage between the work that they are doing and the broader, long-term goals of their organization. The last element of engagement is the creation of well-crafted, high-impact goals that are both challenging and personally satisfying.

If this is a topic that needs to be explored with your team then we suggest that you review Chapter Five, which provides a number of suggestions for engaging participants on this topic, as well as a variety of tools for creating vision statements and team goals.

Create a Team Scorecard

An old adage says, "That which gets measured, gets attended to." We couldn't agree more. Teams that lack effective scorecards end up focusing their attention on activities rather than results. Thus, a corporate training team may brag about the number of hours of training that they provide, yet be unable to demonstrate whether this training leads to improved organizational performance. Scorecards also help teams stay focused on the most important things when they face drowning in a sea of chaos. Finally, scorecards help to motivate teams by demonstrating to them that they are making long-term gains, even when they encounter periods of short-term setbacks. In those situations where a team encounters a severe performance setback, a detailed scorecard can help the team identify what has and has not been working well, which enables them to focus on the root cause of the issue and recover much faster. We recommend that teams take the following four steps when developing scorecards and success measures.

Reach Agreement on What Is to Be Measured It is more effective to create valid and detailed measurements for no more than three key team performance areas than to flood a team with a variety of measures that will simple scatter their attention among competing priorities.

Identify Useful Performance Measures Once again, don't measure your team's activities. Instead measure those products and services that are the team's outputs. The three standard measures for outputs are:

1. *Efficiency:* How productively your team makes use of staff, time, and resources. For a hospital admissions team this might involve the time required for processing new admissions; for a service department it might involve percentage of on-time deliveries.

2. *Quality:* The degree to which your team's work is error-free and meets quality standards. For an automotive service center such a measure might be "percentage of call-backs due to incomplete or faulty service." For a corporate recruiting team it might be based on "quality of hire," as determined by the rating scores on interim performance appraisals for employees at six months after hire.

3. *Customer Satisfaction:* The degree to which your team meets customer requirements and expectations. For an IT help desk such measures might include "time-to-complete" records for service calls or complaint activity trend reports.

Check with Your Internal or External Customers Make certain that these stakeholders agree that you are focusing on the right things and are selecting measures that are valid and reliable. This can save your team a lot of wasted time and frustration. A technical training team was trying to push the implementation of online training to support the creation of a four-level skill certification program in project management and select engineering skills.

The team's initial pitch to its engineering and manufacturing leaders was that this approach would reduce overall training costs. After receiving a lukewarm reception, the team discussed what was important to these stakeholders. The team realized that an organizational "hot button" was the loss of millions of dollars of revenue due to project slowdowns that were incurred while the company scrambled to locate skilled people. Based on this the team changed their success measures to (a) being able to more accurately gauge and identify skill sets within the engineering population, and (b) revenue gains due to fewer project delays caused by staffing issues. With these new success measures in place the team quickly got their funding.

Decide on a Method of Implementation This means determining how and when your team will agree to measure, track, and communicate the results of its performance evaluation. Another important aspect of this stage is determining the types of metrics that the team will use to measure its performance.

1. *Track team improvements over time.* Whenever possible, this should include a baseline measure, so that team members can track significant performance trends over time. From this data, members can isolate factors that are especially important to increasing team performance. For example, corporate recruiting team's data collection showed significant hiring delays were being caused by the time required for processing background checks on job candidates. After partnering with a new vendor that specialized in this area, they were able to make significant improvements in the measure of "time-to-hire."

2. *Identify knowledge gained.* Scorecard reviews should provide team members with opportunity to reflect on what they have learned from performance feedback that can be applied to new situations. We discuss this more completely in Evaluate the Lessons Learned later in this chapter.

Draw Out Others' Concerns and Reservations

People are sometimes hesitant to openly express any concerns and reservations they might hold about their ability to tackle tough projects or initiatives, a situation that could cause these individuals to voice half-hearted commitments that they are not ready to support. One effective remedy for this problem is to model a simple approach for encouraging team members to honestly share their concerns with each other. Start off this discussion by acknowledging that there are certain reasons why it may be difficult to address the issue under review. In facilitating a discussion in which it is important to secure commitment to tough performance goals, you could begin by saying something like the following:

> Before we continue, I think it is important for us to openly discuss any concerns or reservations we might have about our ability to move forward on this plan of action. I know that you have selected a challenging area for review—one that could require a lot of extra time and effort. What I would like to do is go around the room and listen to any concerns you might have. As you talk, I will post your comment on this flipchart for review. If you don't have anything to add for the moment, just say "pass," and we will circle back to you later to see if you have something you would like to add. As a ground rule, I am going to ask you not to respond to any of the concerns you hear until everyone's comments have been posted on the board.

The *Nominal Group Technique* and the *Gallery Technique* are two useful, nonthreatening approaches for drawing out member concerns on projects or initiatives. You could then follow this discussion by using the *One-to-Ten Technique* to gauge the initial commitment levels of participants, and to determine what actions the team can take to address the concerns raised by uncommitted team members. As a final note, if some team members are virtual participants in the session, spend additional time listening carefully to their concerns and comments. This is particularly true if they are communicating over the phone and you are not able to observe their body language.

Clearly Communicate Team Commitments

When team members are accused of "failing to meet commitments" sometimes this situation results from common communication breakdowns. We know of one professional, whom we will call "Linda," who was criticized for "lack of follow-up" on e-mails. Linda continued to assert that she always followed up on her coworkers' requests. The confusion here was in what was meant by the term "follow-up." When Linda received an e-mail request for information she would immediately reach out to other departments to secure that information. However, not wanting to mislead her coworkers, she would wait to reply to her coworkers until she had received and personally checked out the information that they requested. If another department informed Linda that a financial report wouldn't be updated for another week, she might send that department several e-mail "nudges" but would hold off on alerting her own team. From the perspective of her coworkers, Linda would simply receive their requests and fail to respond. This situation, which was quickly cleared up once everyone engaged in an open discussion on the topic, is not uncommon in many organizations.

To minimize communication breakdowns, spend part of your team-building session discussing one selected team responsibility or project that will require a high level of team commitment. Next, invite participants to identify any areas in which they may be unclear on performance standards or expectations. In addition, part of the session could be spent having team members make commitments to each other in support of those areas in which team members depended upon each other for support and to write out their commitments for public review. Table 9.1 shows the difference between a vague commitment statement versus a clear commitment statement. The *Team Support Chart* tool can be useful for engaging in this exercise.

Identify Commitment Gaps

In order for a team to be committed to taking on a project or performance area its members need to be aligned on five points. The *Team Commitment Audit* is an excellent tool for surveying team members regarding their commitment to a proposed work initiative or solution to a business problem. It asks individuals to rate their commitment in four areas:

- *Criticality:* How urgent is the problem or performance challenge under review?

- *Solvability:* How much of this problem or performance challenge can we solve ourselves?

Table 9.1. Difference Between Vague Versus Clear Commitment Statements.

Vague Commitments	Clear Commitments
I will pass the information on to you as soon as I get it from Finance each week.	I will forward by e-mail the budget updates from Finance that I receive on Friday morning by the close of business on Friday. If I get them late in the afternoon, I will check my e-mail over the weekend and forward them on to you.
I will try to make sure that I don't create bottlenecks when I'm traveling on vacation.	I will make sure that my customer notes and related documents are posted on our shared document site before I leave for vacation. I will also give everyone on the team a reminder two days before so that you can talk to me if you have certain actions completed before I leave. I'll also be more diligent about checking my e-mail and texts daily. For your part, I would ask that you hold of copying me on routine e-mails and use your judgment in flagging certain requests as "urgent."
I will do a better job in processing our contracts with external vendors.	We both agree that I am keeping up with the flow of contracts in our department, but I will take on the responsibility of shepherding our contracts through both the Contracts function and our legal team. If either group anticipates delays I will let everyone know immediately by e-mail.
I will try to keep everyone informed of changes to the project.	I will e-mail out to everyone a brief written summary of any changes that come out of our weekly project design meetings.

- *Scope:* How difficult will this area be to address?

- *Accountability:* How responsible does each person feel for personally addressing this area?

This tool is particularly useful when team members give mixed signals regarding their commitment levels to a new project or initiative. In conducting the Audit you might, for example, discover that some team members are hesitant to move forward because they doubt the *feasibility* of the proposed solution. Others may rate the project high on feasibility but low on *accountability* because they feel that the proposed actions fall under the charter of another organizational function.

Identify Commitment Challenges in Advance

It is not uncommon to find that a team starts out being very enthusiastic about tackling a performance problem or taking on a new project, only to have the excitement quickly fade away as team members encounter their first serious roadblocks. For this reason it is useful to invest part of a team discussion in openly discussing potential barriers that could derail team commitment.

One way to do this is to use a modified version of the *Threats Analysis* tool found in your Tool Kit. Let's consider how this tool would be applied to the challenge of getting team commitment for a new project. Further detailed instructions are within the tool.

You would first ask your team to list on this chart the key steps that must be completed to succeed on this project. For each identified roadblock they would then be asked to rate both its probability of occurrence and the impact this roadblock could have on project success. You could then ask team members to identify, within the tool's "Trigger" column, any events that would signal the onset of a given roadblock. The next step would be to reach agreement regarding who, on the team, would be willing to take responsibility for monitoring that situation. Under the columns marked "Preventive Actions" and "Corrective Actions," team members could agree on the steps that they will take to minimize the potential occurrence of a given roadblock, as well as actions they will take to manage that roadblock, should it surface. To ensure commitment we recommend that no more than two team members assume accountability for each identified preventive or corrective action.

Follow Up to Ensure Success

Whenever a team commits to an action plan its members still need to decide how they will follow up on the plan to evaluate its success. During the initial action-planning session, participants are usually excited about the idea of taking concrete actions toward strengthening their team. Over succeeding weeks, however, as work schedules become crowded team members naturally can easily fall behind on the completion of key action steps. That new customer survey is never designed; likewise the industry benchmark study that was promised fails to appear.

If you are the team leader, over the next few weeks meet regularly with your team members to identify project shortfalls and to brainstorm suggestions for addressing these difficulties. If you are a third-party facilitator, use part of the team-building session to engage a discussion on leader-member follow-up.

Follow-up meetings should serve as both a "results check" on what has been accomplished and a "process check" on how team members feel about how they are working together to implement their change plan. A process check might address the following concerns:

- Some team members have begun to feel left out of the problem-solving process

- One individual has made a personal decision to make a significant departure from the team's agreed-upon plan of action—without first informing the other members of the team

- The implementation of the action plan is resulting in changes to business systems, processes, or procedures which are creating problems for other work groups

- Some team members require additional coaching or direction on how to complete certain action steps

- The team is facing severe time constraints, requiring them to either increase their efforts or renegotiate the plan milestones or outcomes

For this next series of recommendations, if you are the team leader, consider these suggestions for managing the follow-up process. If you are a third-party facilitator consider sharing these suggestions with the team leader and members in advance of your team-building session.

Determine the Best Format for the Follow-Up Session Team participants may want to schedule a designed meeting eight to twelve weeks from their commitment point to review the progress that members have made on each action item. This session also provides the meeting facilitator with an opportunity to perform a check-in with participants to see how satisfied they feel about any steps they have put in place to secure follow up on team commitments. A less time-consumptive alternative option is to conduct a brief follow-up session through a phone or videoconference. While this approach is not as robust, it provides a good option when travel and other constraints make it difficult for the team to reconvene on a face-to-face basis. Regardless of the option selected, it is important for participants to commit to the follow-up session and place the date on their electronic calendars before they leave the session. What doesn't get scheduled doesn't get accomplished.

Identify the Outcomes for the Follow-Up Session Prior to conducting the follow-up meeting, reach agreement with team members regarding what they hope to achieve through the meeting. Ideally a follow-up discussion should accomplish five objectives:

- First and foremost, the discussion should allow the team to determine whether its action plan has produced the desired results.

- The discussion should provide the team with an opportunity to gauge their comfort level with any actions they have implemented. For example, do team members feel that everyone is honoring their commitments regarding action plans? Are they pleased with how they have worked together to address team issues?

- In addition, the follow-up session provides members with an opportunity to step back and evaluate what they have learned from their experience about working together as a team.

- The follow-up session should include a review of the lessons captured from this experience that could be applied to future situations. This is represented by the question, "What have we done differently as a team over the past few weeks that works well for us, and that we would like to see carried over to future situations?" These lessons may include how to function more effectively with other work groups, how to track and accurately asses the underlying causes of performance problems, or best practices that can be imported from other work groups or organizations that could be successfully applied to the team.

- Finally, the follow-up process is an opportunity to reinforce the value of making and keeping team commitments. By actually conducting a follow-up session and asking participants whether they have kept their commitments, a strong statement is made about the importance of team accountability.

Use Individual Pre-Meetings to Set the Stage for Discussion Occasionally, it is a smart move to meet individually with the team leader and a few other team members before the follow-up session. During these face-to-face meetings or phone conversations try to get an informal read on the team's mood and identify any issues that could surface within the session. Possible issues that might surface are shown below:

- Team members may be frustrated that their team leader has not been accessible to them during the implementation process, or has not demonstrated his or her support for this process.

- Certain obstacles, such as lack of time or resources or lack of support from adjacent work groups, may have made it difficult for team members to make substantial progress on certain parts of their action plan.

- Team members may voice concerns about the failure of their coworkers to follow up on certain commitments.

- Since the initial team-building session the team might have uncovered certain changes that point to additional, related team-building issues that need to be addressed.

Set a Positive Tone for the Follow-Up Meeting Some team members may be afraid that the follow-up session will take a critical tone, especially if the team has been struggling to make progress on its action plan. To allay these concerns, we recommend setting a positive tone for the meeting.

A good way to begin the follow-up session is to congratulate team members on their progress to date and their willingness to invest additional time on the follow-up discussion. Ask for a volunteer to post the team's action plan on the flipchart or projector. Next, ask for each team member to discuss the progress that they feel that they have made on each of the actions included in the plan. If additional work remains to be done, don't allow the team to shift into blame-casting. Instead, keep their energy focused on what needs to occur now in order to get the plan back on track. If certain team members have fallen behind on their commitments, ask them what "catch-up plan" they have created to bring the project back on track. Also, invite the team to evaluate their progress in terms of the success criteria they established as part of their action plan. All in all, how successful does the team feel it has been in addressing its team-building challenges?

Evaluate the Lessons Learned   During the next phase of the discussion ask team members how they feel about the team-building process that they have just experienced. Find out what they would like to do differently if they were going to engage in additional team-building work over the next few months. One way to conduct this type of evaluation is by using the *Process Check Sheet* tool. This is also the time to invite your team to share with you the lessons they have learned by participating in the improvement experience. The *After Action Reviews* tool provides a great method for encouraging participants to view their follow-up session as a team learning experience.

10

Managing Organizational Boundaries

Changes That Can Lead to Boundary Tensions

It is easy to fool ourselves into believing that teams are self-contained entities that operate independently of their parent organizations. In reality, all teams are permeable. In other words, their very existence depends upon their ability to establish an efficient flow of information, resources, products, and services with other organizational work units. It is not uncommon, however, for teams to feel that they lack the support, assistance, or understanding that they need from other groups. Team members may find their requests for assistance ignored by other departments, hear their work functions criticized in business meetings, or feel that they waste an excessive amount of time trying to resolve petty conflicts between themselves and other work units.

Over the past twenty years we have witnessed the onset of several important changes in our organizational and business environments that make it difficult for teams to work together collaboratively:

Greater Complexity. The increasing complexity of many work functions increases their interdependency. Within your own organization, during the past three years you may have observed continuous changes in your company's budgeting process, performance-appraisal systems, marketing functions, or IT systems. Many organizations undergo such changes on an annual basis, leaving organizational members confused and frustrated about what they view as arbitrary alterations to familiar work methods or processes.

Managing the "White Space." In addition, much of the work that was formerly contained within the walls of functional silos is starting to be performed by cross-functional teams. We see this shift reflected in the creation of temporary team structures in such areas as product development, process improvement, sales, vendor management, and customer engagement. Quite often these temporary teams include representatives from a wide range of work functions. The leaders of these teams are seldom given formal reporting authority over their members. Instead, they are expected to work through difficult issues by relying only on their interpersonal skills and technical abilities. The success of these temporary teams depends on their ability to negotiate outcomes, resource allocations, and work approaches across a wide array of organizational stakeholders.

Orchestrating "Blended" Organizations. Mergers and acquisitions can increase the potential for conflict as work teams and departments are blended together. Overnight, organizational structures are realigned, requiring teams that have never previously worked together to follow the same work processes, procedures, and systems. In addition, reorganizations often lead to the reassignment of team leaders and executives, individuals who may hold very different ideas of how their newly acquired teams are supposed to interface with other work groups. Together these changes can create a great deal of friction between teams. Consider a work team that has been accustomed to engaging in freewheeling brainstorming sessions with other work groups. The team suddenly finds itself acquired by a company whose corporate culture does not encourage the open sharing of information among different work functions. In such a situation, the resulting clash of talent and beliefs can tax the skills of even the most competent team members.

The Standardization of Processes and Systems. In striving for greater efficiency, organizations frequently attempt to redesign fragmented work processes and systems to operate seamlessly and uniformly. This situation is particularly likely to occur in newly blended organizations, which have to make adjustments to antiquated legacy systems. Creating these uniform processes and systems requires compromises between the divergent needs and priorities of different work groups—a situation that can generate a high degree of interteam tension.

Managing Boundary Issues with Customers and Stakeholders

The challenge of managing organizational boundaries also includes doing what it takes to establish strong relationships with internal customers and stakeholders. Visualize a team as a living entity that is connected to its organization via a series of lifelines. Perhaps the most important lifelines are those that link a team to its customers. When a team is unable to respond effectively to its customers' changing needs, its value to its organization is dramatically diminished. From the customer's point of view it doesn't matter whether this problem is due to the deliberate disregard of its requirements, or to such unintentional factors as the absence of an effective customer feedback process. In either case, the results are much the same; the team cuts itself off from critical organizational support.

During periods of rapid change, teams learn that they have to find ways to address the continually shifting requirements of their internal customers. A company's sales function decides to shift away from the sale of individual products to the introduction of product portfolio solutions. In response, the company's training function must figure out how to quickly revise the entire sales training program. Another organization consolidates its back office functions across several subsidiaries. To support this change the finance department finds itself scrambling to build a consolidated financial reporting system. Although these types of events occur all of the time, teams vary widely in their ability to respond effectively to such changes. Some teams are skilled at adapting to these shifts, but others find it difficult to keep pace with their internal customers.

The final component of boundary management is the ability to manage up the organization to secure the support of the team's senior-level managers. Such executive sponsorship is difficult to get and even harder to sustain, but capturing this support is critical to a team's success. If a team fails to secure such support, all of its efforts may go unrecognized as it finds itself cut off from needed direction, information, and guidance. Quite often, a team that lacks senior-level support will find itself groping blindly toward the future, without a clear sense of its organization's changing goals and strategy.

How to Tell When Boundary Management Is a Challenge

Teams that are having difficulty managing organizational boundaries tend to encounter performance issues and greater interteam conflict.

Restricted or Antagonistic Forms of Communication

Stilted and formalized communications between work groups are a telltale sign of interteam conflict and poor boundary management. When team members speak in terms of "us versus them" or stop talking whenever someone from the "enemy camp" approaches their work area, or when teams sever the lines of communication altogether, you can assume the groups are embroiled in conflict. Under these conditions team leaders may caution their members to limit communications with the other team. Some even insist on controlling all communications with the "opposition." Work groups separated by no more than fifty feet of office space begin to limit their communications to e-mails and voice mails. Angry, accusatory e-mails are sent out to other teams accompanied by self-justifying e-mail threads and supporting documentation. Teams waste time debating the "true causes" of their joint problems in an iterative game of revisionist history, as accusations are made and criticisms leveled.

Interteam Conflict Escalation

In some cases the members of different teams "drop rocks" on each other's heads; in other words, they escalate disputes to higher-level managers for resolution. This may involve appealing to management for support against the other parties involved in the conflict, copying senior-level executives on hostile e-mails, or criticizing other work groups in departmental meetings or at senior staff forums. In worst-case scenarios, teams may also make critical comments about other work groups in front of external customers or suppliers ("Sorry we don't have the design changes ready for you, but you know those slackers in our engineering department!").

Conflict escalation can quickly erode a team's time and resources. We are sure that you have observed the following scene play out many times in your own organization. A sales team makes commitments to its customers without first consulting the software design team to confirm the feasibility of those commitments. Members of the software design team respond by remarking that, having been committed to meeting unreasonable delivery schedules, they cannot guarantee that the program's beta version will be bug free. The sales team leader counters by attacking the software team's proposed budget during the annual budget review. The leader of the software team responds by suggesting to senior management that the sales team lacks the technical competence needed to successfully interface with corporate customers. And so it goes, with each new turn of events adding more fuel to the fire. If two teams are locked in an escalating war, you can be sure their conflict has reached dangerous proportions.

Conflicting Goals

Organizations may establish conflicting goals for different departments that result in nasty turf battles. For instance, a sales team wants to sign on the greatest number of customers. At the same time, bonuses for the company's credit department are based on their ability to minimize costs related to late and failed collections. To meet its bonus objectives the sales team becomes overly lenient in their credit screenings of customers. To counter this action, the credit department begins to establish a stringent review process for credit approvals. In the end the organization loses as customers are whipsawed between these conflicting departments.

Likewise, to compete effectively in a niche area such as social networking, an IT team may decide to offer very high salaries to exceptional job candidates. In doing so, the team may encounter resistance from the HR recruiting team, which has adopted a more conservative salary level for those same job candidates as a means of lowering staffing costs. The point is that organizations often set potentially conflicting and demanding goals for different work groups. When this happens one of the real challenges that teams face is searching for common ground in what might first appear to be a highly competitive, win-lose situation.

Ineffective Work Processes

Previously we mentioned that team conflicts sometimes lead to breakdowns in work processes. The opposite can also be true. A poorly designed work process will result in errors, wasted time, deteriorating customer service, and redundant work efforts. In addition, when teams lack effective methods for achieving alignment on important issues, decision-making sessions may degenerate into winner-take-all battles. In a way, work groups are a bit like the proverbial blind men and the elephant—because each group performs a discrete function, the separate teams are rarely aware of the entire process. Hence, when the process breaks down, a team may blame other groups for its performance issues.

Blurred Boundaries

Occasionally teams may operate within highly ambiguous and confusing organizational boundaries, with the result that different teams may need to navigate across overlapping areas of responsibility. In such cases, regardless of the interpersonal skills exhibited by the respective team members and leaders, some degree of interteam conflict is inevitable. A case in point would be an IT team and corporate training team, both of which believe that their functions are responsible for delivering generic software training to their organization's employees. The issue of boundary confusion is magnified when a team's charter and function are significantly changed, requiring it to renegotiate with other groups regarding organizational boundaries.

A clear sign of blurred team boundaries is when two work teams begin to duplicate each other's services, either because they don't trust each other's performance or because they do not want to lose control over important service functions. For example, we know of a marketing team that has repeatedly acquired outside training services as a result of the team's long-standing war with its in-house training department. By circumventing the company's own training department, this team sent a not-so-subtle signal that it did not respect the quality and effectiveness of the department's training services.

The Opportunities Embedded in This Challenge

The results of effective boundary management show up in improved team relationships and decreased employee stress. As a result of improving boundary management, teams frequently find that they can streamline work processes, reduce excessive costs, and improve quality. When work groups are able to jointly work together to reduce boundary confusion, the members of both groups feel more confident to take quick, decisive action and quickly address performance issues. As a result, effective boundary management tends to result in greater member accountability for results.

Teams also create strong opportunities for themselves when they strengthen their relationships with their senior managers and convey their value to upper management. This is important to team survival because senior managers can supply essential coaching and guidance for projects. They often have an in-depth understanding of the inner workings of their organization and can provide a big-picture view that would be otherwise difficult for a team to obtain. Senior sponsors are also in a position to help teams anticipate broader business and organizational changes that can significantly affect their future performance.

Furthermore, they play the vital role of running interference for a team. A sponsor can plead a team's case to the executive staff and make certain that the team's objectives receive a fair hearing. Similarly, they can assist in procuring resources, and ensure that a team's objectives are strategically linked to any other change efforts that may be under way in the organization. In tough times, senior sponsorship can be an especially important survival issue. The backing of senior executives may determine whether teams succeed in the competition for scare resources and talent. Once the budget ax falls or difficult downsizing decisions are made, it is easy to tell which teams have succeeded in winning support from their senior executives.

How to Initiate a Team-Building Session on This Topic

As the team facilitator, your first step is to determine whether this challenge can more accurately be viewed as the need to strengthen boundaries with other work teams, improve performance to internal customers, or gain the support of senior stakeholders. In the following section we will provide separate lead-ins for addressing each of these subissues.

Leading off a Discussion on Boundary Management

If you determine that the team is facing a boundary management issue, work with the team leader to determine which of the following two approaches would be most effective.

Use the Team-Building Meeting as a Team Coaching Session In this scenario the requesting team decides to meet with you "offline" to improve their relationships with selected work groups and to develop guidelines that team members agree to follow when interfacing with those groups. Quite often teams engage in team building based on their "best guess" about how they are viewed by other functions. As with any other improvement strategy, guessing is a poor substitute for hard data. Before they attempt to gather information from other work groups, team members must agree on three points.

First, who will gather the information? As the team facilitator you could complete this step on your own. If you are not a team member the advantage is that you obtain a more balanced perspective on the team's situation. A disadvantage is that team members may feel intimidated by having a third party gather this information. An alternative is to ask pairs of team members to go out and gather information from different organizational stakeholders. This option not only provides team members with firsthand information but also sends the other work group a clear signal that the team is making an effort to resolve joint concerns. To avoid unnecessary overlap it is important that the team be very clear regarding which members will manage each interview.

Second, what data gathering should be considered to be "within scope"? Members may feel that certain issues and concerns are too sensitive for discussion with outsiders. Address this by creating a simple split-sheet list on the flipchart entitled: "For Review" and "Not for Review." Ask team members to use the chart to define boundaries for those issues that they feel should or should not be reviewed with internal customers or senior stakeholders.

Third, what questions will be included in the interview or survey process? The team should establish a written interview protocol or set of survey questions and not vary from them, as making small changes to questions can slant the kinds of responses that they get. Use the *Reframing Technique* found in the Tool Kit to construct a statement that frames the boundary issue in a neutral, nondefensive way. In addition, the *Relationship Audit* provides detailed instructions for gathering information on this topic and the audit form for this purpose.

Armed with this survey and interview data, your team should be in a better position to assess their relative strengths and weakness in managing boundaries across different work areas. As a starting point for discussion, have team members perform a readout on the feedback they have gathered from each identified work group or group leader. The *Relationship Map* is a simple tool the team can use to graphically depict their relationships with other international groups. The *Relationship Map* makes it easier to understand the factors that are driving interteam conflict. After completing the *Relationship Map*, help team members identify those unilateral actions that they can take to improve interteam relationships and those actions that will require the support of those other work groups.

Use the Team-Building Session as a Boundary Management Review The boundary management review is an excellent means of resolving boundary issues with other work groups. The review typically includes the leaders of both teams, as well as representative members, As a general guideline, try to limit the session to no more than sixteen people, as it is difficult to obtain full participation when you extend the session beyond this limit. Be sure to let the other team leader know that as a facilitator you will take steps to ensure that this session does not degenerate into a hostile win-lose confrontation.

Explain to the other team leader that you believe that many of the problems between your teams are not due to deliberate attempts by each team to attack or hinder each other, but by organizational pressures that are affecting both teams. Go on to explain that you hope both teams can use this meeting to (a) agree on which work processes or responsibilities are currently being affected by the actions of both teams, and (b) identify joint solutions to these problems. Finally, assure the other team leader that you and your team members are walking into the meeting with open minds; that is, you're not going to start off the meeting by trying to impose your solutions on them. Ask the other team leader to extend the same courtesy and be willing to consider alternative solutions. You may find it useful to have a third-party facilitator help expedite this discussion. In addition, the *Group Interaction Matrix* in your Tool Kit can help different teams reach agreement on the degree to which boundary-related work processes and responsibilities are interdependent and critical to organizational performance.

Leading off a Discussion on Meeting Customer Expectations

As with boundary management, when working with the issue of improving customer satisfaction it is helpful to first obtain information on how your customers view your performance. Your team can use the *Customer Assessment Matrix* to evaluate the overall importance of different customer relationships to your organization and to determine where you should begin to focus your customer improvement efforts. Once your team has selected a customer for review, the *Customer Requirements Rating Table* and *Customer Satisfaction/Importance Matrix* can be used in advance of your session to gather and graphically display information about how your selected customer views your performance on key accountabilities.

Another option is to invite in the team leader from that customer group to provide real-time feedback during the session. As with the boundary management discussion, if the team chooses to invite the customer to be part of the session, both team leaders should meet together in advance to reach agreement on the following:

- Your facilitation role in the session

- The intended outcomes for the session

- Those issues that are/are not within scope

- Ground rules for managing the feedback process during the meeting ground

A useful step is to invite both team leaders to read Chapters One through Four of this book prior to their meeting.

Leading off a Team-Building Discussion on Securing Stakeholder Support

If the issue is one of lack of stakeholder support, the team-building session will take the form of a team coaching session. As the facilitator you can help the team evaluate the degree to which key senior executives support team initiatives, identify stakeholder support issues, generate ideas and action plans for addressing those issues, and determine how to evaluate the success of those plans. A good lead-in to this discussion is to ask team members to develop a list of situations or events that reflect strengths and weaknesses with key stakeholders. Examples might include situations in which senior sponsors provided or failed to approve needed resources, provided sponsorship of, or blocked key initiatives, made favorable or unfavorable comments about the team in executive meetings, or have taken action to expand or reduce the team's charter.

As the next step, invite team members to identify consistent themes in this list. In other words, in reviewing the list, what does the team appear to be doing to capture stakeholder support? What actions need to be changed? A final step in your lead-in might be to have the team identify those areas in which stakeholder success will be critical to the success of key projects or team accountabilities over the next twelve months. In doing so, use the *Multivoting Technique* to rank these areas by criticality.

The supportive actions identified in the following section include suggestions for more effectively managing stakeholders as well as tools for obtaining feedback from stakeholders. Consider conducting some of these feedback-gathering actions in advance of the team-building session.

How to Take Supportive Actions

In the remainder of this chapter, we provide several suggestions for managing boundary issues with teams, meeting customer expectations, and capturing the support of your senior managers.

Educate Others About Your Team's Organization

Sometimes teams simply don't understand the challenges or pressures that are faced by others in their organization. In addition, they may not have a clear idea of how those other work groups contribute to overall organizational goals and objectives. One way to overcome this problem is to invite leaders from other work groups to sit in on your team discussions, or ask if your team members may visit the work areas of other groups.

An excellent example comes from an international sales and marketing team that decided to educate its company's other work groups on its newly expanded role. To do this, the team produced a type of traveling road show and visited different corporate facilities to share information on its goals, objectives, and work challenges. The team then went further by inviting key executives to travel with team members to selected international sites to meet major corporate customers. These actions greatly improved the team's relationships with its fellow work groups, who developed a greater appreciation of the international team's value to the organization.

The flip side of this action is that teams can also take steps to become better educated about the needs of their internal customers and support teams. The *Listening Post Chart* tool provides a template for identifying and comparing different options for educating your team about different customer groups in your organization.

Improve Underlying Work Processes

Teams frequently experience interteam conflict due to performance problems caused by ineffective work processes. If this is the case for your team, consider creating a cross-functional team to improve those processes and to shift both teams away from faultfinding to joint problem solving. A process improvement team should include representative team members from all teams directly involved in implementing and managing the work process in question. Ask selected members of the process improvement team to meet together in advance of the session, for the purpose of constructing a graphic model, or process flowchart, of how the process is supposed to work.

In advance of the meeting also consider having representatives from the process improvement team conduct joint visits to other organizations that employ similar processes. Their goal should be to identify best practices used by those companies. Taking this step is one way to encourage team members to raise their expectations regarding what can be achieved through process improvement. This action also helps to "depoliticize" the process under review, by helping both teams obtain input from outside organizations regarding potential process changes.

During the session, use the *Traffic Light Technique* to flag process points that are performing as expected (green), somewhat problematic (yellow), or completely broken (red). Spend the remainder of the session reaching agreement on steps that could be taken to identify obvious process flaws, and to identify the underlying causes of those process deficiencies that are not so clearly understood.

It is beyond the scope of this book to outline a systematic approach to process improvement. See Additional Readings for resources on this subject.

Focus on Superordinate Goals

In the pressure of day-to-day firefighting it is very easy to focus exclusively on the conflicting objectives and priorities that place your team in opposition to other work groups. To build strong bonds with other work groups it is useful to occasionally call both teams' attention to those higher-level or superordinate goals on which you are both strongly aligned. Examples might include:

- Strong desire to improve customer service

- Recognition of the need to reduce costs within your organization

- The excitement of entering a new market area

- The imminent threat posed by an outside competitor

Separate Behavior from Intentions

One of the most effective ways to prevent issues from blowing up into interteam conflicts is to separate behavior from intentions. You can easily see another team's behavior and determine whether or not its actions are adversely affecting your team's performance. It is quite a different matter to accurately assess the motives behind this behavior. Many times, what we view as another party's intent to commit harm is nothing more than ignorance on the part of that work group regarding how their behavior is affecting us.

When someone from another work group acts in a way that upsets you, instead of jumping to conclusions, try taking another approach. First, describe the incident in objective terms. For example, you might say something like this: "Tom, I don't know if you remember, but during the project meeting I asked if there was some way your department could free up some graphic support personnel to help us with the proposal that we are working on. What upset me was that your immediate response was to cut me off halfway through my request and tell me, 'No way—we just can't do that.'"

Next, explain how the other party's actions are affecting your team: "As I'm sure you know, we are really under a time crunch and could use some help from your team. I am upset, in part, because you were not willing to offer that support. But what upsets me more is the way you shut me down without even hearing me out."

Communicate to the other party the underlying message in her behavior: "When you did that, it was like you were saying our team is not worth your time and attention."

Finally, check your assumption: "I know that is not what you were trying to communicate, so I thought that it would be good to talk about this with you."

Stay out of the Line of Fire

Occasionally, teams may find themselves sucked into conflicts stemming from personal clashes between higher-level executives. If you feel your team has been caught up in an executive quarrel, try to keep your team members out of the line of fire. In other words, let the other team know that regardless of the personal conflicts taking place at higher levels in your organization, there is no reason why your teams cannot work together effectively. If a member of another team attacks you for something that was allegedly said or done by your manager, offer a response such as: "Before you go on, I need to say that I am not sure exactly what Jerry said or did. I don't really have all the facts. I am not going to waste time bashing my manager, but what I want you to keep in mind is that you and I have always had a good relationship and I want to keep it that way. Now, tell me the whole story, but remember, you're not talking to the enemy here."

Tear Down the Walls

If your team interacts with certain work groups only when conflicts break out, you are setting up a very negative Pavlovian reflex in which team members will come to assume that every meeting between the teams will result in stress and frustration. Unfortunately, situations like this often turn into self-fulfilling prophecies as team members prep for meetings by mentally preparing themselves for battle.

As an alternative, consider proposing taking part in social activities with the other work groups. The occasion could be as simple as ordering pizzas for a joint team luncheon or arranging an informal after-hours get-together. Some companies conduct annual conferences or meetings, which provide perfect opportunities for preconference activities. The only ground rule for these meetings is that there should be no shoptalk; ideally, the purpose is to build relationships and mutual respect. Another twist on this option is for both teams to work together on a community project, such as a walkathon for a worthy charity. We know of one team that invites its internal customers once a year to volunteer to work with them at a soup kitchen for the homeless. There is a lot to be said for having the members of opposing teams walk away from a common experience feeling that they have worked together to make a valuable contribution to their communities.

Construct Service-Level Agreements

Service-level agreements are simple one-page documents recording agreements reached when teams sit down with their internal customers to clearly define the following:

1. The most important services that they provide to those customers

2. How both teams define a level of acceptable service quality

3. The commitments that the internal supplier are willing to undertake to provide an expected level of service quality

4. Any steps that the internal customer could take, such as giving the supplier more lead-time for meeting requests, that would make it easier for the supplier to meet those commitments

The agreement could be as simple as agreeing that "a given document will be updated, fully edited, and available online in a specified shared folder no later than 4 P.M. each Thursday," or as complex as detailing the quality standards that are expected to meet end-user specifications for a new software system.

The use of service-level agreements is based on the assumption that different teams (or different members within each team) might have very different ideas regarding the cost, timing, and quality of deliverables that will be provided to internal customers. Quite often, the simple act of sitting down and negotiating what can or should be delivered to the customer helps both parties find ways to reduce costs, increase efficiency, and prevent misunderstandings.

Several years ago, we were asked to provide team-building assistance to two departments in a public service agency. One department was responsible for acquiring public land bordering on state-regulated bodies of water, and the other was charged with managing the acquired land by performing day-to-day tasks such as clearing away underbrush and constructing dirt levies. For some time, the two departments had been arguing about complaints from the public regarding the agency's failure to properly maintain certain pieces of acquired land.

When we sat down with teams from the two departments to learn more about the steps involved in the purchase of a given piece of land, we quickly located the source of the conflict. Sometimes the maintenance department could not perform upkeep on a piece of property because the acquisitions department had failed to purchase adjacent tracts of land. As the team leader for the maintenance group put it, "How can we be expected to clear a piece of land if it is totally surrounded by private property and we have no way of getting our trucks onto the land?" The maintenance team's proposed solution was that the acquisitions department should consult with them before making land purchases.

For its part, the acquisitions team informed the maintenance team that private land had to be purchased according to a set timetable. Up to this point, the maintenance department's three different subgroups had been providing the acquisitions department with separate reports. Unfortunately, the information wasn't always complete, consistent, or delivered in a timely manner.

During the team-building session we guided these teams in the creation of written service-level agreements. The written agreements specified the type of service each team was requesting from their counterpart, including the minimal performance level that constituted "acceptable service." As part of their service agreements the parties agreed to meet on a routine basis to provide each other with feedback on these specified service areas. Once these guidelines were ironed out, the long-standing problem was eliminated.

Use Your Best Negotiators

Just as every team has certain members who somehow manage to rub other people the wrong way, it usually has at least one or two people who are very skilled in negotiation, consensus building, and conflict resolution. Whenever possible, identify your team's best negotiators and allow them a high level of responsibility for conducting interteam meetings, or representing your team on cross-functional projects. Also give serious thought to identifying those team members who may need to be removed from the front lines, or coached in conflict-management skills. Do you really want a rude and abrupt team member responding to questions from other departments or fielding complaints from outside customers? If not carefully managed, other work groups and customers may form negative opinions about an entire team based on the damage caused by isolated individuals.

Conduct a Diplomatic Exchange

If interteam conflict stems partly from a lack of mutual respect and understanding of respective functions, consider a diplomatic exchange that permits team members to trade places and spend a set period of time in their counterparts' work groups.

Years ago, I (Robert) was employed at an aerospace manufacturing firm. The company sponsored an annual program in which U.S. Air Force officers served one year on-site at our facility to gain a better sense of our business procedures and work challenges. This was excellent program for tearing down walls between our company and our counterparts in government. Not all "diplomatic exchanges" have to be this lengthy. In many companies, customer support representatives are required to make periodic service calls with their company's sales reps, so that both departments gain a better understanding of how their products and services operate in the field. There are a number of options available in this area, limited only by your imagination.

Identify Your Key Stakeholders

When working on complicated, long-term projects, it is likely that there are several senior executives in your organization who could influence the success of those projects. Stakeholders can be divided into three categories. At one end of the spectrum are *supporters* who are willing to take action to move your team's efforts forward. Somewhere in the middle are the *passives* who don't care one way or another about the success of your project. At the other end of the support spectrum are the *blockers* who, because of their particular interests and outcomes, will actively resist your project. The first step in gathering stakeholder support is determining which of these three descriptions best fits the key leaders and work groups within your organization. The *Stakeholder Analysis Chart* is a tool you can use to help your team identify potential stakeholders in these three categories. It provides a graphic form for tracking stakeholders, an illustrated model, and steps your team can take to increase stakeholder support. The *Stakeholder Hats* technique can be used as part of a team session to help anticipate the pros and cons that stakeholders might voice regarding a proposed decision or initiative. The *Team Sponsor Identification Form* can be used to determine which of your stakeholders would make the most effective senior executive sponsor for a particular project. Finally, the *Team Sponsor Evaluation Form* can be completed before meeting with a potential sponsor to help you think through the types of support you are seeking.

Additional Reading

Harrington, H. James. (1991). *Business Process Improvement: The Breakthrough Strategy for Total Quality, Productivity, and Competitiveness.* New York: McGraw-Hill.

11

Working Virtually

The Challenge of Working Virtually

In business, as in society at large, image often lags behind reality. The word "team" tends to make us think of the traditional intact team. This image brings to mind a group of professionals who share the same location and working hours, and who orchestrate their activities thorough face-to-face meetings and personal briefings by the team leader. This image is firmly entrenched in our collective corporate psyche despite the fact that many teams today are essentially virtual teams, whose members may be separated by time and space, and who rely predominately on electronic communication technology rather than face-to-face interactions for collaborating on work. The rapid proliferation of virtual teams is easy to understand when you consider the contributing factors.

The most obvious one is the rise of the global marketplace; this development demands the formation of multinational teams to advance international business objectives, and provide opportunities for new executive talent. Almost every company with a global presence is being challenged to design new virtual team structures that will help link corporate knowledge pools across broad geographic and organizational boundaries.

A second growth factor is the increased corporate emphasis on employing cross-functional teams—to address such issues as corrective action, process improvement, and customer action—as a means of encouraging employee involvement and commitment. The move toward employee involvement is reflected in efforts to include in such teams those who traditionally have been left out of these cross-functional activities, such as second- and third-shift workers and associates at remote field sites. As team membership becomes more diverse, distributed team leaders must search for ways to overcome logistical barriers to project success.

Still another factor behind the spread of virtual teams is the rapid growth of telecommuting to reduce the high cost of brick-and-mortar work units. Corporate cost-containment programs also compel team leaders to identify creative alternatives to the expensive and time-consuming option of flying in team members for face-to-face meetings. Concurrently, we are witnessing rapid advances in technology—for example, the use of embedded videoconferencing capability in smartphones and tablet computers—which make it easier to maintain team connections electronically.

All these factors are forcing many teams to begin operating at least partially within a virtual framework. As a result, we can anticipate that the ability to successfully lead virtual teams will be a critical survival skill for the emerging twenty-first-century manager. As organizations continue to grow globally, in order to create teams that extend beyond organizational boundaries to include consulting partners, suppliers, and customers, and to looking for ways to increase their agility, virtual teams will come to play an even more important role in organizational success.

How to Tell When This Is a Challenge

There are several conditions that can indicate the need for team building within this team development area.

Newly Formed Virtual Teams

All newly formed teams face the common challenges of establishing a common sense of purpose, building trust among members, clarifying member roles, and orchestrating efforts. Unlike traditional teams, however, virtual teams must accomplish these tasks without relying on those face-to-face daily interactions that are so important in building team relationships and a sense of commonality. If you find your team in this situation, it is very important to invest the time upfront to forge strong relationships. Investing time in team building in the early stages of team development can also help you establish team ground rules that can facilitate group efforts in such areas as team communications, decision making, and the setting of member accountabilities.

Team building can also be helpful if you are a traditional, colocated team that has just made the transition into a virtual team structure. When team members are suddenly distributed across time and space they soon discover that the traditional guidelines and assumptions under which they have been operating no longer apply. Some teams never make the necessary adjustments. Their members frantically try to maintain the same types of reporting relationships and communication methods that worked for them in the past—with disastrous results. Members' learn that their e-mails have been countermanded by mixed messages emanating from other team members. Meetings are scheduled, then delayed, then rescheduled, leaving attendance sparse and unpredictable. Project objectives often seem stuck in quagmires, with no solid alignment on goals or outcomes. In the worst-case scenario such virtual teams are experienced as disjointed and dysfunctional, both by their own members and affiliated work groups.

Two useful tools for conducting team building with either new or established teams are the "*Getting Naked*" exercise and the *Needs Checklists for Team Members and Team Leaders*. The *Needs Checklists* are two simple checklists that participants can use for sharing their information and support needs from other team members. The "*Getting Naked*" *Session* exercise helps team members and leaders share the expectations they hold of each other, and flag potential communication issues.

Lack of a Core Identity

Many virtual teams lack the interpersonal "glue" that teams usually depend on to bind members together as a unit. These elements include having dedicated office space that serves as a hub for informal meetings and brief social exchanges, and opportunities for team members to occasionally engage in group social events.

In contrast, for the members of many virtual teams their primary sense of team "identity" is the flow of information and deliverables that flow through the team's electronic communication channels. In some cases the members of a virtual team may never have the chance to meet each other on a face-to-face basis, and may make only sporadic visits to the home office. These frequent, face-to-face contacts have been shown to be essential to building an environment of trust and collaboration (for more information see Cascio, 2000).

Virtual teams may have also difficulty defining who constitutes the actual "team." Should the technical expert who contributes occasional suggestions and problem-solving advice via e-mails or phone conferences be considered a "team member"? How about the work associate who takes it upon herself to provide input to the team's electronic database? This problem is exacerbated for groups such as supplier-management teams or process improvement teams whose members represent different organizations. In this situation, multiple stakeholders may want to have a say into the team's goals, priorities, and decision-making process, leaving members confused about who needs to be contacted or informed regarding key decisions and actions. Without solid answers to these questions, the members of virtual teams will be unable to establish the types of boundaries that support team solidarity, and the team's identity can become diffused and weakened.

Unique Communication Challenges

Due to conflicting work schedules and the need to work from distributed locations, the members of virtual teams have to find ways to provide input on team decisions, tackle problems, and implement team activities with little, if any, face-to-face, real-time communications. Instead, much of the team's communications occur asynchronously through the use of voice mails, e-mails, or inputs to the team's website. For team leaders, this poses the challenge of finding ways to coordinate activities through asynchronous interactions, while building team commitment and minimizing the possibility of communication breakdowns.

The most challenging scenario is presented by those global teams that extend across widely different time zones. In addition, the travel schedules of these team members make it difficult to anticipate the best time and place for team communications. Under these conditions members may walk away from conference calls or videoconferences unsure of what agreements were reached, how decisions are supposed to be translated into team actions, or who is responsible for certain actions.

In addition, when virtual teams rely heavily on electronic tools such as e-mail and phone conferences to maintain communications they miss out on many of the subtle nonverbal contextual clues that they get though face-to-face contact, and which we rely upon to interpret and respond correctly to others' communications. Does a team member's abrupt silence during a phone discussion signal disagreement, anger, frustration, or simply the need to pause and mentally regroup before responding? It is also important to remember that terse and abrupt e-mail messages lacking the subtle context of visual and verbal feedback are more likely to sound aggressive or confrontational. An example is the team member who sends a "flaming," or hostile, e-mail to a coworker without stopping to consider the repercussions.

Similarly, virtual teams can find it challenging to effectively orchestrate their activities. The symptoms of poor coordination are easy to spot:

- Suppliers may receive mixed directions from different team members

- Coworkers waste time by unknowingly duplicating one another's actions

- Tasks fall between the cracks because team members assume someone else is responsible for certain activities

In addition, if effective check-and-control mechanisms are not built into the planning process, virtual team members will be unsure of how far they can stray from group plans without seriously jeopardizing the overall project strategy. The result can be a situation in which the team grinds to a standstill because its members are afraid to take independent action.

Second Class Citizenship

Teams sometimes inadvertently adopt procedures and protocols that create a high degree of mistrust between those members who are colocated at the corporate office and those who are distributed across remote locations. Examples include engaging in the last-minute distributions of documents to those members who are sitting around the table at a team meeting, with a belated apology to those calling in on the phone: "Oh, you didn't get the PowerPoint of our final recommendations? Sorry about that. Here I'll send it now. Oh, you are in your car? Well, could you pull off the road somewhere and jump into your e-mail?" In other cases, professionals who are located at remote sites miss out on all of the rapport-enhancing jokes, stories, and informal discussions that take place in the conference room prior to the start of the "real meeting."

This issue of remote members feeling like second-class citizens is made worse when team leaders are guilty of consistently scheduling team phone or videoconferences at times that are place a high degree of strain on remote-based team members. The authors know of one senior HR leader who consistently held her weekly phone conferences for her global team at noon London time (where she was located). This leader never understood why she did not receive a more enthusiastic response to her suggestions from those team members located in California (who got up before 3 A.M. to be fully awake for, what was for them, a 4 A.M. call)—or from their counterparts in Singapore!

Under these conditions, remote team members may decide that their views and perspectives are not valued. In response they may fail to volunteer their ideas, or fail to speak up and alert the team to emerging problems and issues. In addition, when those sitting around the conference room continually talk over those who are calling in from remote sites, the team leader may falsely assume that everyone is on board with the team's decisions and plans of action. The end result is that work gets bottlenecked, and issues and problems that were supposed to have been resolved in a team meeting are brought up for continued discussion during subsequent discussions. In extreme cases, those team members who feel cut off from the flow of communication may try to compensate for their disadvantages by appealing to friends or colleagues in other work groups to keep them informed of their own team's activities. This scenario can cause a high level of frustration on the part of team members, and a serious erosion in the team's organizational reputation.

Transparency of Team Activities

We use the word "permeability" to describe the transparency of a virtual team's activities to others within the organization. After all, what is said behind closed doors may remain within the team's confidence, but e-mail notes and voice mail messages always somehow manage to find their way to others within (or even outside) the sender's organization. Permeability is a two-edged sword. On the one hand, such transparency puts the virtual team under greater pressure to establish clear guidelines for how, and with whom, information will be shared outside the team. On the other hand, a virtual team that can creatively manage its permeability has greater opportunities for keeping the rest of the organization apprised of its efforts. At the same time it can strengthen its market position within its organization.

As we have said before, many virtual teams are also temporary project, product development, or process improvement teams, whose members report up to different organizational units. A complicating factor here is that the members of these teams have dual loyalties, in that they have a responsibility both to their team and their "real manager." In such cases, the team's decisions, actions, and communications may come under close review by a variety of outside stakeholders.

Diverse Makeup of Teams

As a rule, virtual teams tend to be far more heterogeneous than their intact counterparts. The reasons are readily apparent. Location, time zones, and even organizational identity aren't the primary selection criteria for virtual teams that they are for intact teams. Virtual teams draw from the widest possible pool of talent within the company. In addition, cross-functional virtual teams frequently extend membership to individuals who are external to their organization, such as suppliers, consultants, and customers.

The diversity quotient increases even more when we consider the makeup of international virtual teams, whose members are likely to have different cultural values and languages. For this reason, the challenge of virtual team performance is closely allied with the challenge covered in Chapter Thirteen.

The Opportunities Embedded in This Challenge

For all of the unique challenges they face, virtual teams come with their own set of exceptional opportunities. First, as organizations strive to improve their operating efficiency, agility, and global reach we can expect virtual teams to assume a more important role in organizational life. Given this assumption, those teams that master the ability to perform virtually increase their own value to their organizations, while their team members establish a portfolio of skills that increase both their organizational value and worth in the job market. In addition, a number of research studies have shown that virtual teams that are able to overcome their inherent challenges can obtain several performance advantages. These include the ability to link expertise and talent from across the organization by forming teams that are comprised of the "best of the best" in given technical and business areas. (For more information refer to *Effective Virtual New Product Development Teams: An Integrated Framework* and *Overcoming Barriers to Knowledge Sharing in Virtual Teams* listed in the references.)

Virtual teams can also learn to turn time zone differences to their advantage by maintaining workflow on a 24/7 basis. A common illustration is the team member who completes a project deliverable at the end of her day. She then forwards it electronically to a coworker who is just beginning her day in another corner of the world. This ability to collapse the flow of project deliverables has been shown to play a key role in helping organizations shorten development time and time-to-market cycles. Two research studies noting this phenomenon can be found in this chapter's Additional Reading: *Global Virtual Teams for Value Creation and Project Success: A Case Study* and *Managing Product/Process Knowledge in the Concurrent/Simultaneous Enterprise Environment.*

Still another advantage is when virtual teams engage their members as a widely distributed net of eyes and ears, to help the team obtain input from many parts of their organization. We know of one HR team who effectively used its distributed team members as an advanced listening post to test out proposed ideas related to issues raised on its annual employee engagement survey. Each team member informally reached out to key managers within their own locations to "test the waters" regarding the attractiveness of suggested employee engagement initiatives, before sending these suggestions on to senior management as a formal proposal. Similarly, we know of several other virtual teams who have used their members to effectively track large-scale organizational changes.

How to Initiate a Team-Building Session on This Topic

Initiating Team Building for a Newly Formed Virtual Team

When working with newly formed virtual teams, we recommend that you set aside a day for team building at a location that is most convenient to the team. Solicit team members' questions or concerns in advance of the session. If members have not had an opportunity to meet previously, try to use the evening before the session's start for participants to meet each other in an informal, social context. A typical icebreaker might be to have each participants share with everyone around the table either one interesting or unusual personal experience (climbing a mountain, writing a book, or visiting an exotic local are some of the responses that we have heard in these types of sessions).

Another technique that is sometimes effective is to ask each participant to bring a photo that conveys something important in that individual's life, and then post these on a bulletin board in the area reserved for the social event. Once again, this technique provides members with a wide degree of latitude in determining what they feel comfortable disclosing to each other. Finally, the *Visual Explorer*™ (VE) tool can be very useful during this pre-meeting session, or incorporated into the start-up for the formal session. This exercise can be as simple as asking each participant to pick a VE card that speaks to what they hope the team will be able to accomplish together. Additional suggestions for applying VE can be found in your Tool Kit.

As a starting point for the formal session consider having the team's senior executive sponsor kick off the meeting. Sponsors can briefly discuss the importance of the team's project or focus, provide additional context regarding the need for the project, and provide their own view on factors the team needs to consider to make the project a success. This lead-in also provides an opportunity for the sponsor to make all team members feel valued and acknowledged. The next series of steps will be discussed in How to Take Supportive Actions:

1. Review the team's understanding of its goals, priorities, and outcomes and success measures.

2. Surface any issues that team members might have regarding the feasibility of the team's expected outcomes, or the difficulties posed by potential constraints (such as lack of time, resources, or organizational support).

3. Reach agreement on team members' respective accountabilities.

4. Develop a set of agreed-upon ground rules for managing team communications.

5. Discuss actions the team could take to establish a unifying team identity.

Initiating Team Building for an Established Virtual Team

Once again, we recommend that you select a location for your team-building session that provides members with the best compromise with respect to their different travel requirements. In advance of the meeting inform the team that you will be focusing on actions that the team can take to strengthen its performance, and to establish stronger, more supportive relationships among all members. It would be advisable to provide every participant a copy of this book in advance of the session so that they can explore the challenges that are typically faced by virtual teams, along with suggested actions and tools for improvement. Participants can then use this information to prioritize their concerns and suggestions. In your role of team-building facilitator consolidate this input into a team-building agenda.

There are two ways to facilitate this session. The first is predicated by a scenario in which a team has an urgent need to resolve a critical task issue, such as making a decision on a project or overcoming a performance short-fall. Rather than view the accomplishment of these tasks as falling outside the scope of the team-building session, consider whether the team might be able to use some of the tools found in the Tool Kit to work through this issue during the meeting. This provides the team with a model for tackling such issues. At the session's conclusion participants can discuss whether these tools may be applicable to other team challenges.

The alternative approach is to gather together, in advance of the session, all of the issues voiced by team members and sequence these in a reasonable order of attack. The *Team Alignment Pyramid* in your Tool Kit provides a method for sequencing the review of several commonplace team issues. In creating your agenda be sure that you allow sufficient time (usually ninety minutes to four hours) for the team to explore a given issue and develop an action plan, before moving on to a second issue.

How to Take Supportive Actions

To be successful virtual teams have to leverage available electronic technology while adapting their communication and planning processes to the unique challenges faced by distributed groups. Here are some suggestions for making these adaptations.

Build a Team Identity

Because the members of virtual teams conduct much of their work in isolation with only limited face-to-face interactions, such groups have more difficulty establishing a common team identity. Because of this we say that it is important for virtual teams to "build a human face." Following are a few creative steps you can take to compensate for the lack of rapport and support that are readily available to intact teams:

- If you are leading a temporary, cross-functional team, have members create a name for their group, and ask them to consistently use this name in every team communication and document. Some teams have also found it helpful to create a team symbol or logo that represents their goals and purpose, and display it on their documents.

- If team members have never met, an initial team-building session is essential for helping them build rapport and establish strong work relationships. In addition, some teams have found it helpful to dedicate a separate web page on their team website for social networking. During the team-building event take a group photo that can be posted on this web page. This social page may also include a world map with members' faces posted at different points to show their locations. This page could also include pictures of members on vacation, and recent additions to families (children and pets). Another option is to invite team members to submit two- to three-minute videos of themselves (these can easily be recorded on their smartphones and uploaded to the team's social page). Each recording provides individuals a way to personally introduce themselves to their coworkers. The team's social site can also include a team blog site where members have the chance to share their experiences regarding team or organizational events.

- The *Organizational Social Networking* tool in your Tool Kit provides the names of several commercially available social networking systems. These systems offer teams a means for building social networking sites, within their corporate firewalls, to support faster and more fluid communications among team members and with others in their organization.

- Invite team members to submit ideas for new team projects, or success stories that could serve as interesting features in your company's corporate (hard copy or electronic) newsletter. Consider whether it would be helpful for them to include photos and short bios with these articles. These actions can help team members form personal connections with each other, and provide a way of familiarizing other work groups with those team members who work in remote locations.

- Utilize every opportunity for communication and interaction. For example, periodically call or text members to check in with them regarding potential problems or concerns. If possible, fold meetings with team members into your travel plans when you are planning visits to other company locations. On those occasions when you are able to meet together as a group, include some social activity, such as a team dinner or breakfast. Finally, be alert for team members who seem to be withdrawing from team communications or who appear increasingly demotivated.

Establish Criteria for Team Membership

A virtual team has little chance of success if its members lack the skills needed to perform effectively in a distributed work environment. Some of these skills, such as the ability to self-manage one's performance and a high comfort level in communicating through electronic technology, are obvious prerequisites, with others less so. The *Selection Matrix for Virtual Team Members* can help you evaluate the suitability of candidates for virtual teams.

Another membership challenge is posed by virtual teams that are also cross-functional, whose members come from a variety of organizational functions and business units. In such cases, it is sometimes difficult to determine who is actually a designated member of the team. To remedy this situation we suggest that virtual, cross-functional teams clearly distinguish between those individuals who are considered to be part of their *core team*, and those who are *supplemental* or *support team members*. Core team members are those who are committed to the team throughout its lifecycle, and who have a voice in team decision making. In contrast, supplemental members, such as technical and knowledge experts, flow in and out of the team through as required. Additional differences between core and supplemental team members are:

Core Team Members	Supplemental Team Members
• Invest 20 to 50 percent of their time on the team's activities	• Invest much less time on the team's activities
• Are authorized to develop and change the project plan and deliverables	• Have no decision-making authority
• Are committed to the project throughout its lifecycle	• Are brought into the project from time to time to provide technical assistance or guidance
• Attend most or all team meetings	• Attend only those meetings, e-mail discussions, and so on, for which they are needed to provide technical assistance
• Have final accountability for project results	• Perform a support role in the team, with little or no accountability for team results

Clarify Team Goals, Outcomes, and Success Measures

Compared with colocated teams, the members of virtual teams are more autonomous. They perform their activities at different times and locations, and typically with little managerial supervision. As a result, virtual teams often find that the smooth orchestration of team activities can be a significant challenge. With less ability to comonitor team activities, members depend more on having a shared understanding of the team's objectives. This contention is supported by a study of 54 effective virtual teams by Malhotra and Majchrzak (2004), which found that having a shared understanding of the team's goals and priorities was essential to a virtual team's success.

To address this challenge we recommend that virtual teams spend part of their team-building kick-off session reaching agreement on goals, outcomes, and success measures, and obtaining clarity on members' respective roles and accountabilities. A good starting point for this discussion is to make use of the *Team Alignment Pyramid* found in your Tool Kit. In addition, we recommend that temporary project teams complete the *Human Due Diligence Audit* to obtain alignment on goals, perceived constraints, and expectations. This technique is particularly useful for teams that are comprised of two or more work groups, such as joint venture teams. In addition, project teams may find it helpful to complete the *Customer Satisfaction/Importance Matrix* to determine which team deliverables are most important to internal or external customers, and how those customers view the team's performance against those deliverables.

Additional advantage can be obtained by having participants spend part of the kick-off session preparing and reviewing a *Team Scoping Document*—a two- to four-page summary that explains what the team should consider to be in, or out of, scope for its charter. Details for how to create and review this document can be found in your Tool Kit.

Share the Pain

One way to prevent team members who are operating from remote locations from feeling like second-class citizens is to "share the pain" involved in having to overcome the barriers of time and distance. Steps that can be taken include holding team meetings at different times so that each member has at least a few meetings conducted at a time that is convenient to his or her schedule. In addition, as a means of encouraging all team members to feel equally accountable for the team's success, consider having team members rotate responsibility for hosting phone or videoconferences.

Finally, try to vary the locations for your face-to-face meeting. This spreads the travel burden among all participants. Taking this action also gives remotely based members opportunities to host the session, and introduces the team to key managers who are located at their sites. When possible, plan meeting start times to minimize jet lag for those who will be traveling great distances.

Clarify Expectations with Members' Managers

If you are leading a cross-functional virtual team whose members report to different organizational managers, you face a unique set of challenges. Because a cross-functional team places more responsibility on team members to self-manage their activities, it is important to get the full support of your members' managers.

To help team members avoid being caught in a tug-of-war regarding competing time commitments, clarify the estimated time commitments in advance. At the same time, discuss how you intend to keep managers posted on any changes to these time commitments. In addition, before launching the project try to get these managers to commit to allow their direct reports to attend all planned face-to-face meetings. At the same time, clearly communicate whether travel costs for these meetings will come from a central pool or will need to come from the manager's function.

Address Potential Communication Issues

Do not wait until your team is experiencing severe communication breakdowns to explore potential obstacles to team success. As soon as possible, encourage your team members to provide input on potential communication issues. Ask them:

- What communication avenues would work best for you?

- What unique technology or equipment restrictions do each of you face? (Example: Some telecommuting members may not have access to portable printers or faxes, and others may not have required project software.)

- When could you make yourself available during the next few weeks for regularly scheduled e-mail or phone discussions?

Ask team members to take on the role of team troubleshooter to help you identify potential communication obstacles and suggestions for addressing these obstacles. As a starting point, the *Telecommuting Check Sheet* can help you anticipate some of the unique issues that accompany telecommuting arrangements. The *Alternative Communication Options* tool in your Tool Kit can help your team compare the applicability of different communication options.

Establish Guidelines for Managing Communication

Invest a few minutes of your team-building session brainstorming a list of guidelines for strengthening team communications. Here are a few suggestions.

When faxing information, take the time to send out originals instead of photocopies, and keep the type size large enough for readability. This is especially important when conveying financial or other numerical data, since blurry faxes can lead to transposition errors. Also, be sure to date and number all document revisions (reports, project schedules, and the like) transmitted back and forth electronically for repeated review to ensure that team members reference only the most recent editions.

When communicating by phone, check to confirm mutual understanding. If an extended silence occurs during a phone discussion, explain that you do not know how to interpret the team's reactions and you need their feedback. Because you cannot see who enters and leaves a room during a phone conference, ask members to be courteous enough to announce when they are joining or exiting a phone conference. As a ground rule, ask members to identify any nonparticipants who may (unknown to the rest of the team) be sitting in on the call at remote locations.

When sending out a communication, always spell out the type of responses that you are looking for from others. Never assume that the recipients of your messages automatically know what to do with the information you are sending them. Is your e-mail simply meant to inform or are you looking for an answer to a specific question? When you announce that you will be discussing a topic at your next meeting, will you simply be performing a "data dump" of information on the topic, are you looking for input before making the final decision, or will you be asking the team to make the final decision? Make your intentions known.

Whenever possible, consolidate communications. Between the two of us we typically receive over a hundred e-mail messages a day. Many team members contribute to this problem because they are guilty of engaging in a kind of "stream of consciousness" e-mailing. That is, they send off a brief e-mail message, only to follow up over the next few minutes with a second and third e-mail, as additional ideas or queries come to mind. For the e-mail receiver this scenario can be extremely frustrating. We have all experienced situations in which we have responded to e-mail messages, only to find our comments instantly preempted by the sender's next message. To eliminate this problem, ask team members to think through their comments and send out e-mail or voice mail messages as consolidated "chunks" rather than as an iterative stream of short questions or comments on the same topic. In addition, ask team members to refrain from distributing e-mails to everyone in the company.

Highlight the major points in your e-mails. Use color and bold fonts to highlight key information in your message, and to help recipients immediately identify the main points in your e-mails. Another option is to send out an e-mail that provides very brief summary explanation, and then include additional details as a series of attachments.

During phone or videoconferences there are times when it is advisable to ask participants to hold back on discussions during the conference and continue their conversations with you offline, immediately after the call is concluded. Examples would include the following situations:

- A team member is becoming very upset during the call and could probably benefit from a one-on-one "venting session"

- A team member has started to mention a sensitive topic that should not be discussed with the entire team

- Someone wants to provide an information briefing on a project or work area that is only of interest to one other person on the call

- Two team members are locked in a heated conflict on a topic which they could more easily resolve on their own

Make Optimal Use of Communication Avenues

Team leaders who are accustomed to directing colocated teams have a difficult time weaning themselves from face-to-face team meetings. We often find that such leaders respond to every new project roadblock or organizational change by scheduling another meeting. As a set of general guidelines we recommend that you substitute the use of e-mails, faxes, or individual phone contacts for meetings whenever you are attempting to:

- Assess the status of tasks performed by individual team members

- Pass along team documents, research, or status reports for input from the team

- Obtain initial input project deliverables

- Assign tasks to individual team members

- Clarify technical issues that pertain only to isolated team members

- Provide background data to accelerate your team's thinking about project obstacles or problems

Managing the preceding types of tasks with alternative forms of communication enables you to utilize your scarce face-to-face meeting time for the following:

- Develop your team's game plan for completing key objectives

- Resolve critical team management issues, obstacles, and problems

- Recalibrate and make midcourse corrections to team plans

- Assess the impact of any large-scale changes that have occurred since your last team meeting

Establish Ground Rules on Member Accountability

Work with all participants to establish useful ground rules for meeting team commitments. These ground rules might be subsumed into several categories. For example, one area for discussion might be the steps that team members are willing to take to keep project activities on track when they are widely dispersed. Supportive ground rules may include:

- Team members are expected to attend all meetings and to have all required deliverables (spreadsheets, reports, and so on) prepared in advance of the meeting. Team members will try to arrange travel schedules to virtually attend meetings. If, for some reason, a member cannot attend a meeting, they have the responsibility of alerting the team leader twenty four hours in advance and convey to the team leader all deliverables required for the meeting.

- It is important to give team members ample time to review detailed financial documents or other reports for review in advance of team meetings. Accordingly, individuals will electronically distribute such information to all team members (or load it into the team's shared folder) no less than twenty four hours before the meeting start date.

- No team member will change milestone dates for key projects without first consulting the team leader.

- Team members will respond to each other's e-mails within twenty four hours of receipt.

- Team members will flag as "critical" only those e-mails pertaining to urgent requests, problems, or emergency situations.

- When providing others with documentation, team members will flag any information that is incomplete, out of date ("The information that I am sending you will be supplemented by an updated report that should be out next Friday") or not yet confirmed.

- No surprises: if members have not alerted the team leader to delays or obstacles, it will be assumed that members are still on target to meet all project goals deliverables.

- Team members agree to take certain steps to inform one another of outside changes that could affect the operation of their team.

- The team will identify those team members who will be responsible for keeping executive stakeholders updated on the team's activities.

- No "hit-and-runs." A hit-and-run is an e-mail message sent at the last minute, that informs the project leader that a certain team activity will not be completed as promised. People who "hit and run" assume they have fulfilled their team commitments once they have sent an e-mail message and dropped their problem into someone else's lap.

- Track team decisions and actions on project planning sheets or through a decision log.

- Establish a clear protocol for how you will update documents that are located on the team's shared workspace to ensure that all team members are working from the latest documents. When submitting and revising documents, each document revision should be numbered in sequence with the date of posting, to ensure that members can follow revisions.

Another step a team can take to encourage member accountability is to identify those activities and project milestone that are most prone to slippage, and will therefore require the closest attention. These project activities tend to:

- Be located along the "critical path" of major project plans, and delays or errors could hamper the completion of all downstream activities

- Require precise coordination from all team members and are most vulnerable to miscommunications

- Require inputs in the form of approvals, software, data, and so forth from other departments, customers, or suppliers

- Are highly variable and susceptible to any large-scale changes that could ripple through your organization

To illustrate this last point, assume that your IT department is frantically trying to keep pace with an extensive project backlog while your project requires the creation of a customized software program. In this case, a potential point of vulnerability is the scheduling delay you might encounter if the IT group decides to downgrade your project's importance on its priority list.

Once you have identified points of vulnerability, your team should discuss strategies for addressing potential obstacles or delays. It is particularly important for a virtual team to determine the degree of initiative and personal accountability that each team member can take to individually resolve problems or revise schedules, without obtaining prior approval by the team or team leader.

Use Electronic Tools to Maximize Team Efficiency

There are a few simple steps that teams can take to increase the efficiency of their use of electronic tools:

- Create a group mail list in your company's e-mail system so you can distribute a single e-mail message quickly to all team members.

- Become acquainted with the relevant features of your company's voice mail system, such as the ability to distribute messages to multiple addresses.

- Many e-mail systems feature an electronic prompt that automatically notifies team members of key dates, for example, meetings and executive briefings.

- Make use of your company's electronic calendar system. Team members should have their calendars on this system to expedite the scheduling of meetings and events.

- Many videoconference centers now offer electronic whiteboards that display written information at both the sending and the receiving video sites.

Coordinating milestones and activities is extremely important when you are working on projects that involve high cost, a wide range of resources, and a time period of several weeks or months. There are many good software tools on the market to support project coordination. An example is Microsoft® Project, which enables team members to link related tasks so that they can understand how delays at one point of activity will affect the entire project. It also allows you to assign team members and resource support people to projects. Furthermore, by loading the hourly pay rate of team members into the project spreadsheet, you will be able to determine the total staffing cost for a given project. You can also quickly determine when a given staff member is approaching 100 percent allocation to a given project. In addition, the software enables your team to link the activities of several different projects, allowing you to identify such problems as scheduling conflicts when the same individual has been assigned to two or more activities for a single time period.

The *Asynchronous Work Spaces* tool provides a great summary of some of several other electronic communication tools that are particularly useful to virtual teams, such as group workspaces, online survey tools, and video conference systems.

Develop Electronic Facilitation Skills

When conducting phone conferences take steps to facilitate discussions. Before distributing documents prior to a meeting confirm that everyone has the software needed to open those documents, or to import them into a readable format.

If you are going to be conducting a webinar or videoconference it is a good idea to ask one remotely located team member to volunteer to call in several minutes early to confirm that your systems are working properly. Nothing is more frustrating for participants than experiencing extended "dead time" during the first minutes of a conference while the facilitator is attempting to resolve technical issues.

At the start of the meeting take roll call to identify missing team members who may require individual follow-up calls. Facilitation basics include keeping track of time, helping participants maintain their focus during discussions, and acting as a monitor to prevent verbal collisions when team members try to talk at the same time.

Some participants may be overly assertive and verbose during phone conferences. Because they lack the visual feedback that normally serves as a "stop sign" during face-to-face meetings, you must be able to rein them in. At the same time, you will need to draw out those quieter team members who may be reluctant to speak up. Keep in mind that in a phone conference others may not be able to see the document that you are referencing, and that you may be referencing several documents during the discussion. Avoid confusion by identifying each document by its correct title, and by referring to page numbers as needed.

If you are leading a cross-functional team, its members probably represent different technical groups, functions, and even organizations. If this is the case, avoid or clearly define all specialized jargon and acronyms. If your team makes extensive use of such terms, consider creating and maintaining a jargon dictionary for team review.

When you are on a team phone call and place yourself on speakerphone, be sensitive to the fact that all noise in your work area (your typing on a keyboard, shuffling of papers, conversations next to your desk) can be picked up by others. In such instances, when you are not talking, place your phone on mute.

If you are a team leader directing a phone conference take a roll call at the beginning of each meeting to confirm who is at the other end. Have a check sheet in front of you to check off who is contributing and who has not yet had a chance to speak. Later call on those silent individuals by name.

When conducting videoconferences in which members will be calling in from a wide range of time zones keep in mind that you will encounter a time lag between video and audio responses. When you say something provide an additional few seconds to hear others' responses before continuing to speak.

When conducting face-to-face meetings:

- Check national and religious holidays, which vary widely by country and culture, to prevent scheduling a meeting on a date that would present a conflict for certain team members.

- Confirm the start and stop time for participants who will be flying in. Let them know if the closing time assumes a "hard stop," that will require members to schedule travel arrangements to accompany it. At the very start of the meeting reconfirm that all team members will be able to stay until the close of the meeting.

- To accommodate those team members for whom English is a second language, distribute all materials, including PowerPoint slides, in advance of the meeting.

Extend Your Reach Through Social Networking

Teams are coming to realize they can dramatically improve their collective performance by leveraging the knowledge, contacts, and expertise that are available through social networks. Facebook and LinkedIn provide two of the most common examples of open social network systems that have gained great followings in the past few years. We use our Facebook pages to keep our customers and associates updated not only on our products and services but also to build relationships and provide thought leadership through our blogs.

LinkedIn provides an excellent means for extending your circle of contacts, and for keeping those contacts updated on your professional activities. Moreover, the many discussion groups that are nestled within LinkedIn allow your team members to take part in communities of learning that are based on specialized areas of interest. For example, the two of us follow, and occasionally contribute, to discussion threads within several subgroups, including those posted by our affiliated universities, as well as international leadership development and organizational development forums. Participation in these groups helps us track emerging trends in our field. In addition, posting questions is one of the fastest ways of gaining diverse perspectives on almost any topic of interest.

Many teams have found that such open social networks also provide an excellent means of staying connecting with their customers. Such networks have also been successfully used in lead generation for potential customers who might be interested in the team's products or services. Other organizations have found that they can use social networks to accelerate learning and knowledge creation. As an illustration, an *Organization Science* article entitled "Social Networks, Learning and Flexibility: Sourcing Scientific Knowledge in New Biotechnology Firms" discussed how some biotech firms have used social networks, particularly those extending to university scientists, to expand their knowledge bases and keep abreast of developments in their field.

Many organizations are attempting to balance the desire for intra-organizational collaboration with concerns about privacy and the protection of intellectual property. The result is the use of enterprise or organizational social networking systems that operate within the organization's IT firewall. These systems allow individuals to build social networks based on areas of common interest, such as new product development or technical educations, and to reach out across the organization when they need to solicit advice on work-related challenges.

A recent *Harvard Business Review* article entitled "What's Your Social Network Strategy?" noted the impact that Cisco's internal organizational social network platform has had in collaborative decision making, and as a communication vehicle for keeping employees posted on each other's project activities as well as organizational news. The same article discusses the impact that Clorox's organizational social network, *Clorox Connects,* has had in enabling its employees to brainstorm with suppliers and customers on new research and development efforts. A recent *Economic Times* article entitled "How India Inc Uses Social Networking for Business" cites the case of CSC India, which employs business social networking systems for the large majority of its 91,000 employees. In doing so, CSC was able to reduce their response time to proposals from 45 to 30 days, by supporting faster and more agile collaboration among its employees. The trend in the corporate adoption of social networking appears to be growing. In his August 2011 correspondence with us, Matthew Cain, research vice president at Gartner, Inc., suggests that "within the next few years, social networking services will replace e-mail as the primary vehicle for interpersonal communications for some business users."

Another advantage in the use of such systems is the preservation of organizational knowledge and expertise, in the form of information on the organization's customers, systems, procedures, and products. This occurs, in part, because valuable knowledge lies hidden away in some departmental silo, where it remains completely unknown to the rest of the organization. An additional problem is when knowledge walks out the door whenever employees leave the organization. For virtual teams these issues are exacerbated by the fact that, being distributed across time and space, members lack access to the even informal sharing that constitutes the unwritten "tribal knowledge" gathered by most teams.

Over the last few years teams have attempted to overcome these problems by migrating key documents from PCs, laptops, and tablets to shared databases that can be accessed by all team members. Other formal "knowledge capture" systems, such as customer relationship management (CRM) systems represent another attempt to capture this information. The problem is that all such systems rely on the willingness of members to contribute content to these systems and ensure that this content is continually upgraded and complete.

Organizational social networking systems take the preservation and distribution of organizational knowledge a step further. They typically include search features that enable associates to search for specific information in the system according to "tags" or content titles, or through key words. These features enable team members to troll through a broad base of organizational knowledge without knowing exactly where such knowledge resides.

In addition, the search often uncovers knowledge experts who can provide advice on the topic in question.

The broader implications of social networks is that they are causing us to extend our view of "teams" to include those people who participate in communities of interest and learning, based on specific topics of interest. The products of these communities, be it the content found in Wikipedia or conversation threads related to an associate's question regarding an emerging market, become increasingly robust and valuable as participants continue to provide their collective input. The *Organizational Social Networking* tool in your Tool Kit provides additional information on the possible applications of enterprise social networking, as well as a summary of several social networking services that can be obtained by organizations.

Make Use of Bonding Experiences

No, we are not talking about group counseling sessions or campfire rituals. Bonding experiences are any set of team tasks that enable team members who typically would not be able to work together to spend face time together working toward a common goal or learning activity. These experiences need not involve the entire team but could instead involve a few selected members of the team.

One such bonding experience is a joint learning activity. One of our corporate clients provided their managers with a leadership development program that was conducted at different global locations throughout the year. Savvy managers would sometimes request that two of their team members be sent to the same workshop so that these individuals had a valuable opportunity to spend both learning and social time with each other.

Another bonding experience might involve sending selected members off together to conduct best practice reviews. We know of one company who used this approach to have different team members work together to arrive at joint comparative reviews of different vendors for an enterprise-wide project involving the outsourcing of many of the company's HR business processes. Still another example involves having selected team members travel together to visit customers or suppliers, or to conduct best practice site visits to other companies.

With a little forethought such activities can be used to help team members bridge cultural differences and gain a stronger appreciation of each other.

Additional Reading

Badrinarayanan, V., and Arnett, D. B. (2008). Effective virtual new product development teams: An integrated framework. *Journal of Business and Industrial Marketing, 23,* 424–428.

Cascio, W. F. (2000). Managing a virtual workplace. *The Academy of Management Executive, 14,* 81–90.

Lee-Kelly, L., and Sankey, T. (2008). Global virtual teams for value creation and project success: A case study. *Journal of Project Management, 26,* 51–62.

Liebeskind, J. P., Oliver, A. L, Zucker, L. G., and Brewer, M. B. (1996). Social networks, learning, and flexibility: Sourcing scientific knowledge in new biotechnology firms. *Organization Science, 7,* 428–443.

Malhotra, A., and Majchrzak, A. (2004). Enabling knowledge creation in far-flung teams: Best practices for IT support and knowledge sharing. *Journal of Knowledge Management, 8,* 750–88.

Rosen, B., Furst S., and Blackburn, R. (2007). Overcoming barriers to knowledge sharing in virtual teams. *Organizational Dynamics, 36,* 259–273.

Singh, Shelly. (2011). How India Inc uses social networking for business. Retrieved August 2, 2011 from http://economictimes.indiatimes.com/quickiearticle show/9451727.cms.

Sorli, M., Stokic, D., Gorostiza, A., and Campos, A. (2006). Managing product/process knowledge in the concurrent/simultaneous enterprise environment. *Robotics and Computer-Integrated Manufacturing, 22,* 399–408.

Wilson, H. James, Guian, P. J., Parise, Salvatore, and Weinberg, Bruce D. (2011). What's your social network strategy? *Harvard Business Review* (July-August, 2011), 23–25.

12

Overcoming Setbacks

The Challenge of Team Setbacks

Eventually, every team runs into an obstacle it cannot overcome. These road-blocks take a variety of forms, ranging from projects that are dismal failures, to changes that the team can't quite manage, to sharp, unanticipated declines in work performance. The great paradox is that teams with the greatest drive for success are also the most likely to encounter setbacks. After all, the laws of probability suggest that the more we attempt, the more opportunities we have to fail. The only way we can ever truly insulate ourselves against failure is to take no action at all, thereby removing ourselves completely from the game of life.

Although every team encounters setbacks, teams (like individuals) respond very differently to difficulties and disappointments. When faced with rever-sals, some team leaders can rally their troops, quickly reassess the situation, and regroup. With renewed effort these teams overcome and learn from dam-aging setbacks and then move forward, often emerging from their trials even stronger than they were before. Other teams respond to setbacks by lowering their performance expectations. They pull their collective energy inward, redirecting their efforts away from constructive activities toward blaming one another or succumbing to self-recrimination. These ineffective behaviors may further weaken a team, making it less prepared to deal successfully with subsequent roadblocks. Without action, such a chain of events may turn into a self-fulfilling prophecy, with the team drawn down into a debilitating whirlpool of failure.

How to Tell When This Is a Challenge

A team that is struggling with disappointments or setbacks often provides clues to its state of mind. Ask yourself if you have observed any of the following behaviors exhibited by your own team.

Risk Avoidance

The first sign to look for is when team members appear discouraged and defeated. They seem to lack confidence in their ability to tackle tough challenges, and are far more reluctant to set tough performance goals for themselves. After falling off the high wire, team members prefer to stay at ground level and do everything they can to avoid the possibility of failure. Such teams tend to shy away from any goal that is not 100 percent attainable and totally risk-free.

Some time ago the authors provided team-building assistance to a sales team that had the responsibility of securing large-dollar contracts with their corporate clients. The team's leader had called us in because he was frustrated with the fact that during the past eighteen months he had seen a significant decrease in the number of contracts secured by the team. During our team assessment interview process, team members shared with us the underlying problem. Each time they submitted a proposal and did not get it they were soundly berated by their manager for not only failing to gain a potential contract, but also for driving up expenses through the expensive and time-intensive bid and proposal process. How did team members respond to these consequences? They decided that it was better to take the heat for going after fewer contracts than to lose on the proposals on which they had bid. In other words, they set their sights lower with the intent of aiming only at those targets they were sure to hit. As one member summed it up, "We learned that getting three out of four was a lot better than getting six out of ten."

Continually battered teams tend to do everything they can to avoid the possibility of future failure. This may include "sandbagging"—the process of padding project plans with extensive time and resource buffers. Sandbagging not only costs an organization excessive project delays and increased costs, but it also makes it more difficult to establish an accurate baseline for future project planning. Another self-protective action is hiding business problems or work process deficiencies from other team members or team leaders, based on the fear that the team member who exposes these issues will be held accountable for correcting them. In the same way, members will be less likely to point out potential business opportunities, under the belief that such opportunities translate into simply "more chances to fail." When presented with new projects they may also develop the habit of immediately listing a variety of potential project risks or barriers, in the hope of eliminating or postponing these new challenges. These are just some of the tactics that teams may use to set the performance bar low enough to guarantee success.

Once a team becomes preoccupied with avoiding failure, it inevitably loses its ingenuity and flexibility and concentrates more on protecting itself from risks than on successfully performing its functions. As more signatures are required to approve decisions and more meetings are called to distribute accountability across a larger group of people, the team begins to grind to a standstill and underperformance becomes a certainty.

Focusing on Blame Instead of Solutions

When teams experience setbacks or disappointment they may try to shift the responsibility for these situations onto others. If this becomes a team's habitual response to setbacks, over time more attention will be placed on assigning blame, leaving less energy available for overcoming reversals and moving forward.

When directed inward toward other team members this kind of behavior can quickly divide a team. Eventually this type of blame-casting can result in communication breakdowns that compromise the team's ability to perform effectively. When interacting with other work groups, members may begin to distance themselves from their team. In backroom gossip sessions and coffee-break chats, individuals who do not want to be associated with the team's setback will describe themselves to others as totally separated from "those losers." The result is not only a demoralized team, but also a loss of the team's credibility with other work groups and organizational leaders.

One final concern is that when a team is focused on avoiding failure rather than on seeking solutions, its members miss valuable opportunities to use reversals as learning opportunities. As a result they increase their vulnerability to future problems. Teams that direct their blame-casting to other work groups will inevitably increase the conflict level with those groups, and cut themselves off from needed support. If these trends continue, a team can eventually lose the support of its senior stakeholders.

Preoccupation on the Past

Some teams fall prey to rearview-mirror vision, or preoccupation with the past. They waste a lot of time on "if only" discussions rather than dealing with the realities of the present. For example, "If only we had obtained better marketing research *before* we brought out the new product, none of this would have happened." When a team's energy is absorbed in recriminations about past events, less energy is available to meet emerging challenges. This problem also reveals itself when it is evident that a team is repeating past mistakes. If late project time lines, inaccurate sales or budget forecasts, or poorly conceived product designs continue to surface as repetitive issues then it is likely that a team has not been able to learn from the past.

When teams appear to have difficulty learning from setbacks it is usually because of one of two reasons. The first reason is fear of failure. As mentioned, if team members are terrified of the consequences of failure than they will tend to hide, minimize, deny, or rationalize setbacks. What they will not do is bring these performance failures out for open discussion in the hope of uncovering contributing factors and learning from these problems.

As a result, underlying causes for setbacks, such as resource misallocations or broken work processes, are never identified or corrected.

The second factor is time urgency. Team members may feel that they are under such time pressure that they have no time to stop, carefully evaluate, and learn from performance setbacks when they occur. Instead, they are immediately thrown into the next project. Once again, the team rolls on but the underlying performance issues are ignored.

A Short-Term Perspective

Some teams have difficulty moving past setbacks because they find it difficult to stay focused on the big picture. Instead, they develop a myopic, short-term view of their efforts. In this situation every obstacle or detour is blown out of proportion and assumes the team's full attention. The only way out of this trap is to take steps to maintain a long-term perspective.

Anyone who has ever undertaken an intensive training program, such as training for a marathon, knows what we are talking about. If you begin a running program you are likely to find that your performance level will fluctuate each day. Without a clear reference to your long-term progress, when you hit a bad workout day, it is easy to convince yourself that you aren't making any progress. Serious runners (or weight lifters, or golfers, for that matter) keep themselves motivated over the long term by maintaining a written record of their performance. That way, they are not thrown by day-to-day variations because they can clearly see that over a period of weeks their performance level is steadily moving up.

In the same way, teams require clear, well-defined measures for assessing success and a reliable scorecard for tracking their efforts against these measures over a long period of time. With these elements in place, team members will be less likely to be thrown by temporary setbacks or performance shortfalls.

The Opportunities Embedded in This Challenge

Today many organizations are undergoing periods of rapid and unpredictable change that take the form of disruptive business models, tough, new competitors, and an increasingly uncertain economy. Organizational teams soon discover that these changes are translated into tougher performance targets, severe resource constraints, and conflicting demands and priorities from senior leaders. Facing such conditions, teams are more likely to encounter repeated setbacks. The only question is their ability to adapt and respond to these situations.

When teams tackle this issue head-on they strengthen their resiliency as a work unit. Over the past twenty years a lot of applied psychological research, as evidenced by such books as *Learned Helplessness: A Theory for the Age of Personal Control* (1995), has centered on the subject of learned helplessness; a condition in which individuals come to assume that they are helpless in the face of harmful or destructive circumstances. People who are caught up in a state of learned helplessness tend to quick give up when placed in difficult situations—a tendency that creates a self-fulfilling prophecy.

More recent research, as revealed in such resources as Seligman's *Learned Optimism* (2006) and West, Patera, and Carsten's *Team Level Positivity* (2009), show that the opposite is also true, in that those individuals and teams that develop greater resilience find it easier to bounce back from setbacks, increase their chances of survival, and ride out successive waves of change. Teams that increase their ability to overcome setbacks become tougher when faced with new challenges, and more confident in their ability to manage difficult change. In the process they take aggressive steps to develop the skills, experience, and capabilities needed to raise their performance levels.

How to Initiate a Team-Building Session on This Topic
Why It Is Important to Move Quickly

A Japanese saying defines success as "fall down six times, get up seven." We believe the truth in this saying; quite often the key to successfully overcoming a setback is being able to quickly get the team back on its feet. The speed and effectiveness of a team's recovery depend on its responses during the first few critical days and weeks following a reversal. A team that waits an extended period of time to respond to setbacks instills a deeper feeling of passivity and helplessness on the part of its team members, and creates a scenario in which team performance will only continue to deteriorate. For these reasons, don't allow a setback to fester over time. Instead, set a goal of quickly mobilizing your team to action by conducting a team meeting within forty eight hours of the setback event.

Open the Door to Discussion

As noted earlier, setbacks often produce a lot of fear on the part of team members. This is particularly likely to be the case if a team is operating within an organization that has been suffering from significant performance difficulties. That said, if you are the team leader and the setback in question is related to performance issues on the part of individual team members, these issues are best addressed through one-on-one discussions in advance of the team-building session. Starting off the session with criticisms of individual members will only demoralize your team and inhibit participants from voicing their concerns and ideas.

Start off by suggesting two intended outcomes for this session:

- To establish a recovery plan for this particular setback

- To agree on a series of steps that can be taken to help prevent the occurrence of future similar situations

Following your introduction, honestly present the facts that you know about the current setback situation. If you are the team leader, don't feel that you have to mask your own concerns. Share your thoughts honestly with your team, but at the same time explain why you feel the setback is surmountable.

Open the door to a frank discussion by acknowledging the natural human reaction of withdrawing when confronted with a nasty obstacle. Encourage team members to talk openly about their concerns and frustrations regarding the setback, and be prepared to give them some time to vent. While acknowledging these concerns, redirect team members back to the need for a corrective action plan. Challenge them with a statement such as, "We all agree that this situation has created some real difficulties for us. The important question is, what are we going to do about it? I would like to hear your opinions."

Develop a Plan for Reversing the Setback

Ask participants to help you sketch out on the flipchart or whiteboard the following components. Ask participants to clarify whether their responses are based on solid information or untested assumptions:

1. The severity of outcomes produced by the setback—a cost overrun, disgruntled customer, lost contract, and so on.

2. Any potential opportunities that could be an eventual byproduct of the setback. (The *Opportunities/Threats Matrix* can be a helpful tool for outlining these first two steps.)

3. The current trend line for the setback. Is the current situation stable, slowly improving without intervention, or getting worse? What is the prognosis if the situation is not quickly addressed?

4. Use the *Mind Maps* tool to identify and prioritize all factors that are believed to be contributing to the situation, and those unknowns that need additional research.

5. Discuss and agree on options for dealing with the setback. The *Decision Matrix* can be a useful tool at this point if the options are clearly known and simply need to be weighed (in terms of their comparative cost, timeliness, feasibility, and so forth). If the options have not been clearly identified and you want to engage the team in creative problem solving, or you are facilitating a fairly large (twenty+) group, you might consider making use of the *Mix and Max* technique.

6. Identify in writing the action steps that each participant will commit to take to reverse or contain the setback. Include in these actions all steps that may be taken to ensure damage control with internal customers and senior stakeholders. The various tools, such as the *Stakeholder Analysis Chart,* can be very useful at this step.

7. Make sure that clear priorities are set for actions so that participants know where to direct the focus of their attention.

Plan to Anticipate and Meet Future Setbacks

Following the team's completion of the preceding task, it may be helpful to spend additional time identifying those actions that could be taken to prevent the occurrence of future similar setbacks. At this point you, as the team-building facilitator, need to make a process decision regarding whether the team has the time and energy needed to move ahead to this topic. We find that teams will typically require two to four hours to complete the review of the current situation. On the one hand, if you have planned this session as an all-day meeting and your team's energy level is still high, we suggest you move immediately into second phase of discussion. On the other hand, if time and energy are in short supply and the team appears to be emotionally taxed from their discussion to this point, you would be advised to wait for several days before proceeding to this step.

One way to build a team's resilience is to provide them with applied tools that can make members feel better prepared to anticipate and manage future setbacks. Chief among these skills is the ability to help your team establish early warning systems for uncovering emerging work problems before they reach "critical mass," quickly determining those change factors that are within or beyond your team's control, and systematically analyzing and preparing for broad-scale changes. Chapter Eight includes a number of good suggestions and tools for strengthening team change management. In addition, the *Mind Maps* and *After Action Reviews* tools can prove very useful at this stage of the discussion.

How to Take Supportive Actions
Assess the Damage

If you have ever watched reruns from any of the old *Star Trek* television shows you have seen a great model of how a high-performing team deals with setbacks. Almost every week, we would watch the Enterprise (or Voyager, depending upon the series) as it was attacked by alien craft, or dealing with some other galactic catastrophe. The crew's first reaction would always be to assess the damage: How badly were they hit? What weapon systems were still online? Could they continue to navigate? Were the crew's life-support systems still functioning? The ship's captain would quickly synthesize this information and then meet with the crew to determine their options.

In the same way, a good team leader will immediately assess a nasty setback event, taking into consideration such potential impacts as cost variances, schedule delays, and public relations damage. The aim of this assessment is to form an objective, balanced picture of the fallout from the situation, and the team's ability to execute against its objectives. With this picture in mind, the team can formulate plans for surviving and moving past the current situation.

A damage assessment is particularly important when the setback is still under way and some recovery action is still possible. Examples would include a customer service problem that is severe enough to potentially lose a corporate account, or the failure to meet critical milestones on a major project. If some ability to salvage the situation is still on the table, a quick damage-assessment meeting is in order. During the session the team will need to determine how best to reallocate work priorities to meet the crisis, what team talent to put into place to handle the developing situation, and those stakeholders who need to be immediately apprised of the situation and proposed recovery plan.

During this team huddle you may find it help to do an exercise of constructing a control chart. (This simple exercise is not presented as a tool.) Have team members list on sticky notes (one item per note) all of the factors that will affect their ability to turn the current situation around. Next create a two-column chart, with one column labeled "Within Our Control" and the other column labeled "Beyond Our Control." Now ask team members to place the sticky notes in the appropriate columns; in other words, you are asking what factors do participants view as being under their control?

While this exercise may seem simplistic, we have seen that this activity can be very powerful. First, the usual reaction when faced with this question is that people automatically begin to focus their thoughts on the "uncontrollables." It is only when the "Beyond Our Control" column is packed with sticky notes that participants come to realize how much they are adopting a mindset that automatically frames the solution as being beyond their control. Through continued discussion, team members often discover that with a little creative thought they can extend their range of control over their setback, even if that is limited to influencing key stakeholders to support required actions. The second payoff that participants get from engaging in this exercise is that it puts in perspective situations that initially may appear to be overwhelming problems. As an analogy, think about a person who is worried about her personal financial situation. A good financial planner helps the client accurately itemize her assets and liabilities and identify options for getting her finances under control. In going through this process the client begins to see that the situation is potentially manageable.

Work with your team to use this damage report to realistically assess the effect of the setback on their long-term performance. Armed with this information, team members can determine any necessary adjustments they need to make to their objectives and work processes. The *Closing the Gap Chart* found in your Tool Kit can help your team compare different options for overcoming setbacks.

Place the Setback in the Context of Success

Major setbacks often cause teams to focus primarily on their failures. Though it is important not to gloss over failures, take the time to remind your team of past victories. Rather than engaging in a superficial cheerleading session, consider performing a different kind of split-sheet review. In this procedure, team members list their many small and large successes of the past year on one side of a flipchart, and on the other side, the setbacks and disappointments they have experienced. Using the lists as the basis of your discussion, pose these two questions:

- "In terms of our overall performance scorecard, how would we rank this setback? That is, to what degree is it truly representative of our long-term performance?"

- "If we were to think in terms of a footrace, over the past few months would you say that we have been running downhill, on level ground, or uphill? If we have been running uphill and are attempting to tackle tougher goals, isn't it natural to assume we would expect to encounter more setbacks as we pursue those tougher goals?"

Agree on How to Discuss the Setback Outside the Team

An important part of dealing with a setback is reaching consensus on how all team members will agree to frame the setback when discussing it with those outside the team. This does not mean masking problems or minimizing difficulties. It does, however, mean accepting the fact that to some extent every member must assume the role of team ambassador. For example, if you have just finished a project that did not achieve the desired results, there is a big difference between saying, "We did not accomplish everything we hoped for, but in the process we have learned a lot about the steps we can take to perform better in the future" and "We really blew it this time—I don't actually know how we are going to get back on our feet." Discuss openly with your team how you would like the group to be perceived by others, and seek agreement on the best way for members to respond when presented with difficult questions about the recent setback.

Position the Setback as a Learning Experience

During your first discussion with team members, they probably will not be ready to view their setback as a learning experience. Only after they have had an opportunity to voice their concerns, assess the damage, recalibrate objectives, and refocus on past successes will they be able review the reversal with a dispassionate eye. You can set the stage for this phase of the discussion by suggesting that it is possible to garner valuable lessons from this experience that will enable all of you to perform more effectively in the future.

Some military forces conduct regular *after action reviews*, in which leaders of military actions are asked to perform a detailed comparison of whether or not that action met its stated objective, and ways in which that action went according to plan or veered off course. In the same way, the *After Action Reviews* tool found in your Tool Kit can be helpful in shifting team attention away from blame-casting and toward solution setting. As a start, ask your team the following questions:

- "Moving ahead, what steps can we take to ensure that this kind of problem doesn't happen again?"

- "What have we learned from this situation that we could use to our advantage?"

- "What do we need to do differently next time around?"

Temporarily Suspend Limitations

Sometimes teams have difficulty making commitments because short-term obstacles appear large and intimidating. One way to overcome this constraint is to temporarily suspend these limitations. Ask team members to list the most limiting constraints—time, money, staff, lack of information—that could potentially stand in the way of reaching their goals. This discussion might focus on the ideas that they have developed for solving a major problem, for exploiting a new opportunity, or for implementing a new project. List these constraints on a flipchart and explain that you will come back to them eventually. For the next thirty minutes, however, you want your team to pretend that these limitations do not exist. For example, if "lack of funds" was previously identified as a principal constraint, you might say to your team, "If money were *not* an issue, what would be the ideal solution to our problem?" After you have identified all potential ideal solutions, go back and ask how they might be modified to meet actual constraints. The *Creative Whack Pack*® tool can serve as a useful tool to help your team move away from routine solutions to more creative problem solving options.

Act to Regain Momentum

When faced with a setback it is important to quickly regain any lost momentum. As a rough analogy, picture your team competing in a race. Although all team members are temporarily out of action on the shoulder of the road, you have convinced them to get back in the race. Now you have to figure out how to close the gap, or make up for lost time and distance. Here are four options to regaining momentum. Once again, the *Closing the Gap Chart* provides a way of capturing solutions that link to these options.

Deploy Additional Resources　This is the most frequently used catch-up strategy in a team's arsenal. Unfortunately, it is also the most misused. Many people automatically assume that the easiest way to overcome a problem is to throw more resources at it. Before requesting additional resources, confirm the validity of your improvement strategy and assure yourself that additional resources will make a real difference in your team's ability to overcome the setback.

If you decide you can justify your request for additional resources, do not limit yourself to addressing the problem by requesting additional team members. Consider every possible option for adding to your project resources, including the use of outside experts, part-time help, college interns, volunteers, and personnel loaned from other departments or company subsidiaries. In addition, find out whether it is possible to acquire more time from team members who are already assigned to your project.

Reframe the Problem Another approach to regaining team momentum is to reframe, or redefine, the nature of your setback. Quite often, our perception of a problem determines the types of solutions we are able to identify. A few years ago we heard about a marketing team that was having difficulty finding the funds to evaluate customer interest in a new product, an innovative design for a wheelchair. Faced with budget cutbacks, the team first redefined its problem, changing the question from "How can we get additional resources or staff? to "What other avenues are available for testing the receptiveness of potential customers to our product?" The answer to the second question involved using Internet discussion groups frequented by wheelchair-bound individuals who were potential end users of the team's product. The team posted a series of queries to gauge the level of interest in proposed product features. Within forty eight hours, the team had received hundreds of responses from prospective customers. The *Reframing Technique* provides additional details on how to reframe problem questions in ways that open up additional possibilities for creative solutions.

Redesign Your Implementation Strategy If your setback involves significant schedule delays in key projects, revise your implementations strategy for managing the project. This could require such actions as simultaneously performing activities that are now performed sequentially, reducing the completion time for projects by assigning subteams to different project sections, or identifying steps that can be eliminated from projects.

Renegotiate Project Parameters Your final option is to renegotiate with your project stakeholders and sponsor. We can understand why you might be a little skeptical about attempting to implement this option. Most of the team leaders with whom we have worked have responded with something like, "But you don't know our executives! It is impossible to negotiate with them." If this is your concern, take heart—it is not as hopeless as it seems. You *can* negotiate with your senior managers if you're willing to follow a few simple guidelines:

- First, know the facts. When you walk into a room to renegotiate, come armed with all available information. If you expect that a probable delay will slow down your project, be precise in explaining its extent and projected impact. If you have discovered a fatal flaw in your attack strategy, be ready to justify your conclusions on how this flaw will likely affect your performance.

- Next, ask for an independent audit. If your stakeholders are reluctant to renegotiate it may be that they do not fully understand the problems you are facing. Invite them to learn firsthand about these problems by encouraging them to perform an informal audit and review of your project. This could include sitting in on team problem-solving sessions, reviewing your project plan, or inspecting your budget. It could also mean having a third party provide a different perspective. For example, it may be that you want to sell your managers on the advantages of outsourcing a functional area to a vendor. In this case your procurement department could provide a good third-party assessment of the attractiveness of the outsourcing contract.

- Finally, realize what can and cannot be negotiated. Accept the fact that some aspects of your project are etched in stone, while others are negotiable.

Manage Your Own Stress Level If you are the team leader or an influential team member, then the one behavioral change that you can personally make to help your team out during setbacks is to manage your own stress level. Team leaders and influential team members tend to be "weather vanes" for the other members of the team; during difficult times everyone on the team carefully watches these individuals to try to determine clues that provide some assessment of the team's overall health and viability. A team leader or member who complains a lot in public about a setback, who appears overly anxious, and who privately confides in other team members his or her doubts regarding the team's chances for survival will quickly raise the stress level of the entire team. Here are a few suggestions for managing your stress. Don't behave in ways that generate needless stress. Avoid adding needless stress to an already stressed-out team. Take a look at the following behaviors and note any that pertain to your own professional communication style.

- Vacillating on decisions, procrastinating on decisions, or rushing to judgment without first having sufficient information

- Creating arbitrary deadlines for projects without taking into account real job requirements

- Generating conflicts by encouraging win-lose behavior among other team members

- Criticizing members in public rather than private

- Making comments that cause other team members to feel threatened about the loss of their jobs

- Intentionally withholding information from other team members

- Using force and threats to win discussions with other team members

- Gossiping about members behind their backs

- Withdrawing your support, assistance, and energy from your group

- Creating conflicts between your team and other work groups, and then thrusting other team members into the middle of those conflicts

- Becoming loud and vocally abusive when you discover a work problem

Monitor your stress level. You probably know those subtle warning signs that clue you in to the fact that your stress level is going up. Like us, you might be aware of a facial tightening sensations around eyes, mouth, and jaw. The feeling that accompanies this is a sense of urgency—everything needs to be done NOW! Over time we have learned to track the first signs of a stress build-up and take a few simple steps to unwind. These include shutting the door of our offices and taking a quick mental break, breathing slowly and deeply, taking a short walk, and listening to some of the relaxing songs that we've have programmed into our smartphones. We also began the practice of mindful meditation, which we both strongly recommend. As a beginning guide to this area we recommend *Mindfulness for Beginners* by Jon Kabat-Zinn. The point here is that stress is a lot easier to manage if you can detect its buildup at its earliest stages. Waiting until your stress level is through the roof before you take action is a bit like standing in the middle of the road to stop a high-speed bus—it's a scenario that just doesn't end well.

Keep things in perspective. When people become chronically anxious and stressed out they tend to view all irritations and problems as critical. If you become emotionally drained over small, inconsequential problems you will deplete energy resources that would normally be reserved for dealing with critical challenges. In this respect, you will perform like a marathon runner who exhausts herself by running a series of high-speed sprints immediately before the big race. If you would like suggestions on how to keep things in perspective we recommend *Don't Sweat the Small Stuff—and It's All Small Stuff* by Richard Carlson and *Full Catastrophe Living* by Jon Kabat-Zinn.

Make key decisions during low-stress periods. Although it is impossible to predict with 100 percent certainty the types of situations that will trigger excessive stress, if you carefully track your stress level over a period of days or weeks you will probably find that you experience a stress cycle of predictable highs and lows. For example, your stress level may build immediately before you meet with your manager, or you are about to engage in a potentially confrontational discussion with a certain team member. Highlight on your weekly calendar any upcoming events or responsibilities that are likely to create stress for you. If possible, avoid making key decisions or taking critical action during these periods, Save important decision making for times when your stress level is moderate and your attention is fully focused on the task at hand. Be ruthlessly honest with yourself about recognizing situations when you are not emotionally and mentally prepared to wrestle with difficult work issues.

Additional Reading

Carlson, Richard. (1996). *Don't Sweat the Small Stuff—and It's All Small Stuff.* New York: Hyperion.

Kabat-Zinn, Jon. (2009). *Mindfulness for Beginners.* Louisville, CO: Sounds True.

Kabat-Zinn, Jon. (1990). *Full Catastrophe Living: Using the Wisdom of Your Body and Mind to Face Stress, Pain, and Illness.* New York: Delta Books.

Peterson, Christopher, Maier, Steven F., and Seligman, Martin E. P. (1995). *Learned Helplessness: A Theory for the Age of Personal Control.* New York: Oxford University Press.

Seligman, Martin E. P. (2006). *Learned Optimism: How to Change Your Mind and Your Life.* New York: Vintage Books.

West, Bradley J., Patera, Jaime L., and Carsten, Melissa K. (2009). Team level positivity: Investigating positive psychological capacities and team level outcomes. *Journal of Organizational Behavior, 30,* 249–267.

13

Managing Across Cultures

The Challenge of Cross-Cultural Teaming

Over the last few years many organizations have expanded internationally, as they strive to penetrate new markets, cross national boundaries through mergers and acquisitions, or form creative partnerships with global suppliers. We are also witnessing a dramatic increase in the number of organizations that are extending their international reach to become truly global enterprises. The movement is not limited to the corporate sector, but also includes educational sector and nonprofit organizations. An example of the latter is World Vision, a faith-based relief organization that provides such services as emergency relief in times of disaster, food relief, and agricultural support to over 100 million people in 100 countries (see Additional Reading for the URL).

Today, as almost every industry sector struggles to keep up with its ever-changing business landscape, speed and agility become critical to organizational success. A great example can be found in the mobile phone industry.

As mobile phone services providers and manufacturers attempt to make rapid inroads into an increasingly crowded international markets, they face the challenges of ever-shrinking product life cycles, complicated supply-chain dynamics, aggressive moves by competitors (one currently getting a lot of attention is patent purchase and litigation), rising customer expectations, and increasingly unpredictable patterns in the worldwide economy. Teams that are caught up in these changes soon discover that they are expected to hit the road running, without a great deal of time available for building international relationships and bridging cross-cultural differences.

To be successful, professionals who work within cross-cultural settings must contend with the challenge of cultural blindness. By this we mean that each of us operates from a set of implicit cultural assumptions that are so embedded that they largely operate implicitly, outside of our awareness. There are several subtle ways in which these assumptions shape how we interpret our interactions across cultures.

How We Interpret Communication Cues

Think for a moment about the following: how fast do you talk, what is the degree of eye contact that you feel is appropriate when conversing with others, what constitutes a "comfortable distance" for you when you are standing and talking to others, and how formal or informal are you when addressing others in a business context? These are parts of those implicit communication patterns that can be subject to misinterpretation when you make the transition from one culture to another.

Our cultural assumptions also influence how we interpret moments of silence in a conversation. What does it mean when, in response to something you have said, you encounter an extended silence from a team member? Before you answer, think for a moment about how you define an "extended silence?" The fact is that, depending upon our cultural backgrounds, each of us adheres to a set of unspoken norms that governs the flow of our communications. People in some Latin American countries such as Brazil tend to respond faster than we do here in the United States, whereas people in certain Asian countries may engage in longer pauses before responding. Complicating matters are the regional variations in communication patterns that occur in many countries. (Anyone who has relocated from New York City to Dallas, or vice versa, has probably experienced this firsthand.)

These differences play out in the "meaning" that we ascribe to silence during conversations. We feel that others are rude if they jump in too quickly with their comments. In the same way, when we experience (what we view as) an extended lapse in the conversation we may draw the conclusion that the other party is only partially attending to what we have to say, may not fully understand what we are saying, or is hesitant to speak up.

In summary, think of communication as a kind of verbal "dance" that takes place between people. When we dance to different beats or are unfamiliar with the dance steps, we are more likely to misinterpret each other's signals—increasing the chances that we will collide with each other on the dance floor.

The Degree to Which We Attend to Context

In *Understanding Cultural Differences* (1990) cultural researchers Edward and Mildred Hall explain that people from different cultures vary a great deal in how much they attend to contextual cues in interpreting communications. Individuals from low-context cultures, such as Germany, tend to be more direct in their communications and focus much more on the content of the message. In contrast, professionals within high-context cultures, such as Japan, tend to be more indirect when communicating. Communicators from high-context cultures also pay more attention to contextual cues, such as tone of voice and body language, when interpreting communications.

The impact of these differences is when people from low-context and high-context cultures interact, they may experience communication difficulties because of the degree to which they attend to contextual cues. As an example, visualize two team members reviewing a project plan. One member (from a low-context culture) is outlining the proposed project milestones. At one point she suggests completion dates for some of the project milestones, and asks if these dates are feasible. Her worker says "yes." Unfortunately while the first speaker hears these words, she fails to note the subtle nonverbal signals and the wording of the response—both of which suggests that the completion dates might not actually be achievable.

How We View Power Differences

One of the most widely referenced research studies has been cultural researcher Geert Hofstede's excellent book *Culture's Consequences: Comparing Values, Behaviors, Institutions, and Organizations Across Nations* (2001). To develop his research, Hofstede surveyed thousands of professionals to establish a comparative review of the cultures of over seventy countries. One of the cultural dimensions that emerged from these studies is that of power distance. Individuals who come from countries such as Russia that have been found to be high in power distance tend to acknowledge and accept power differences based on title and authority. Hofstede's work showed that national cultures vary widely along this dimension, and those individuals who come from countries that are low in power distance (such as the Sweden) are more egalitarian and place less emphasis on power distinctions.

The implication for teams is that team members from cultures high in power distance might be less likely to challenge bad ideas if those ideas emanate from their team leader. In the same way, they would be more resentful of actions (such as eliminating offices and moving team members into cubicles) that reduce symbols of status or power, and more likely to expect those people in lower reporting levels to work through the chain-of-commend when taking actions or making decisions.

As a different example, think of a manager from a low-power distance culture who takes on a team leader assignment within a high-power distance culture. Trying to be friendly, the new leader attempts to develop informal, relaxed relationships with her team. She stops by their work areas for chats, and when they ask for directions, instead of giving orders she attempts to solicit their views. When problems arise she trusts them to take the initiative. Given this scenario it is likely that the team may interpret the leader's actions as indicating a lack of confidence or inability to lead.

How We View Time

Cultures vary in terms of the attitudes that people have toward time. What does "being on time" to a meeting mean to you? If you called a team meeting or phone conference and some team members were ten minutes late, would you be upset and consider the behavior to be unprofessional, or would you relax a bit and make small talk with those in attendance until the late arrivals finally show up?

Hofstede's research on culture found that another cultural aspect of time involves the degree to which we prefer to focus on one thing at a time (monochronic) or to engage in multiple activities at the same time (polychronic). Individuals who have a monochromic time orientation prefer to focus on one thing and complete it before moving on. Those who are polychronic feel comfortable engaging in several things at once (such as talking to someone and then stepping aside for a moment to take an impromptu question from someone else, and then come back to the original discussion). Polychronic individuals are more comfortable with distractions when they are working on a task, and are less likely to view interruptions as rude behavior.

How We Make Decisions

Let us start with the understanding that people from different cultures may hold very different assumptions about what it means to "reach a decision." Team members from some cultures, such as the United States, tend to view a verbal decision as a firm commitment that signals a move to action planning and implementation. Professionals from other cultures, such as Saudi Arabia, may view the "decision" as a first step toward further negotiations.

Professionals in the United States tend to move faster toward reaching decisions and expect to "hash things out" in the meeting room. Japanese professionals tend to spend more time upfront working behind the scenes to gather support from other team members and stakeholders for decisions, before settling on a course of action. In this scenario it is expected that when the team convenes much of the negotiation process for decisions has already taken place.

Another factor that can affect decision making is the value dimensions identified by the cultural researcher Geert Hofstede is that of "uncertainty avoidance" (UA). Team members from high-UA cultures, such as Greece, are likely to want more details about the decision before acting, a more careful assessment of risk management, and a greater reliance on rules and procedures to guide decision making. At the other end of the spectrum, according to this model, team members from low-UA cultures, such as Denmark, would be less concerned about having every detail spelled out in the decision process.

How to Tell When This Is a Challenge

If your team is performing in a multicultural environment then we are certain that you have encountered many of the difficulties that we have just discussed. By "multicultural" we mean, of course, not only international organizations but also those teams in countries whose domestic workforces are becoming increasingly culturally diverse. These challenges are more likely to form under any of the following conditions.

Global Team Structures

Although all teams that extend across cultures have to deal with the challenge of cross-cultural teamwork, there are several reasons why these challenges are amplified for teams that have a global reach:

- Global teams operate within complex and confusing work environments.

- Such teams are often larger than their domestic counterparts, making it more difficult for members to orchestrate activities and maintain effective communications.

- Teams that stretch across many countries have more extensive language issues. Though the members of your team may be fluent in the English language, that is not always the case for their lower-level reports and location-based executive stakeholders. The result is that team communications are continually translated and filtered by team representatives, with the occasional by-product of communication mishaps.

- For members of global teams the challenge is not simply making an adjustment to team members from a different culture; it is creating team communication patterns and processes that serve as the "glue" to bind members together despite the challenge posed by multiple cultural differences.

- Global teams are, by definition, virtual teams and so must contend with all of the unique challenges facing such teams (see Chapter Eleven).

- Quite often international expansion occurs, not through organic growth, but through mergers and acquisitions. When this happens a new dimension has been added, as each acquired company will have evolved its own unique organizational culture.

- Many global teams have matrix organizational structures; that is, team members report up to the team leader on a full- or part-time basis, while simultaneously reporting up to another leader within their location. This situation can produce conflicting loyalties among team members. Moreover, teams must deal with the issue of influential senior stakeholders who may be operating behind the screen, out of view.

- When global teams are created in such areas as product development, human resources, IT, or finance it is often with purpose of building uniform enterprise-wide systems and processes to replace what were previously inefficient, redundant, patchwork operations. Common examples include the installation of enterprise-wide learning management systems or financial reporting systems. These represent highly complex projects that involve huge resource investments and an accompanying high level of risk.

We would posit that in tough economic environments, such as the current global situation, teams that can effectively bridge cultural differences will have a strong competitive advantage in addressing these challenges.

Lack of Cross-Cultural Experience

You may have people on your team who have had little prior experience in working cross-culturally. Such situations pose challenges not only for the cultural neophyte, but to the rest of the team as well.

Consider the following situation. As we write this, the authors know of one executive who is about to relocate from the United States to France, in what will be his first major international assignment. This executive has a very direct communication style, and prides himself in speaking directly without "bothering with the niceties." Based on his few preparatory visits to his new location, this leader has quickly come to realize that the company's corporate managers are more nuanced in their speech. His concern (which we think is justified) is that if he is not careful they will view his blunt style as reflecting a lack of finesse and sophistication. Moreover, in his new role this leader will be directing a team of several people who represent different nationalities. Finally, this leader will have to take on the role of change catalyst in overhauling many of his department's work processes. In summary, this leader must quickly position himself as being a strong change agent, while at the same time adapting to a new set of cultural norms and building credibility with his new work team, peers, and senior stakeholders.

In such a situation there are no second chances. When people lack experience working in cross-cultural settings they can, with the best of intentions, take actions that can lead to communication breakdowns, damaged work relationships, and substandard work performance.

Us Versus Them

Be on the lookout for the following signs that your team may be dividing into culturally aligned camps:

- Team members talk about "we" (the people in our cultural group) versus "them" (team members in other cultural groups).

- They describe individuals from other cultures in terms of cultural stereotypes.

- During team meetings members consistently side with other members within their culture on key work issues.

- During meetings you observe cliquish behavior. Team members within the same cultural subgroups eat together and take breaks together. They shift into silence (or into their native language) when others approach their discussions.

- Members are more angry about *how* decisions are made then the actual *content* of those decisions. (You might hear a comment such as, "Well yes, she was right about those supplier issues but did you see how *pushy* she was on the call?")

Organizational Fault Lines

The "us versus them" issue will be exacerbated if your team is structured in a way that generates damaging fault lines. According to researchers Kelly Hannum, Belinda McFeeters, and Lize Booysen and editors of the book *Leading Across Cultures* (2010), fault lines are those interface zones where different cultural subgroups within the team are responsible for managing different parts of the team's tasks, responsibilities, processes, or systems. Under these conditions it is easy for team members to attribute any performance issues they may be experiencing to problems that are intentionally created by those "on the other side." In other words, fault lines amplify cultural conflicts because they can polarize the team into different camps.

As an example, a global HR team may have its corporate leadership development group housed in one country, while most of that team's HR business partners are located in several other countries. This situation can produce a high degree of tension between those corporate team members who design programs and those field associates who are left with the responsibilities of selling these programs to their managers, securing funding for participants, and managing training. If a development program is poorly received or logistical issues are encountered, the resulting tensions can turn these subgroups into opposing camps.

The Opportunities Embedded in This Challenge

We said in the introduction to this section that large-scale business and economic conditions are driving organizations to expand rapidly into international settings. Teams who are adept at bridging cultural differences are able to help their organizations effectively make these transitions, while simultaneously increasing the market value for individual team members. In addition, when teams become stronger in cross-cultural team management they are able to benefit from the different perspectives and viewpoints provided by their culturally diverse membership. Cross-cultural teams also allow organizations to export best practices from different national locations to other organizational sites.

Teams that can effectively bridge cultures see the results in improved performance. This happens in part because the team's energy is directed toward the accomplishment of team goals, rather than dissipated in stressful conflicts. When team members achieve a better understanding of each other's cultural perspectives they are also less likely to encounter the types of quality issues, customer service problems, and project delays that are a natural outcome of communication breakdowns.

Such teams also learn skills that are readily transferable to management relationships with customers and suppliers across their cultural settings. Many teams work within cross-cultural, culture-sensitive areas of the world— locations where a professional's personal behavior reflects strongly on his or her organization. In such circumstances, team members who have developed cross-cultural skills will be less likely to engage in behaviors that offend local sensibilities and that will subsequently damage the organizational brand.

How to Initiate a Team-Building Session on This Topic
Planning for the Session

More care needs to be taken in planning for the facilitation of a team-building session when team members represent different cultures. As part of your planning process, go back and review the suggestions that we provided for planning sessions with virtual teams (see Chapter Eleven). Another suggestion is to avoid scheduling the session during dates that fall on religious holidays.

Also note any logistical adjustments that you might need to make in order to accommodate participants' cultural values. These adjustments could include such things as providing both vegetarian and meat dishes, serving both tea and coffee during breaks, or even setting aside special break times and a separate room for those participants who need to observe daily prayers. If you are not sure what arrangements may be suitable, discuss this with the team leader. In addition, when working with team members who may have difficulty with English, review the suggestions provided in the section Make Language Accommodations, later in this chapter.

If you are a third-party facilitator who will be working with a team leader during the team-building process, the following caveats apply. First, make certain that the team leader and members fully understand the role that you will play as a team-building facilitator. Members who come from high-power distance cultures are more likely to view you as an "expert" who will weigh in on team decisions, or step in at times to provide the team with advice or direction. Similarly, when dealing with team leaders from high-power cultures, confirm that the leader is comfortable with your involvement as a facilitator. Make a clear distinction between the supportive role you will play and the direction and guidance that this manager will provide.

A universal ground rule for team building is everyone has an equal chance to voice his or her opinions. When working across cultures, power issues sometimes emerge that can run counter to this ground rule. In some cultures, more established and higher ranking members may feel that they deserve more "air time" during the meeting. Similarly, women participants who come from male-dominated cultures may be more hesitant to freely voice their opinions during the session. Under any of these conditions you may find that certain team participation tools, such as *Group Brainwriting and Electronic Brainstorming*, the *Nominal Group Technique*, or *Gallery Technique*, can encourage team members to fully participate in the session. Another facilitation option for encouraging the brainstorming of issues is to divide the team up into subgroups, with each subgroup made up of people within the same power or status level. Similarly, the *Multivoting Technique* and *Traffic Light Technique* are both useful approaches for encouraging participation during decision-making discussions.

In addition, when working with members made up of both low- and high-context cultures, participants from low-context cultures might have difficulty understanding how activities that are intended to engage team members on a personal level (such as those described in the following section) are relevant to the "true purpose" of team building. In such cases it is often useful to discuss how these activities are intended to support mutual trust and collaboration.

Conduct a Pre-Meeting Social Event

Staging an informal social gathering the evening before the full-day team-building session is essential to building relationships, and to making sure that team members feel comfortable contributing during the session. As we have previously mentioned, cross-cultural teams are, by definition, virtual teams. We therefore recommend using the same pre-planning process that is outlined in Chapter Eleven.

Apart from these suggestions, the pre-session gathering is a great opportunity to introduce team members. One approach we have seen work well is to ask team members to present brief bios (a page or less). Ask them to include in the bio a few key professional or career changes that have resulted in their becoming a part of this team. Once again, this approach gives participants great latitude in determining how much personal information they wish to share with the rest of the team. It is also a great way for team members to gain a better appreciation of their coworkers' special skills, capabilities, and work experiences.

Initiating the Team-Building Session on This Topic

We have developed the following focal areas for discussion with the newly formed team in mind. Having said that, we believe that many of these issues are equally applicable to established teams. We believe this because we have frequently found that team leaders tend to overestimate the degree to which even experienced members have a clear understanding of, and full alignment on, such things as the team's mission, success measures, and member accountabilities. We have arranged these issues according to what we view as their logical order of attack.

Because it could require two or more days to cover all task and process issues covered here, if only one day is available for the session, you should talk with members in advance to identify which issues are most relevant to their needs. One way to obtain this feedback is ask participants to complete the *Team Building Assessment Questionnaire* in advance of the session. Another option is to start the session by asking participants to provide their views on where their team currently stands in relationship to the categories presented in the *Team Alignment Pyramid*. As we have mentioned previously, before moving into a discussion of team issues, have participants agree on the communication ground rules they would like to follow throughout the meeting.

Exploring the Team's Task Issues

Team building issues can be divided into those focused on task-related team challenges and those focused on process issues. Task issues involve such factors as team reporting structures, organization, member roles, and guidelines that members are to adhere to with respect to meeting performance goals and standards. The following are suggestions for helping teams to address such task issues.

Review Organizational Factors That Have Spurred Team Creation Quite often, not all team members fully understand the broader organizational and environmental factors that have led to the creation of their team. A global sales team may already know of a competitor's intrusions into the company's markets. At the same time, some team members might not make the connection between that competitive shift and the company's decision to combat this move by converting what were formally separate products into bundled product/service offerings that might be more attractive to large global customers. One way to approach this part of the team-building process is to use the *Mind Maps* tool found in your Tool Kit to have participants identify those external factors (changes in customer requirements, resource constraints) that directly influence the team's performance.

Clarify the Team's Mission and Charter Consider the members of a cross-cultural employee engagement team. Some members might feel that their team was launched to identify, from the annual engagement survey findings, those key factors related to employee retention and job satisfaction. Others may believe that they are expected to go beyond this analysis to recommend engagement actions that can be implemented at the discretion of their individual business units. Still others might see their mission as developing a uniform set of engagement actions that will be (upon approval of the executive team) mandated for implementation across the organization. The *Team Vision Summary* can be useful at this point. If you are working with a temporary project team the *Team Scoping Document* can be very useful in defining the team's efforts.

Identify Critical Stakeholder Issues. This step is particularly important when the team is organized through a matrix structure, with participants reporting up to two different lines of management. The *Stakeholder Analysis Chart* in your Tool Kit can be useful for mapping those stakeholders who are "blockers," "supporters," or "neutrals" and to determine actions for gaining stakeholder support. In the same way, the *Customer Satisfaction/Importance Matrix* provides a great method for comparing participants' perceptions of the team's current performance in terms of customer requirements.

Clarify Team Members' Roles and Accountabilities The team leader should start out this phase of the discussion by clarifying each team member's role and accountabilities, with emphasis on any recent changes in these areas. If the team is large and complex it often helps to have organizational charts available, with members' photos placed next to their names. As part of this discussion, review team boundaries and discuss members' roles in managing boundary issues. The members of cross-functional teams have to manage boundaries with other teams and work groups, as well as external customers and suppliers while simultaneously managing cultural differences. For these reasons it is important that participants have a clear understanding of how they are expected to address problems with other work groups, and the conditions under which they are expected to escalate issues to the team leader or senior stakeholders for resolution. This is also an opportunity for team members to jointly resolve any boundary management issues they may be having with other work groups. Use the *Relationship Map* and *Group Interaction Matrix* to fully explore this topic.

Exploring the Team's Process Issues

Team process issues are those that relate to how team members interact and communicate with each other on a daily basis. Representative issues involve how members come together to make decisions or resolve disputes, or the guidelines they following in keeping each other informed on performance issues or organizational changes. The following suggestions may prove helpful when you are working with teams to address process issues.

Establish Ground Rules That Support Ongoing Communications Just as teams can identify the ground rules they would like to follow throughout the team-building session, they can also take the time to generate ground rules that they would like all members to abide by to strengthen day-to-day communications (e-mails, the management of conflicts, and so on) within the team. The first step is to ask participants to create a three-column list. Starting in the left-hand column, ask them to identify those aspects of communications that might be problematic. In the middle column they should describe (without focusing on particular members) any problems they are encountering in these communication areas. After the first two columns are completed participants can note proposed ground rules or improvement suggestions in the right-hand column.

Map Cultural Values Mapping cultural values involves having team members note differences and similarities in the cultural values represented within the team. One way to do this is by having team members divide into subgroups by culture. Ask each subteam to create a separate list of those values and behaviors that best describe the culturally influenced approaches they and the other subteam take to manage interactions and relationships. Detailed instructions for alternative approaches to this technique, as well as sample "culture value cards" and "behavior cards" can be found in an excellent book entitled *Facilitating Cultural Teams: A Practical Guide* (2007).

In conducting these kinds of discussions it is easy to focus on cultural differences that can pose issues. Though this type of learning is certainly useful, it is also helpful to point to those areas in which all team members are aligned on underlying goals and objectives, in case they fail to see this alignment because they approach those goals in very different ways.

To illustrate this, think about two professionals who share the same underlying concern about the importance of responding quickly to an urgent request for a new program. The difference is that one team member interprets "responding quickly" as moving as fast as possible to produce certain project deliverables, with less upfront analysis of risks. The second team member might argue in moving more slowly at first, wanting to engage in a more thorough assessment of risks and potential risk mitigation actions. For the second team member "responding quickly" means avoiding the types of errors and rework that could result in having to redo many of the project deliverables.

Work Through Mock Scenarios Another approach that can help participants discover how cultural differences can result in potential communication mishaps or faulty assumptions is through the use of mock scenarios. Compared with the discussion of recent work problems, this approach is more likely to shift a team's attention from blame-casting to engaging in joint problem solving.

To use this approach, several weeks prior to the session work with representative team members to create a hypothetical work scenario. The scenario should describe in detail a work situation that, if it occurred, would test the ability of team members to communicate effectively across cultures. Examples might include the need to quickly introduce a change strategy, or to coordinate actions in resolving a problem with a corporate client. During the session members divide into subgroups by cultural background. Each subgroup is asked to do the following:

- Determine how they would respond to the situation

- Anticipate how the other subgroups would respond to the situation

- Identify any potential communication breakdowns that could arise as the respective groups attempted to orchestrate their tasks and decisions

During the debriefing session, ask each subgroup to provide a brief summary of what they concluded. After each subgroup has completed this phase ask all participants to identify the major themes that emerge from this discussion. The focus here should be on identifying culturally based breakdowns in communication. The final stage involves getting the team to develop suggestions and guidelines they could follow for addressing these types of communication issues. This process also gives team members an opportunity to discover the culturally based assumptions that others might hold about them.

This approach can be modified by constructing a hypothetical scenario that is actually completed as a simulation during the session, as different subgroups are asked to work together in making decisions or resolving issues related to the scenario. Such interactions can also be videotaped to aid the team in observing their own behavior.

Several years ago one of the authors (Robert) used this approach to support team building with a global sales team. The simulation in question involved the hypothetical acquisition of a smaller U.S. competitor by a second, larger global competitor. Team members were required to (1) develop an impact assessment for the situation (this was a move that would radically expand the competitor's product offerings and customer base), and (2) develop a plan detailing the first series of actions that they would need to take in response to this situation. The debriefing period allowed the entire team to discuss what worked and didn't work during their interactions, and arrive at steps for strengthening team communication. The great irony here is that six months later the "hypothetical" situation actually took place, with the result that the team was better prepared to deal with the aftermath of this change.

Explore Process Support Issues Cross-cultural teams often find that they can achieve great inroads by exploring the following question: "What do we need to create or strengthen in terms of communication vehicles, groupware, or organizational structure that could help us work together more effectively as a team?"

We know of one team whose members were beginning to feel isolated and cut off from each other. Phone conferences were addressing only part of the problem and cost constraints made it difficult to conduct face-to-face meetings. While the corporate office had videoconferencing facilities, it was difficult for some team members to link up to these conferences from their remote locations. At one point one team member suggested that they use the Skype Manager function of Skype software (which allows up to ten people to simultaneously videoconference) but their IT department didn't allow

Skype inside their corporate firewall. The solution they came up, which worked out well for them, was to use this system on their personal laptops and tablet computers.

For another team the process support issue was one of conflicting loyalties. Some team members reported up, through a matrix structure, to both the team leader and their local area managers. The team was working on a global project that required 50 percent of everyone's time, but some local area managers were pushing back on this requirement. After an intense team discussion the resolution came when the team leader appealed to the team's senior sponsor to work with the company's team to clearly communicate to all company leaders the high priority that had been assigned to this project.

It may be that there are no "work-around" solutions for the process support issues that are facing your team, but you will never know until you invest some time in exploring this issue during your team-building session.

How to Take Supportive Actions
Make Language Accommodations

If English is a second language for some team members, prior to conducting a meeting, send participants a brief summary of the major points that will be covered during the meeting. This will make it easier for participants to follow you during your presentation, and will give them additional time to formulate their questions. In addition, whenever possible use graphics, illustrations, or photos to help members visualize your ideas. Two good resources that are very useful when considering how to apply visual methods in conveying information are *Facilitating Cultural Teams: A Practical Guide* (2007) and *The Back of the Napkin: Solving Problems and Selling Ideas with Pictures* (2008).

Apply Cross-Cultural Collaboration Methods

Certain specialized group collaboration methods have been shown to be very applicable across many national cultures. Each summer, we train and educate graduate students in our respective graduate programs in four of these techniques, in an one-week course on *International Organizational Collaboration* conducted in Dublin, Ireland (for inquiries write to disputer-esolution@smu.edu). These techniques are Appreciative Inquiry, the World Café, Future Search, and Open Space Technology. Though each of these methods involves a different approach, they share certain commonalities:

- They are not intended to improve relationships among team members or address dysfunctional team dynamics. Instead, they provide communication vehicles through which participants can productively explore critical issues (issues about which participants feel very strongly, and to which they are fully committed).

- Although these techniques are not designed for team building, quite often participants find that these techniques provide constructive collaboration models that can be applied to other organizational issues.

- These approaches have been applied to both small teams and large (100+) groups. In the latter case they provide methods for "getting the full system in the room"; for example, engaging a broader base of organizational stakeholders.

- In advance of the session a lot of effort goes into having participants word the title for the session in the form of an engaging and provocative question—one that provides a positive entry into discussion.

- For each method, much time goes into the selection of participants who truly care about the issue under discussion. Participation is always voluntary.

- The setup for these methods (seating, room environment, use of ground rules, and so on) is designed to provide participants with a safe, comfortable environment for entering into dialogue. Each participant's voice carries equal weight in the discussion.

- Within each method participants are, at some point, broken up into small groups to give each individual an opportunity to present his or her views. Participants are often given the opportunity to shift into other groups at different times in the sessions, to encourage them to gain the broadest spectrum of perspectives.

- These discussions are largely self-managed. Facilitators enter into the process to ensure that participants understand the purpose of the technique, introduce the process, provide overall direction—and then they step out of the way.

- Each of these methods involves a search for common ground. Participants attempt to identify those major themes and points on which they agree, with little emphasis (and no facilitator mediation) in forcing parties to consensus on those "sticking points" in which there appears to be little agreement. Conflict is acknowledged and parties may attempt to resolve such conflicts, but facilitators do not play the role of mediator or negotiator in these discussions.

While we lack the space in this section to go into additional depth on these collaborative group methods, two useful resources for additional development in this area are *The Change Handbook: The Definitive Resource on Today's Best Methods for Engaging Whole Systems* (2007) and *The Handbook of Large Group Methods: Creating Systematic Change in Organizations and Communities* (2006).

Develop Cross-Cultural Competencies

There is little evidence to suggest that there is a fixed set of leadership competencies that are transportable across all cultures. With that caveat in mind there is substantial research to suggest that certain abilities are necessary prerequisites working effectively across cultures. These include developing cultural sensitivity, and the ability to cope with ambiguity and deal with complex, unstructured situations.

Research studies such as that produced by Yoshitaka Yamazaki and D. Christopher Kayes (2004) indicate that several key competencies, including the ability to demonstrate flexibility in one's work and learning approaches, to deal with complexity and ambiguity, to remaining resilient in the face of obstacles, to be change adaptable, and to learn from and interact with very different types of people, are closely related to success in global leadership positions and expatriate assignments.

We consider these abilities to be a part of a mega-competency that has commonly been referred to as learning agility, and which can be defined as an individual's ability to quickly adapt to new situations and to learn and profit from experience. My (Robert's) previous book, *How to Accelerate Your Development as a Leader* (2010), reviews relevant research on this topic, describes a few things to look for in performing an informal self-assessment on one's learning agility, and provides suggestions for becoming a more flexible and adaptable leader.

Before leaving this section, we want to point out that one cultural consulting company, ITIM International, has created an iPad and iPhone application that is, according to the company website, based on Hofstede's research model. The free "light" version of this app, CultureGPS Lite™, provides a summary of Hofestede's five culture dimensions, along with a lookup feature that reveals the culture profiles for ninety eight countries. CultureGPS Professional™, a paid application, includes a self-assessment for determining one's own culture profile along with a method for comparing the profiles of any two countries in the set. (Note: At the time of writing, the authors have not been able to obtain any independent reviews of these products.)

Decide on How to Decide

When teams are colocated, a large part of how they make decisions lies in the informal interactions that occur outside of formal team meetings. Members will drop by each other's work areas to discuss common issues, or small subgroups may meet over lunch to hash out critical points pertaining to an upcoming decision. Virtual teams face a much more difficult challenge. It is easy for those team members who are sitting around the conference table in the team's office to dominate the conversation, shutting out team members who are participating from other locations.

The challenge becomes even greater when cultural differences cause team members to hold very different ideas regarding what it means to "make a decision." In some cultures, such as in the United State, we often assume that agreements made by the end of the meeting imply a commitment to implement those decisions. In other cultures, whatever conclusions are reached, the meeting may be regarded as representing only the first of several steps in an ongoing negotiation.

One way around this constraint is for the team to agree in advance of a meeting on what they hope to obtain as an outcome by the end of the session. In addition, before engaging in the decision the team should set aside time to agree on the process that they will use to reach the decision. This could involve "majority rule," total consensus, or the application of one of the decision-making tools that are included in your Tool Kit, such as the *Multivoting Technique*, the *Plus/Delta Technique*, and the *Decision Matrix*.

Manage Organizational Fault Lines

As mentioned earlier, fault lines are those interface zones where different cultural subgroups within the team are responsible for managing different parts of the team's tasks, responsibilities, processes, or systems. One way to effectively manage fault lines is to ask your team to arrive at ways in which responsibilities are comanaged by subteams of members who represent different cultures and nationalities. If this issue is an obstacle to collaboration within your team, consider incorporating this discussion into your team-building session.

Additional Reading

Bunker, Barbara Benedict, and Alban, Billie T. (Eds.). (2006). *The Handbook of Large Group Methods: Creating Systematic Change in Organizations and Communities.* San Francisco: Jossey-Bass.

Coleman, Peggy, Devane, Tom, and Cady, Steven (Eds). (2007). *The Change Handbook: The Definitive Resource on Today's Best Methods for Engaging Whole Systems* (2nd ed.). San Francisco: Berrett-Koehler.

Hall, Edward T., and Hall, Mildred R. (1990). *Understanding Cultural Differences.* Boston: Intercultural Press.

Hannum, Kelly, McFeeters, Belinda, and Booysen, Lize. (Eds). (2010). *Leading Across Differences.* San Francisco: Pfeiffer/Wiley.

Hofstede, Geert. (2001). *Culture's Consequences: Comparing Values, Behaviors, Institutions, and Organizations Across Nations.* Thousand Oaks, CA: Sage.

Hogan, Christine. (2007). *Facilitating Cultural Teams: A Practical Guide.* Philadelphia: Kogan Page.

Roam, Dan. (2008). *The Back of the Napkin: Solving Problems and Selling Ideas with Pictures.* New York: Penguin Books Ltd.

Yamazaki Yoshitaka, and Kayes, D. Christopher. (2004). An experiential approach to cross-cultural learning: A review and integration of competencies for successful and expatriate adaptation. *Academy of Management Learning & Education, 3,* 362–379.

World Vision website: http://www.worldvision.org/content.nsf/pages/sponsor-a-child-innocent?Open&campaign=1193512&cmp=KNC-1193512&open=

Section Three

Tools and Techniques for Team Building

THIS SECTION INTRODUCES SEVENTY tools and techniques that you can use when facilitating team-building sessions and when managing teams or groups. Guidelines and tips for each tool are provided for effective application, and a variety of forms and templates are also included.

14

THE TOOL KIT

THE SEVENTY TOOLS and techniques within this chapter are presented in alphabetical order. See the Table of Contents' "List of Tools" for a complete list.

Action Planning Chart

One way to ensure that your proposed solutions are actually translated into action is through the use of this *Action Planning Chart*. The chart's purpose is to identify the actions that need to be taken to complete a project or initiative, who will be responsible for completing them, and the completion and review dates for each action. The final section of the exercise requires agreement on the dates when team members agree to report back to the group regarding their progress on each action.

Here are some suggestions for completing the chart:

1. Ensure that everyone on your team has input into the chart's construction.

2. Try not to tackle too many initiatives at once. Focus each action-planning chart around a single problem/solution set.

3. Examine the chart to confirm that team members have taken on their fair share of responsibilities.

4. Make certain that one team member is assigned as lead coordinator or director for every action.

5. Consult your appointment calendars when you are completing the chart. Check for potential conflicts—for example, deadline dates that fall on weekends, holidays, or days when team members simply won't be available.

6. Scan your appointment books to confirm that team members who have agreed to complete action items will actually be on-site on those days.

7. Save the chart electronically for e-mail distribution to your team and to any outsiders who will be involved in implementing the final action plan. That way, you can easily update the chart as needed.

Action-Planning Chart

Action to Be Taken	Team Member(s) Responsible for Action	Date to Begin This Action	Date to Complete This Action	Date for Team Review

After Action Reviews

What Is an After Action Review (AAR)?

Today's teams are under incredible time pressure. As a result, many teams find that they jump from one project to another without having the chance to stop to reflect on what went right or wrong in a particular situation. Unfortunately, if this becomes a team's standard way of working then its members never take the time to learn from their experience.

An AAR is a formal method for addressing this issue. Many military forces use AARs to analyze the effectiveness of certain critical military decisions and events. Unlike a performance management discussion, the focus here is not on critiquing and evaluating the performance of particular team members. Instead, an AAR requires a team to compare what was ideally supposed to occur in a situation with what actually occurred, to note key differences between "planned" and "actual," and to clearly identify the "lessons learned" that could be applied to future situations.

The Advantages of Completing an AAR

An AAR offers a team several unique advantages:

- An AAR forces team members to pause and review the event while it is still fresh in their minds, and their recollection of events has not yet been distorted through lost information, memory fatigue, or self-justification.

- An AAR uses the collective eyes and ears of the team to identify all pertinent aspects of the situation. In the same way, it uses the team's collective creativity and knowledge to generate more powerful and durable solutions.

- AARs are particularly useful for virtual teams, or temporary teams such as cross-functional process improvement teams. In these situations AARs can strengthen the team's communication channels.

- When the situation under review is a complex, long-term project, an AAR can be used as a critical milestone discussion to help a team determine the recovery actions that need to be taken to bring the project back online.

- An AAR provides a valuable learning experience for all team members. In engaging in this exercise many people discover aspects of the situation that had previously been either poorly understood or were completely unknown to them. In addition, less experienced team members learn a great deal by trading off ideas and suggestions with their more experienced coworkers.

- AARs encourage team accountability. The message is "regardless of how we got to this point, we are all responsible for finding a way out."

After critical project milestones or work situations have occurred leaders have a tendency to discuss the effectiveness of the situation with team members on a one-on-one basis. The problem here is that performance problems or successes are seldom solely tied to the actions of a single team member. Conducting an AAR brings the entire situation into focus. Consider the following situation. One team member, Linn, fails to prepare a financial forecast report in time for an important project milestone. During the AAR the team discovers that Linn was waiting on a spreadsheet from Carlos, a professional in another department. Carlos had previously given Linn incomplete information, and part of the delay involved the additional time he needed to correct the first version of his spreadsheet and resubmitting it. Through continued discussion the team discovers that Linn never actually spoke to Carlos directly, but left him a rushed voice mail indicating what she needed. Carlos had misinterpreted her request and sent the wrong information. Moreover, when she had mentioned that she needed it "Friday" he assumed that it would be acceptable to get the information to her by close of day on Friday. At this point in the discussion the team might ask itself, "Are there other situations in which we are getting inaccurate, incomplete, or delayed information because other work groups don't fully understand our requirements and deadlines?"

It is worth bearing in mind that AARs do not have to be focused on failure. If a sales team suddenly finds that its ramping up sales in one of its sales territories, or a team has uncovered a great "work-around" for a long-standing process problem, why not conduct an AAR to ask the question, "What new and effective actions did we undertake within this situation that could be applied to other areas of our work?"

How to Conduct an AAR

The following steps will guide you in completing an AAR:

1. In advance of the review the team facilitator should set the focus for the review; that is, a single significant project or event that needs to be explored. In an invitation e-mail to team members, the team leader should explain what an AAR is and what the team hopes to gain from it.

2. Begin the meeting by reaffirming the meeting's purpose and positive focus.

3. Confirm everyone's understanding of the hoped for outcomes of the project or event under review.

4. Confirm participants' understanding of what actually happened. At this point it is helpful to construct a graphic split-sheet on the whiteboard, with the two columns entitled "Planned" and "Actual." In soliciting input from participants ask them to stick to the facts and whenever possible, reference hard data.

5. Ask: "What are the critical differences between what we hoped to see happen versus what actually happened?"

6. Ask: "What are some of the factors that contributed to these differences or variances?" At this point, it may be helpful to create a process flow diagram or other similar graphic, especially if the situation under review involved many people or functions in several activities.

7. If there are certain differences that are unaccounted and for which team members have no explanations, visually flag these areas for later review. Someone on the team will need to takes steps to determine the underlying root causes of these situations.

8. If the situation under review represents a less than satisfactory outcome, ask, "What can be done the next time around to improve the situation?"

9. Ask: "How can we apply what we have learned here to future situations?"

Additional Reading on AARs

Barner, Robert. (2010). *Accelerating Your Development as a Leader.* San Francisco: Pfeiffer/Wiley.

Alternative Communication Options

When you are leading a virtual team, you may be challenged to find the most effective means of communicating within your team. The *Alternative Communication Options* table below reviews the advantages and disadvantages of four communication methods: e-mail, phone conferences, video conferences, and face-to-face meetings.

Alternative Communication Options

Options	Advantages	Disadvantages
E-mail	Fast Saves time with online editing Provides an audit trail or team record Supports asynchronous communications	Impersonal Absence of contextual clues may lead to flaming or censoring of message Some systems have no option for e-mail conferences
Phone Conference	More personalized than e-mail Easier to administer than video Easy access for all team members while on the road	More difficult to facilitate than videoconferences (cross-talking) Fatigue factor sets in after 60–90 minutes Greater chance for communication breakdowns for team members who don't speak English as primary language
Video Conference	Most personalized electronic communication option Simultaneous review of video and text Provides a stronger team experience than phone or e-mail	Rental systems are often three times the cost of phone conferences Irritating lag time between sending and receipt of message More difficult to administer (do all members have access to system?)
Face-to-Face Meeting	Strongest option for team building Full context (opportunity to read between the lines and interpret visual clues) Less fatiguing than phone, video, or e-mail	Low-status team members can be intimidated by high-status members (studies show this occurs less in e-mail communications) Major time and cost factors for setup and delivery Unfeasible for teams separated by large geographic areas

To apply this tool, complete the following steps:

1. Send this *Alternative Communication Options* table to your team to review before your discussion.

2. Ask team members to identify the advantages or disadvantages on this checklist that are especially important to them.

3. Invite members to note additional communication opportunities, concerns, or considerations that are not mentioned in this list.

4. Use team members' feedback to determine which communication approach(s) will work best to maintain communication within your team.

Asynchronous Work Spaces

Contributed by Daniel Rainey

Traditionally, group work or teamwork has been thought of as a synchronous, face-to-face activity, with perhaps some individual or small-group work conducted between face-to-face sessions. Increasingly, work tools available in the cloud are changing the conception of how teamwork or group work can be accomplished.

For purposes of illustration, think of three common scenarios for group work. First, consider traditional team or group work, where the bulk of the activity is scheduled in a face-to-face environment, with the possibility of "homework" between face-to-face sessions. Second, consider a mixed face-to-face and online environment for group work, where a significant amount of the work is done while not meeting face-to-face. Third, consider an all-online environment, where the work is done with no face-to-face meetings at all.

There are many online tools to assist in all three scenarios. Perhaps most useful are comprehensive group workspaces (such as Central Desktop or Share Point), mind-mapping tools (such as MindMeister or FreeMind), online survey tools (such as Survey Monkey or Zoomerang), and web video tools (such as WebEx or Skype).

Comprehensive work-spaces offer an array of functions, including calendars, task managers, document sharing, and discussion forums. In my work in Online Dispute Resolution (ODR), I refer to them as "virtual table" applications because they offer the capability to do asynchronously most or all of the things one can do around a conference table. For dispersed groups who have to make a great effort to meet, using a comprehensive work site allows scheduling, discussing agendas, and sharing information in advance of face-to-face meetings, so that all of the face-to-face time is spent in real work, not in administrative work that can easily be done online ahead of time. Between sessions, the workspace can be used to codify decisions made during face-to-face work, to extend the work and prepare for the next face-to-face session, or to begin work that can be concluded in the next face-to-face session. For groups who may never be able to meet in person (such as groups with international members or members scattered geographically within one country) the comprehensive workspace forum can be used to discuss items posted in the workspace, and other online tools can be linked to allow for a full group work experience.

Mind maps, surveys, and web video sites can be linked from the comprehensive work spaces as noted above, or they can be used as stand-alone applications to assist with work in primarily face-to-face processes. In mixed face-to-face and online work, group workspaces are particularly useful for distributing information and furnishing the entire team the same information in preparation for discussions. Group workspaces are also very helpful at the end of work sessions when single-text editing capabilities can be used to draft agreements or to draft information that the work group wants to share with its constituents at large.

Mind maps, as noted elsewhere in this book, allow groups to generate and visually manipulate ideas. Online mind maps allow for the process to extend over time, with group members accessing the mind map multiple times over an extended period. The primary advantage of mind maps is for the members of the working group who are offering ideas and trying to make sense of multiple options. However, it is possible to open the finished or near-finished mind maps for viewing by larger constituent groups as a way to forecast potential organizational changes.

Online surveys allow for collecting detailed information from group members, conducting multivotes, and for rating and ranking ideas generated by the group. It is usually assumed that surveys are a way of assessing agreement with or support of items by members of a large group, or by constituents of work groups. That certainly is a common use of surveys, both internally and externally by work groups. But it is also possible to use online surveys alone or in combination with "view only" mind maps to push information to constituent groups at the same time that work groups are getting real-time feedback on potential organizational changes.

Web video programs, particularly those that offer document sharing, allow for group members to "meet," discuss, and share documents as if they were together face-to-face. Applications like WebEx that allow for the sharing of e-documents in a real-time format come as close as possible to the dynamics of a face-to-face meeting.

All of these tools—group work spaces, online surveys, online mind maps, and web video and audio sites—can be obtained either free or at very low cost, and all are password protected so that only those group members invited into the work can access the online information.

General Advantages

- Cost: Use of online tools can eliminate or greatly reduce the cost of travel and lodging for dispersed groups and can eliminate or limit the need for time away from the office.

- Convenience: All of the tools mentioned are easily accessible from any Internet-capable computer, and all allow for group members to work at any time that is convenient.

- Increased Processing Time: Use of online tools, alone or in conjunction with face-to-face meetings, allows group members to consider ideas, and consider their responses, in a way that is not possible in an immediate, face-to-face environment.

Intercultural Advantages

- Translation: In situations where multiple languages are used, or where some of the participants may feel disadvantaged by the use of a dominant language, using online tools allows for time to process information, seek clarification, and consult translators in a way not possible in face-to-face environments.

- Anonymity: One of the major differences between face-to-face work and online work is the ability for participants to be truly anonymous when offering ideas, seeking clarification, or responding to ideas. In many cultures, the "normal" North American approach to problem solving (naming the problem as the first step) is very uncomfortable. Using online tools allows for direct input, but allows for it in a way that reduces the discomfort of direct confrontation.

- Expanding the "Table": Although generalizations are dangerous, in individualist cultures like the United States, we tend to expect that the individuals "at the table" should have the authority to discuss issues and make decisions. In most collectivist cultures, the individuals at the table feel an obligation to include members of a family, community, or organization in a way that is not expected in individualist cultures. Using online tools in an asynchronous or partially asynchronous environment allows for group members to take time to consult with others in their community who are, really, extended participants in the decision-making process.

Tools and Resources

1. Comprehensive Group Work Spaces

   - Central Desktop—www.centraldesktop.com—Central Desktop offers calendars, task managers, discussion forums, document sharing, and single-text editing in an easy to use package. Discussion administrators control access by inviting group members into the site, and by setting and monitoring levels of access and security. Central Desktop is available in a free version without encryption and with a cap on the number of workspaces that can be set up simultaneously, or in a paid version with full encryption and virtually unlimited workspaces.

   - Share Point—www.microsoft.com/sharepoint—Share Point operates much as does Central Desktop, and it can be bundled into the Microsoft Office suite. There is no free version of Share Point.

2. Mind Maps

   - MindMeister—www.mindmeister.com—MindMeister is a web-based application with a free version that limits the number of simultaneous mind maps that can be open, and an inexpensive paid version that offers essentially unlimited open maps.

   - FreeMind—http://sourceforge.net/projects/freemind—FreeMind is a free download that is resident on a desktop or laptop, not in the cloud.

3. Surveys

- Survey Monkey—www.surveymonkey.com—Survey Monkey is available in a free version with a limited number of surveys that can be open at once, and with limits on the reporting capability, or in an inexpensive paid version with unlimited simultaneous surveys and robust reporting.

- Zoomerang—www.zoomerang.com—Zoomerang also offers a "downsized" free version, and a paid version that has a remarkable array of tools in addition to pure surveys.

4. Web Video and Audio Conferencing

- WebEx—www.webex.com—WebEx is a subscription application that can be purchased by the year, month, day, or project. It is a secure application, used by security conscious organizations like the Department of Defense, with full real-time document sharing, application sharing, and screen-sharing capabilities.

- Skype—www.skype.com—Skype is a free service when used computer-to-computer, with voice and video, and paid versions have add-on that allow for multiple connections and document sharing. Skype also offers "Skype Out," a paid service that allows for very inexpensive calls from a computer to land line or cell phones anywhere in the world.

Note: There are an amazing number of applications in each of the categories mentioned above. The list of examples does not constitute an endorsement of any particular application. Sites are accurate as of July 2011.

Baby and Bathwater Technique

When people voice criticisms, they frequently make the mistake of "throwing the baby out with the bathwater" as the saying goes. That is, they make sweeping criticisms of everything they have heard rather than being specific. The following technique enables team members to reflect on those areas on which they have reached consensus and to avoid making generalized critical statements.

The *Baby and Bathwater Technique* is deceptively simple. Quite often, both parties will discover during the final step that they have overestimated the scope and severity of their disagreement. This technique also helps redirect conflict away from a personal tug-of-war and toward a joint review of topics for discussion.

Follow these six steps to complete the procedure:

1. Preparation: For two participants, prepare a flipchart with columns and headers as shown in the model table below. If there are more than two people, revise the flipchart accordingly.

2. Getting Started: Make the following statement to your team members: "I'm going to ask you to individually explain your views on this situation. However, before telling us about those points on which you disagree, outline those points on which you feel you are in agreement."

   • Share the following example: "I agree with you that we need to have the software in place before we can go further on the project, and that, ideally the most effective software package would be one developed internally by our own IT department. The point on which you and I disagree concerns the *feasibility* of doing this. Our IT department is so backed up that going this route will slow our project down by three months."

   • Ask both parties to allow you to complete the chart before either one offers comments.

3. Agreements: Start with one speaker and ask, "With regard to this issue, on which points do you feel the two (or three, and so on) of you are in agreement?" List these points on the flipchart for review.

4. Disagreements: Then ask, "On what points do you disagree?"

5. Repeat Steps 3 and 4 with the second and any additional participants.

6. Review: After the entire chart has been completed, ask, "Looking at the flipchart, what do you see as your strongest points of agreement? On which points do we need to try to seek alignment?"

Linda's Point of View	Janet's Point of View
Points on Which We Agree	Points on Which We Agree
Points on Which We Disagree	Points on Which We Disagree

Change Analysis Chart

To help your team navigate through stressful situations, you must first be able to identify change indicators that act as a type of organizational "weather vane" by indicating significant changes in your company's direction. The *Change Analysis Chart* shown here identifies nine key indicators that tend to signal the onset of organizational change. This process begins by inviting each member of your team to take a day or so to respond individually to the questions presented in the chart. At a later date, set aside two hours to meet as a group and discuss your responses. During your team discussion, compare your individual observations and look for any recurring patterns in the data.

Change Analysis Chart

The change event you are tracking:

Change Indicators	Your Observations
Topics of Interest What topics currently capture the attention of executive-level leaders in their meetings? On what issues is your manager beginning to spend an increasing amount of time?	
Paths of Influence To what functions have your most influential managers been reassigned? Which functions have been handed off into mediocre performers? Which functions have recently been given approval to hire "A players" from the outside?	
Sources of Organizational Pride Which programs/functions have been highlighted in your company's newsletters or annual report? Which programs/functions have been recently paraded in front of key customers, the media, or your board of directors?	

(conitnued)

Change Analysis Chart (Continued)

Change Indicators	Your Observations
What Is Rewarded Which functions are now receiving top priority from your senior managers? Which functions/projects receive the greatest weight on your managers' bonus objectives? In which functions are budgets rapidly growing or shrinking?	
Shifts in Skills Emphasis What leadership and technical competencies are being aggressively sought by your company? What new technologies/products are being closely monitored? Which functions have recently received increased funds for training?	
Organizational Pioneers Who within your company would you consider as at the cutting-edge in your field? Where are these individuals currently focusing their attention?	
Outside Influences Which consultants are being courted by your senior managers? What feedback on impending changes are you receiving from external customers and suppliers? What trends are being avidly discussed in leading technical and business journals?	
Areas of Sensitivity Which work areas are being micromanaged by your boss? What topics are suddenly off-limits to your inquiries? Within which functions/projects do people quickly jump on emerging problems?	
Organizational Indicators What world-class corporate performers are your company attempting to track? What are these companies currently pursuing that is of such interest to your senior managers?	

Change Events Technique

Some of the tools to which you are being introduced in this book involve discrete change events that are at least partially within the control of your team. By contrast, the *Change Events Technique* begins with a review of large-scale changes that lie well beyond the control of your team and then moves inward to assess how these events could influence your team's success. Because this technique forces teams to shift their focus of attention from external events to team performance, we sometimes refer to it as the outside-in exercise.

The following *Change Events* chart illustrates how this technique has been applied by a cross-functional management-associate team that has been given the responsibility for introducing self-directed work teams to a selected plant site. Self-directed work teams are groups that are trained to function as semiautonomous and self-managed teams and whose members gradually learn to take on responsibilities that are traditionally reserved for managers.

To lead your team through the *Change Events Technique* process, complete the following five steps:

1. To begin, introduce the three component change areas. We find it easier to analyze large-scale changes if they are first broken down into these three areas. Also, indicate that the "what," "how," and "who" for each of these areas will be discussed.

   - *Functional* changes that affect the operation of discrete work functions

   - *Technological* changes that become a factor

   - Broader *organizational and business* changes that must be addressed

2. What: Next, have your team brainstorm the "what" or types of changes associated with each change area. In the example *Change Events* chart shown, one such change concerns the imminent introduction of computerized sorting machines.

3. How: Once your team has finished brainstorming, ask members to complete the "How" column by describing the possible effect of each identified change event on the project. Include both potential obstacles and opportunities.

4. Who: Complete the "Who" column, indicating the person(s) within or outside your organization who is considered the most knowledgeable about, or responsible for, each change event.

5. As the final step in the exercise, ask team members to circle the changes they feel are most likely to affect the team's long-term success. Then consider whether it is feasible to use some of the other tools in this book to better prepare your team to address these changes.

Change Events Technique Model Chart

Change Area	What?	How?	Who?
Functional	New plant manager will be coming on board	Does she support the program? Same priority?	Carlos Gonzalez, Manager
	Safety certification program coming online	Will this slow down our training effort?	Gary Smith, HR Director
Technological	Introduction of automated sorting machine	New responsibility for SDWT members	Nicky Hanson, Operations Manager
Organizational and Business	HR is planning a new quality incentive system	May encourage SDWT membership	Gary Smith, HR Director
	Major contract is anticipated for second quarter	Could take focus away from the SDWT project	Marta Sloan, CFO

Change Management Grid

Your team can use a change management grid to identify critical information gaps about an emerging change event, and determine the steps you can take to manage it. The completed *Change Management Grid* model shows how this grid might look if it were filled in by a hypothetical corporate training team that has just learned its company will soon be expanding into a new market area (auto sales).

Note that the top row of the grid contains three categories: Known, Unknown, and Sources.

- Known aspects are solid facts, not assumptions or guesses on the part of your team. In our completed example, the training team knows a number of facts, including the location of the new sales office (Auburn Hills) and the time frame for the staffing of this office (six months).

- Unknown aspects of the hypothetical change event in the completed example include the types of customer-based training that will be required as part of the corporate contract and the amount of funds allocated for training.

- Sources provide necessary information for your team. In our example, the training team identified the company's director of contract administration as the best source for information on specialized training, since this individual will be closely involved with contract compliance.

The second row of the chart covers three additional considerations for change: Within Our Control, Subject to Our Influence, and Beyond Our Control.

- The first category, Within Our Control, covers aspects of the change event that are completely within the team's control. In the completed example, members of the training team included the format of training delivery as one of the items they felt they control.

- Although unable to control certain events, a team may still be able to influence the decisions and actions of other individuals and work groups. In our example, the training team has decided that although they will not be in a position to determine whether training components are outsourced to another supplier, they can influence the selection of such vendors.

- Finally, some aspects of the change event will be beyond the team's control. In the completed example, the training team knows they have no control over training programs that are mandated by the contract.

Change Management Grid for Expansion into a New Market

Known	Unknown	Sources
Our company is planning to expand into the U.S. auto market over the next 6 months	What training will this group require over the next year?	New VP of auto market
		Director of contract administration
We have secured a contract with Ford Motor Company	What customer-based training (for example, completion of customer's quality assurance course) will these employees be expected to complete?	VP of human resources
This market sector will be based in Auburn Hills, MI.		Director of contract administration
First year of operation will involve a staff of 150	What is the expected staff size in year two?	New VP of auto market
No training needs have yet been identified for this employee group	What training (ISO 9000) will be mandatory? What will be optional?	New VP of auto market
	What training funds have been budgeted for this department?	VP of human resources
	Which managers will be heading up this operation?	

Within Our Control	Subject to Our Influence	Beyond Our Control
Selection of staff allocated to this project	Timing/scheduling of training	Training requirements mandated by the contract
Delivery format for training	Criteria we use to evaluate training	Amount of auto staff time available to participate in training
Design and delivery of corporate-mandated training	Our recommendations regarding outsourced training supplier	
	Recommendations for supplemental budget to meet these needs	

Closing the Gap Chart

Teams can lose momentum or experience performance setbacks. This tool provides a structure for members to determine how to close the gap between where they are to where they want to be. Using the *Closing the Gap Chart*, members explore solution options that are applicability to their needs.

Apply this technique by completing the following steps:

1. Next to each option, briefly describe the challenge the team is experiencing.

2. Describe how each of the four options outlined in this chart could be applied to your team's current setback.

3. Invite an objective third party from outside your team to play the role of troubleshooter as your team selects the most applicable options for regaining momentum.

Solution Options	Applicable to Your Team?
Deploy additional resources: Obtain additional staff or resources to raise your level of work activity.	
Reframe the problem: Redefine your setback in a way that makes it easier to overcome.	
Redesign your implementation strategy: Revise your project plan through such actions as dividing into subteams or looking for ways to eliminate nonessential steps from your project.	
Renegotiate project parameters: Determine the possibility of renegotiating elements such as scope of the project, final delivery schedule, or deadlines for completion of key milestones.	

Creative Whack Pack®

The *Creative Whack Pack®* is a problem-solving discussion tool developed by creativity consultant Roger von Oech, the author of two best-selling books on creativity, *A Whack on the Side of the Head* and *A Kick in the Seat of the Pants*. The pack is a deck of sixty four cards divided into four different suits. Each suit contains sixteen cards that pose questions about a different phase of problem solving:

- *Explorer* cards pertain to alternative ways of extracting information that relates to the problem at hand.

- *Artist* cards address the process of merging available information into creative combinations.

- *Judge* cards relate to analyzing potential solutions and deciding on the best way to apply them.

- *Warrior* cards apply to thinking through the implementation of potential solutions.

There are many ways to apply the *Creative Whack Pack*, some of which are described in a miniguide that comes with the card deck. We have outlined below one approach that has been useful for us.

Divide the cards into their four suits, and then use them to supplement brainstorming as your team moves through the four stages of problem solving. If your team has been engaged in creative brainstorming regarding potential solutions to a problem, take out the Artist cards and ask team members to draw one card each and read the question on the card aloud. The team could then discuss how each question could be applied to the problem at hand. For instance, Card 19 of the Artist suit, entitled "Challenge the Rules," offers the example of Alexander the Great, who solved the problem of untying the Gordian knot by cutting it in half with his sword. According to von Oech, the deck's creator, Alexander made up his own rules to the game represented by this problem. Card 19 poses the question "What rules can you challenge?" After reading this card aloud, challenge your team to list all the rules or assumptions they have imposed on the problem at hand, and ask them to determine which ones might be subject to change.

The *Creative Whack Pack* is not a problem-solving process; it is a tool that embeds creative thinking into a team's problem-solving discussion. The pack may help your team develop innovative thinking toward unique solutions and ideas.

For more information, contact Roger von Oech at Creative Think, Box 7354, Menlo Park, California 94026 (telephone 650–321–6775).

Customer Assessment Matrix

We like to think that all of our customers are of equal importance. Yet some have more impact on the success of your organization and your team than others. So, assuming that your team has limited staff, time, and resources, it makes sense to understand how the team can focus their attention on meeting the needs of crucial customer groups. To do this, you must determine which of your customers are truly "gold customers." The *Customer Assessment Matrix* can help your team identify these customers.

The completed *Customer Assessment Matrix* model represents a hypothetical sales team discussion. Let's walk through the seven steps of how this sales team created their matrix and how you and your team can create your own.

Customer Assessment Matrix

Customer	Customer Rating Factors					
	Current Sales Volume (8)	Projected Sales Volume (10)	Strategic Importance (7)	Investment Requirement (5)	Gateway Potential (7)	Assessment Total
Alpha Co.	2/16	3/30	3/21	5/25	4/28	120
Beta Co.	3/24	2/20	3/21	2/10	5/35	110
Delta Co.	4/32	5/50	5/35	4/20	3/21	**158**
Theta Co.	4/32	4/40	2/14	3/15	3/21	122

1. Customers: List all customers served by your team.

2. Factors for Evaluation: Agree on the distinguishing factors that will characterize a gold customer. The top row of the sales team's completed model shows five factors you could also consider:

   - Current total sales volume for a customer

   - Projected sales volume for a customer over the next three years

   - Customer's strategic importance to the company's long-term business plan

- Investment requirement, that is, the amount of resources that will be required to service the account

- Gateway potential, that is, the likelihood that the account will lead to additional business

3. Importance Scale: Use a 1 to 10 scale (10 = highest) to determine the relative importance of each factor. Write these scores next to the corresponding factors in the top row. For example, in the completed model "Projected Volume" is the most important factor as 10, whereas "Investment Requirement" is lowest as 5.

4. Evaluation Rating: Evaluate your customers in terms of each factor on a 1 to 5 rating scale. Write these ratings to the left of a hash mark ("/"). As shown in the model, "Projected Volume" for Delta Co. was rated high with a 5 and Beta Co. received a 2 rating. Note that rating numbers may be used more than once within the same factor. To minimize evaluative bias, we highly recommend that the team evaluate one customer at a time across all factors (moving across), rather than evaluate all customers within one factor. We also suggest that a customer's completed ratings be set aside (out of sight, out of mind) when starting another customer's evaluation.

5. Score: Next, use a little math to create an assessment score. Multiply the customer's evaluation rating number by the factor's relative importance score. Place this number to the right of the hash mark ("/"). For example, in the model "Projected Volume" has an importance of 10. Delta Co.'s high rating of 5 was multiplied by 10 and the assessment score of 50 was noted—5/50 is Delta's rating/score for that factor. Similarly, you can see that in the "Project Volume" column each customer's rating was multiplied by 10.

6. Assessment Total: For each customer, add the scores for each factor and enter that number in the Assessment Total column. For example, Alpha's factor scores (16, 30, 21, 25, and 28, respectively) totaled 120.

7. Results: The customer(s) receiving the highest assessment score is your team's gold customer. Within the model, Delta Co. is the most important customer with a 158 total assessment score. If the resulting assessment scores are numerically close, you and your team may want to search for more definitive differences. Two options for doing this are to (a) revisit an evaluation of each customer, going more in-depth into the discussion, and/or (b) identify additional factors that will help distinguish gold customers.

Customer Relationship Audit

Your customers might feel you do an excellent job when it comes to your work output, yet still feel that there are opportunities for improving the interpersonal relationships between your respective groups. One way to evaluate the quality of your customer relationships is to perform a *Customer Relationship Audit*. This process involves sitting down with your customers and identifying opportunities in five key areas:

- Accessibility: How available is your team to your customers?

- Responsiveness: How quickly, and with how much enthusiasm, do your team members respond to customers' requests and inquiries?

- Listening skills: How much attention does your team pay to customers' inquiries and concerns?

- Information sharing: How open is your team about sharing information with customers?

- Collaboration and conflict resolution: How effective is your team at being collaborative, especially when resolving problems or conflicts?

Use the *Customer Relationship Audit* to obtain feedback on these five factors. The audit is a questionnaire containing fifteen questions that address behaviors related to these five factors. The audit also includes two additional open-ended questions to help your team identify which behaviors work for your team and which ones need to be changed. To complete this audit, follow these guidelines:

1. Ensure Confidentiality: Because the questionnaire pertains to somewhat sensitive performance factors, consider giving multiple questionnaires to one of your customer groups and then having one member of that group provide you with the team's averaged scores and collected comments. By offering respondents this confidentiality, you increase the amount of feedback you can obtain.

2. Ensure Understanding: Once you have received your customers'
   feedback, you will want to ask for their help in interpreting it.
   If your customers are unable or unwilling to describe specific inci-
   dents of problem behaviors, suggest that they provide hypothetical
   examples. For instance, a customer might say, "We don't feel your
   team listens completely to us. For example, if we were to ask for an
   exemption to company policy, we feel you would refuse our request
   on the spot without even discussing or considering it."

Customer Relationship Audit

Relationship Factors	Customer Ratings Low. . .Moderate. . .High
Accessibility 1. You can reach us easily by phone or e-mail. 2. We are readily available for face-to-face meetings. 3. We take the initiative to arrange meetings with you.	1. . .2. . .3. . .4. . .5. . .6. . .7 1. . .2. . .3. . .4. . .5. . .6. . .7 1. . .2. . .3. . .4. . .5. . .6. . .7
Responsiveness 4. We make an effort to respond quickly to your requests for assistance. 5. If we are not able to respond to your requests, we try to direct you to others who can help. 6. We convey a high level of enthusiasm when responding to your requests.	 1. . .2. . .3. . .4. . .5. . .6. . .7 1. . .2. . .3. . .4. . .5. . .6. . .7 1. . .2. . .3. . .4. . .5. . .6. . .7
Listening Skills 7. We give you our full attention during discussions. 8. When you leave a discussion with us, you feel we clearly understand and have not misinterpreted what you have said. 9. We present ourselves as being open-minded and willing to listen to different points of view.	 1. . .2. . .3. . .4. . .5. . .6. . .7 1. . .2. . .3. . .4. . .5. . .6. . .7 1. . .2. . .3. . .4. . .5. . .6. . .7
Information Sharing 10. We freely share important information with you (we are not reluctant to disclose information you need to perform your job). 11. We provide timely information about changes that could affect your department. 12. When sharing information, we communicate clearly and succinctly.	 1. . .2. . .3. . .4. . .5. . .6. . .7 1. . .2. . .3. . .4. . .5. . .6. . .7 1. . .2. . .3. . .4. . .5. . .6. . .7
Collaboration and Conflict Resolution 13. We make an effort to work harmoniously with you. 14. We look for win-win solutions to problems. 15. When involved in a conflict, we conduct ourselves professionally (no yelling, personal criticisms, and so forth).	1. . .2. . .3. . .4. . .5. . .6. . .7 1. . .2. . .3. . .4. . .5. . .6. . .7 1. . .2. . .3. . .4. . .5. . .6. . .7

Other
16. What one behavior should we continue to strengthen relationships between our teams?
17. What one behavior do we need to change to strengthen relationships between our teams?

Customer Requirements Rating Table

The *Customer Requirements Rating Table* tool will help you pinpoint your customers' key requirements and evaluate your team's effectiveness in relation to those requirements. The word "requirements" refers to the features of your team's products and services that are especially important to your customers. Requirements come in all shapes and sizes. Common examples of customer requirements (such as, timeliness, responsiveness, cost, quality) are described below to help your team get started.

Some requirements are more important than others. For example, your customer may care more about the timely delivery of their financial report than their report's attractiveness (such as a four-color layout with high-end graphics). It is essential for a team to know the relative importance of different requirements in order to make the best trade-offs, when necessary, between competing requirements. Going back to the financial report example, this customer may be willing to work from a well-organized spreadsheet, minus graphics, if it means getting this report earlier in the month. In fact, the ideal solution may be to offer the customer the ability to pull financial data, as needed, by placing the report on the company's intranet.

To complete the *Customer Requirements Rating Table* for your team, follow these steps:

1. First, we recommend completing the *Customer Assessment Matrix* to identify gold customers. Then, use that list as a starting point for working with this tool.

2. Select a Customer. Identify the primary customer for which this *Customer Requirements Rating Table* will be completed. If your team could address their performance for just one customer, which customer would it be? Write this customer's name(s) in the space provided in the table.

3. Identify an Output. Select one of the most important outputs your team provides to this customer. An output is a specific product or service outcome. Briefly summarize this output in the space provided. For instance, the following teams might identify these vital outputs:

- Help desk: a service call
- Design team: a software program
- Training team: a training program
- Finance team: a financial report
- HR team: phone responses to inquiries regarding company policies

4. Compile Requirements List. "Requirements" are those performance factors you and your team believe are especially important to your customer. These are the expectations your team must meet when generating its outputs. List these requirements in the left-had column of the table.

5. Rate Importance to Customer. Using a scale of 1 to 7 (7 is highest importance), ask your team to rate the relative importance of each requirement to that customer. This is your team's best guess as to how your customer would rate the relative importance of each requirement for the selected output. Record the score for each requirement in the "Importance to Customer" column.

6. Rate Performance of Team. Using the same scale of 1 to 7 (7 is highest performance), ask your team to rate its current performance in fulfilling each requirement. Record the score for each requirement in the "Performance of Team" column.

7. Obtain Customer Feedback. You are now ready for the moment of truth—asking your customer for feedback. You may obtain this feedback from discussions with your entire customer team, team leader, or representative members of the team.

   a. Provide your customer with a partially filled *Customer Requirements Rating Table*—include the output and requirements information, but no ratings. Do not share your team's ratings to avoid influencing how your customer rates the factors of importance and performance.

   b. Ask your customer to use the scale of 1 to 7 to indicate the relative importance of each requirement; then, to rate your team's performance on each requirement. Place these ratings in their respective columns, Importance to Customer column and Performance of Team.

8. Discuss Team and Customer Ratings. Discuss the comparison between your team's and the customer's ratings of the requirements. What gaps are indicated? Discover in which area(s) you have an opportunity for improvement and develop a plan accordingly.

Customer Requirements Rating Table

Customer Requirements Rating Table		
Customer:		
Output:		
Customer Requirements	Importance to Customer	Performance of Team
1.		
2.		
3.		
4.		
5.		
6.		
7.		
8.		

■ ■ ■

Common Examples of Customer Requirements

Timeliness	The degree to which your team provides products and services in a timely manner. A computer manufacturer that requires the completion of an elaborate purchase order before shipping the product via snail-mail would be rated as poor in this area, while a competitor that offers direct ordering through the Internet and guaranteed overnight delivery would be rated extremely high.
Responsiveness	The degree to which a team responds quickly and with enthusiasm to customers' needs. The team that makes it a point to answer all phone calls on the first ring and immediately takes action on customers' concerns would score high in this area. In contrast, a team that lets their phones ring off the hook and fails to follow up on voice mail messages would score very low in its ability to meet this requirement.
Cost	"Cost" doesn't mean the actual price of a product or service but the degree to which customers perceive value obtained for their investments. Consider a video production department that bills its marketing department $20,000 to create a ten-minute infomercial. If the marketing department believes a well-known external production house is prepared to provide the same service for half this price, the video team will receive a low rating on this requirement.
Friendliness	The degree to which your team is viewed as friendly and helpful. A team that responds to a request with "No, we can't help you" would score low on this requirement. A highly rated team might respond with a statement such as "We can't provide that service, but I can put you in touch with a department that can help you. If you'll stay on the line, I'll see if I can connect you."
Quality	The degree to which a requirement is error free and meets all necessary specifications. A software design team that produces a program with few glitches would be rated high in this area, while a team that has to go through several versions of a program to keep debugging it would receive a poor rating.
User-friendliness	The degree to which a product or service is easy for the customer to use and apply. A tax guide that's only a few pages long and clear enough to eliminate alternative interpretations would be rated high on this requirement. In contrast, the complex guidelines provided by the IRS are generally rated low in this area.
Reliability	The degree to which a product or service can be used repeatedly without flaws, errors, or deviations in a consistent fashion. A cleaning team that is assigned to service an office at 8 P.M. and frequently arrives late would be rated poor on this requirement, but a team that shows up promptly and consistently would be scored high.

Customer Satisfaction/Importance Matrix

The *Customer Satisfaction/Importance Matrix* helps your team identify perception gaps or differences between your team's view of their performance and your customers' views their performance on an important output. We recommend that your team obtain customer feedback using the *Customer Requirements Rating Table* tool and then visually interpret your findings by creating a *Customer Satisfaction/Importance Matrix*. Let's review a completed model from a hypothetical team to understand how this matrix is laid out, completed, and interpreted.

The layout of the matrix reflects the same information as that in the *Customer Requirements Rating Table* tool, and then aligns rating data into quadrants for further interpretation. The top area is where the customer's name and the selected output are placed. The vertical axis, "Importance to Customer," shows how important the selected requirements are to the customer. "Requirements" are those performance factors you and your team believe are especially important to your customer for a specific output. The horizontal axis, "Customer Satisfaction of Team Performance," reflects the customer's rating of the team on fulfilling those requirements. Both axes reflect a 1 to 7 rating scale (7 is highest).

The completed model displays all requirements for a hypothetical team responsible for installing cable television, and the specific output under review is the service installation calls. The team has received feedback on four service requirements from a sampling of their customers within the "ABC region." These requirements and their ratings are indicated on the matrix as A, B, C, D and are described as follows:

1. A: Dependability. Does the team arrive at the customer's house as scheduled and complete the job in a timely manner?

   Model rating: 6 = Importance to Customer and 2 = Customer Satisfaction

2. B: Quality. Is the installation completed effectively without the need for a second service call?

   Model rating: 5 = Importance to Customer and 4 = Customer Satisfaction

3. C: Friendliness. Are the installation technicians courteous and professional?

Model rating: 3 = Importance to Customer and 3 = Customer Satisfaction

4. D: Education. Are the installation technicians providing their customers with education and information on their digital cable technology?

Model rating: 2 = Importance to Customer and 6 = Customer Satisfaction

Customer Satisfaction/Importance Matrix							
Customer: Sampling of Region ABC Customers Output: Digital Television Cable Installation							
High **7**	Gold Mine Quadrant			Satisfaction Junction Quadrant			
6	**A**-Dependability (6/2)						
5				**B**-Quality (5/4)			
4							
3	Who Cares? Quadrant			Consider Effort Quadrant			
			C-Friendly (3/3)				
2						**D**-Education (2/6)	
1							
Low	1	2	3	4	5	6	7

Importance to Customer

Customer Satisfaction of Team Performance   **High**

Once the rating data are plotted on the matrix, it is time to interpret the results. In this model's scenario there are several points to note. Begin with the customer's most important requirement and how the team performed in fulfilling this service. In this case, customers are very dissatisfied with the team's performance in the area of dependability (A, 6/2). This quadrant is named "Gold Mine" as it represent a critical improvement opportunity that can be mined to yield increased customer satisfaction.

Second, customers rate the team fairly high on quality (B, 5/4). This quadrant is called "Satisfaction Junction" because these requirements represent important service features on which the team is performing well and indicates opportunities for continued satisfaction enhancements. Third, the team's service technicians may not be perceived as the world's friendliest (C, 3/3), but this requirement is of average importance to their customers. This quadrant is "Who Cares?" to remind the team that these items represent less significant service opportunities, as the importance of the requirement is low. Finally, the customers rate the team's performance on customer education as high while the requirement's importance is low. This quadrant, "Consider Effort," reminds the team to consider whether continued effort and time on this requirement should continue as is or be revisited to open opportunities for the upper quadrants.

In summary, in this model, customers indicate the team's primary focus for improvement should be in "Dependability." The team needs to determine how to refocus or change work processes to enable an on-time arrival and service completion at customers' locations.

Finally, the *Customer Satisfaction/Importance Matrix* can be enhanced by including additional data values on how your customers view the performance of your competitor(s). This information would be extremely valuable in helping the team determine what steps they could take to surpass their competitors.

Decision Matrix

This tool is one of the most commonly used methods for analyzing solutions options and improvement ideas. The first step in creating your matrix is to ask your team to help determine criteria for evaluating their ideas. The completed model is by a hypothetical team reviewing solution options to drive innovation. This model includes examples of frequently used criteria entered into the "Criteria" column:

- Effectiveness: Will the idea actually have a positive impact on the team's work performance?
- Cost: How much will it cost to implement the idea?
- Customer impact: Will the idea help, and not have a negative effect on, internal or external customers?
- Feasibility: Is the idea easy to implement?
- Time: Can the idea be implemented quickly?
- Control: Can the idea be put into action directly by the team?

After team members identify the criteria they wish to use, they should determine the "Criteria Importance Rating" or relative importance of each criteria. A simple way of doing this is to assign values to each criterion based on a scale of 1 to 10 (10 is essential, 1 is unimportant). Have team members score the criteria individually first. Afterward, arrive at the team's overall importance rating for each criterion by adding the individuals' scores and then dividing by the total number of individuals. The model shows that "Effectiveness" criteria is most important (10) and "Feasibility" has second importance (9).

Next, indicate the "Solution Options" the team is reviewing in the top row of the *Decision Matrix*. The model shows that the team has identified four potential solutions to this opportunity. Now ask each team member to rate each solution option, using a 1 to 5 scale (5 is highest), in terms of its ability to meet the team's criteria. In the model, the five members have rated their four solutions against the criterion of "effectiveness." For each solution option, the individual scores are listed along with the average score (average scores are 4.8, 3.2, 2.2, 3.0, respectively).

Remember that the team also rated the relative importance of each criterion, and "effectiveness" received the highest possible rating. By multiplying each importance rating by each solution option's average score, you arrive at the team's final scores for the four solutions. In the model, "Effectiveness" has "Solution Options" final scores of 48, 32, 22, and 30, respectively. Have your team continue this process for each criterion to determine total scores for all solution options.

Finally, total the solution options' scores within each column. The solution with the highest total score will generally be the team's selected solution. If, however, several solutions receive similar scores, this would suggest that the team should engage in further discussion before ending its evaluation. In addition, your team may decide to pursue more than one solution simultaneously.

Decision Matrix—Driving Innovation

		Solution Options			
Criteria	**Criteria Importance Rating**	**Perform external benchmark studies**	**Attend technical conference as a team**	**Submit team improvement project to annual corporate continual improvement contest**	**Form learning consortium with other local companies**
Effectiveness	10	5, 5, 4, 5, 5 = 4.8; **48 total**	4, 2, 2, 5, 3 = 3.2; **32 total**	4, 1, 1, 2, 3 = 2.2; **22 total**	3, 3, 3, 3, 3 = 3; **30 total**
Cost	6				
Customer impact	8				
Feasibility	9				
Time	4				
Control	8				
Total					

Early Warning Chart

Use the *Early Warning Chart* to help your team establish its own monitoring system—an early warning process for addressing potential challenges. Schedule time during a team meeting to complete the following five steps:

1. Areas for Monitoring. Use the first column to list the types of tasks and project areas that should be closely tracked for changes and potential problems by team members. When attempting to define areas for monitoring many teams have found it useful to consider the following criteria:

   - Importance: Teams should give special attention to work areas that have the greatest impact on their performance.

   - Volatility: Teams should closely monitor those work areas that are subject to sudden, unpredictable changes.

   - Past Experience: Teams should identify past situations in which they were caught off guard by sudden problems or changes and try to determine why they were unable to anticipate these events.

2. Red Flags. In this step, your team identifies "red flags," or indicators that signal sudden changes or problems. Common indicators might include:

   - Sudden increase in customer complaints

   - Sudden increase in delayed payments from a major account

   - Loss or gain of a major corporate contract

   - Proposed large-scale changes for a function's work methods or processes

3. Suggested Guidelines. Ask your team to establish agreed upon guidelines for monitoring key work areas and red flags. Team guidelines usually address the following factors:

   - Will a single team member or the entire team be responsible for monitoring selected work areas?

- Should the team leader be the only one alerted to emerging problems or changes, or should the entire team be placed on alert?

- At what point should the team or team leader be alerted to changes? In other words, what degree of urgency do we assign to the change areas we have identified?

4. Suggested Follow-Up Actions. Finally, your team should develop procedures for following up on the actions and guidelines you identified in Steps 1 through 3. During the follow-up session, your team should review the success of your tracking system by asking the following questions:

- Have we improved our ability to anticipate and plan for problems or changes within this work area? Are we still encountering nasty surprises? If so, what do we need to change about our monitoring system?

- How quickly are we able to alert ourselves to problems? Are there ways of further reducing the time between the occurrence of problems or changes and the point at which our team is first alerted to them?

- Are we supplying the right people within and outside our team with necessary information?

- Are we getting accurate information on problems and changes?

- Are we getting complete information on problems and changes?

- How could we further improve our early warning system?

5. Document and Post Chart. Ensure that the *Early Warning Chart* is understood and available to all team members. Review the chart as needed to maintain accuracy and effectiveness.

Early Warning Chart

Areas for Monitoring	Red Flags	Suggested Guidelines	Suggested Follow-Up Actions

Follow-Up Team Building Questionnaire

The *Follow-Up Team Building Questionnaire* can be used to evaluate the success of a team-building session, to help a team learn from these shared experiences and assess the need for additional team-building work in the future. The questionnaire consists of six open-ended questions.

Open-Ended Questions

1. Looking back on it, what worked for you about our team-building session?

2. What was one thing that you personally gained from this session?

3. Out of all of the commitments that we made at the conclusion of the session, which ones have we met? Where have we taken concrete action?

4. In your mind, which of these actions still remain to be accomplished? What steps do we need to take at this point to accomplish these actions?

5. What was different about how we worked together during our team-building session that you would like to see replicated in our future interactions? In other words, what worked that you would like to see more of in the future?

6. Has our team-building session helped to reveal any additional issues that our team needs to address or opportunities that we need to explore?

Three Implementation Options

There are three options for completing this follow-up questionnaire.

Option One: Confidential Feedback Allow 90 minutes for this follow-up process. The questionnaire can be e-mailed to team members with the request that they send their responses back to the team facilitator. The facilitator compiles the responses without referencing respondents' names, and then e-mails the consolidated list back out to the entire team for discussion during the follow-up session.

This option provides the following advantages:

- It makes it easy to obtain feedback from virtual members.

- It gives team members additional time for critical reflection before submitting their initial responses, and additional time for reflection in having the opportunity to review all of the team's comments before entering into the team-building session.

- It provides a safe avenue for the sharing of perspectives.

- It saves some initial time during the team-building session by beginning data collection prior to the start of the follow-up session.

Option Two: Real-Time Review Allow three hours for this follow-up process. In this option the questions are simply posted on a flipchart or board at the beginning of the follow-up session. Each question is discussed in turn and responses posted. Members are advised to refrain from evaluating others' comments until all are posted for review.

This option provides the following advantages:

- It may support team collaboration since team members engage in the simultaneous discussion of their team-building experience.

- It may encourage a greater feeling of openness and transparency since all concerns and issues are openly aired.

- As team members hear others' comments they have opportunities to add to those comments.

Option Three: Modified Gallery Technique Allow three hours for this follow-up process. In this option the team employs a modified version of the *Gallery Technique* found in your Tool Kit. In advance of the session, the facilitator writes each of the six questions at the top of a separate piece of flipchart paper. These questions are then posted on the walls for team review. Participants are then given marker pens and sticky notes, and encouraged to take 30 minutes to stroll through this "gallery." Using their sticky notes they can post their comments to any questions, as they wish. During this time members are not allowed to discuss their own responses, nor are they allowed to comment on others' comments posted. After all comments are posted, the facilitator reviews each question along with the posted answers. The team members are encouraged to share additional comments and those comments can be noted on the flipcharts.

This approach offers the following advantages:

- It may support team collaboration by allowing team members to engage in the simultaneous review of their team-building experience.

- By insuring that all concerns and issues are openly aired, it may encourage a greater feeling of openness and transparency.

- It gives team members additional time for reflection, by giving them the opportunity to review others' posted comments before engaging in the discussion.

- It provides a relatively safe venue for the sharing of perspectives.

- It gives participants the chance to respond to those aspects of the team-building process that were relevant to their personal experiences.

Forecast Grid

Sometimes teams hesitate to undertake a major business initiative because they fear the potential difficulties and negative repercussions that might ensue from innovative actions. One way to keep these fears in check is to encourage your team to explore all the possible implications of tackling a major project or initiative. To explore this area, use the *Forecast Grid,* which encourages your team to think through a variety of effects that could result from new business initiatives, ranging from ripple effects for other organizational functions to the cost implications of taking on a new initiative.

The *Forecast Grid* tool has four useful applications. First, it can help your team determine whether the potential payoffs outweigh the potential problems associated with the new initiative. Second, it can guide your team in anticipating and eliminating obstacles that might be encountered in undertaking the new initiative. Third, it provides a means of obtaining alignment on project goals, outcomes, and roadblocks well before you undertake the project. Complete the grid's troubleshooting questions and then share the results with your manager or any other important stakeholders who will play a strong role in your proposed business initiative. Finally, you can use this chart to compare the likely payoffs and problems associated with implementing two or more alternative projects. Such an assessment is especially useful when your team has limited time and resources and must select just a few new areas for innovation.

The grid's first column lists four "Potential Repercussions"—Ripple Effects, Cost and Revenue, Team Relationships, Work Efficiency—as a starting point for your team discussion. To complete the grid, take the following steps:

1. Discuss the troubleshooting questions that are provided for each potential repercussion. Record your team's conclusions to each question in the "Team Response" column.

   - Use these questions to identify all potential positive and negative repercussions that could ensue from this project.

2. Impact Rating. Use a rating scale of 5 to +5 (5 is negative impact and +5 is high positive impact) to rate the impact each repercussion will have.

3. Odds Rating. Use a rating scale of 1 to 5 (1 is unlikely and 5 is very likely) to rate the likelihood that a given area or repercussion could actually occur.

4. Total Score. Multiply the two rating scales to arrive at a total score. Note that a given score could be either negative or positive. Record this score in the "Total Score" column.

Once the *Forecast Grid* is completed, facilitate a team discussion on monitoring two areas of potential repercussion:

1. The potential repercussion that has the *highest positive* total score.

2. The potential repercussion has the *highest negative* total score.

Forecast Grid

Potential Repercussion	Troubleshooting Questions	Team Response	A: Impact Rating (−5 to +5)	B: Odds Rating (1 to 5)	Total Score (A × B)
Ripple Effects	Will this project create additional problems for other work functions? Will this project eliminate efficiency, quality, or staffing problems for other functions?				
Cost and Revenue	Will the completion of this project require a heavy initial investment? Once completed, will this project help you reduce costs or generate additional revenue?				
Team Relationships	Will this project produce a strain in your team's relationships with other work groups? Does it involve an area of great political sensitivity? Will this project provide opportunities for your team to work with and strengthen relationships with other functions?				
Work Efficiency	Will this project involve temporary disruptions to work flow or customer service? Once completed, will this project increase overall work efficiency or customer service?				

Forecast Guide

When we think about what to do to develop change-management skills, we tend to focus on accommodating large-scale changes that lie well beyond our control. At the same time, we frequently forget to consider how major change events initiated by our team might affect others in our organization. To explore this, ask your team to select one upcoming business initiative for review. Next, have the team review and answer the questions in the *Forecast Guide* tool.

In addition, we strongly recommend that you invite several key stakeholders to participate in the forecast discussion with your team. By taking these steps, you will accomplish several things. First, you will begin to identify potential obstacles that could derail your project. Next, while developing greater alignment among team members and stakeholders regarding your project implementation strategy, you will also be encouraging stakeholders to accept some degree of ownership for the success of your business initiative. Finally, by treating stakeholders as representatives of your overall organization, you will be able to identify opportunities and concerns that may be addressed when you present the initiative to other groups in your organization.

Forecast Guide

Briefly describe a significant, future business initiative for your team:	
Implications for Your Business Initiative?	**Decision Criteria**
	Ripple effects? Could this business initiative produce a strong, negative ripple effect in other areas of your organization? Example: The revised hiring system your HR department is proposing requires additional time and paperwork in other departments.
	Uncertain, unpredictable changes? Does the success of this business initiative depend on unpredictable large-scale factors? Example: You discover that the electronic database your team is trying to create must be compatible with the PeopleSoft® system your company is currently installing. The timetable for your project might be contingent on the timetable for the PeopleSoft® system.

(continued)

Forecast Guide (Continued)

Implications for Your Business Initiative?	Decision Criteria
	Permanent and difficult to modify? Once the initiative has been implemented, how difficult will it be to modify the changes you've made? Example: The business initiative you are considering requires a substantial redesign of facilities and equipment.
	High level of resistance? Are your managers and associates likely to react to this change initiative with a high level of resistance? Example: The initiative calls for specific functional responsibilities to be shifted from one department to another, and you're sure certain managers will oppose what could be interpreted as a loss of status and power.
	Complicated and requires coordination? Does the change initiative require coordination with other departments and/or external suppliers, as opposed to being something your team can accomplish entirely on its own? Example: Your revisions to the format of your company's annual conference require the cooperation of departments that handle events and travel, training, purchasing, and marketing.
	Uncertain financial payoffs? Are the financial returns for this initiative relatively uncertain? Could the investment turn into a financial black hole? Example: Your initiative involves your company's first entry into mobile advertising. Has your team developed an adequate cost-and-revenue model that predicts your financial break-even point, or are there too many variables to assess the financial payoffs for this endeavor?
	Affects internal or external customers? Will the implementation of the business initiative adversely affect your customers? Example: Your IT team is recommending major changes to your company's intranet server. Does this mean internal customers will experience an extended server shutdown?

Gallery Technique

The *Gallery Technique* is an evaluation process that resembles the structure of an art gallery. The tool is useful whenever team members are entering into an extremely sensitive problem-solving situation and may have some difficulty remaining open to one another's points of view. The premise behind the gallery technique is to enable team members to carefully articulate their solutions before posting them, to consider all solutions before commenting on any of them, and to express their concerns in writing. This latter point is especially important, because people tend to provide a more balanced perspective when asked to put their ideas in writing, as opposed to saying the first thing that pops into their minds.

To initiate this technique, complete the following steps:

1. Provide each team member with a sheet of flipchart paper and ask them to write out a statement or two (in large print, so the flipcharts can be read easily) describing a tentative solution to the problem under consideration by the team.

2. Ask team members not to sign their names—all solutions should be anonymous. As soon as team members finish describing their solutions, they should scroll up their flipchart pages and hand them in to you.

3. Next, dismiss the team and post all solutions on the wall.

4. Reconvene your team and ask them to walk around and silently review all of the posted solutions. They should refrain from making comments during this time.

5. Give your team 15 minutes to read and review all solutions, and then invite them to identify those on which they wish to comment.

6. Give your team an additional 15 minutes to write at the bottom of the flipchart pages they've selected any clarifying questions (when they're having difficulty understanding a solution), any suggestions for strengthening the solution, or any concerns regarding the solution. Tell them they may respond on as many pages as they wish, as long as they stay within the time limit.

7. At the end of this thirty-minute review and responding period, start at one end of your "gallery" and read aloud both the posted solution and the subsequent commentary.

8. At this point, the owners of the solutions are free (if they choose) to identify themselves and respond to any questions, suggestions, or concerns.

"GETTING NAKED" SESSION OR NEW TEAM ASSIMILATION
Contributed by Samir Gupte

Trust is a key to success for any team whether it is a short-term project team or an existing and ongoing entity. Transparency from the leader and amongst team members engenders and enables trust at an amplified rate. The greater the amount of information about the leader that becomes available as early in the process of forming any team for any reason, the higher the level of perceived transparency and ultimately greater level of trust is formed. This could permit a team to achieve their desired result in a shorter period of time.

The *New Team Assimilation* process, which a French client referred to as "Getting Naked," is designed to achieve just that. It is a creative collaboration process—a systematic, structured approach by which the leader of a team shares openly the information or questions from the head and heart of the members of the team. This technique has been used across the globe, in a variety of industries and organizations, at and across all levels, departments, and functions. Ideally this technique would be employed approximately four to six weeks after a new team has been formed or a new leader appointed to lead an existing team.

The first step is to align with the leader on the importance and benefit of attaining an accelerated depth and speed of trust attainment within the team and between the team and leader. Next you must find a facilitator to lead the session. The most important quality to consider when selecting the facilitator is someone who can immediately engender trust with the group that will undergo the facilitation. There are too many variables that will factor into that decision. Using the ability to engender trust as the basic criteria, the team leader along with the group's HR partner should be in the best position to consider and select the most appropriate individual to facilitate from inside or outside the organization.

Selecting the correct venue is an important element of the set-up process. If at all possible, select a meeting space that is physically away from the team's work area. In many cities there are creative spaces that are designed for meetings such as these. You will want to find space that can accommodate your group size, placement/hanging of flip charts, and basic refreshments.

Allocating a half-day to this event as well as a team celebration with either lunch or dinner is smart from a planning perspective. You could schedule a half-day block that would end with lunch or begin after lunch with a team dinner or happy hour after the event.

Basic materials for the session are at least two flipcharts with easels, flip-chart markers, tape (flipchart paper with adhesive on the back is best) or tacks, and drinks/snacks.

So, you have decided that this is an important technique to enhance creative collaboration and have found a trustworthy facilitator. An interesting venue has been procured and post-meeting meal is arranged. It is time to invite the team to attend. When you send the meeting invitation it is great to provide the purpose or objective for the meeting, but don't feel like a detailed agenda is necessary. There is a benefit to more top-of-mind responses during the actual meeting than having people prepare too much in advance.

The agenda for the *New Team Assimilation* process is as follows:

- Welcome, introductions, and expectations
- (Team leader departs)
- Facilitation
- (Participants depart)
- Debrief with team leader
- Team leader discussion with participants
- Team celebration

Welcome

The team leader begins the meeting by thanking the group for attending this session, explains the importance and their desired outcomes for the session. The most important aspect of this agenda item is for the team leader to state unequivocally that open, candid, constructive answers, and feedback to the questions that will be posed are the key to success for this process. The facilitator should ask the group for their expectations or desired outcomes, record those on a flipchart, and post in a visible place.

Facilitation

Once the team leader departs, the facilitator should ask the group if they have any questions or concerns about the process. The facilitator should also reiterate the confidentiality point and enlist the support of the group to maintain that after the meeting. Then, the facilitator will ask the following questions and record the answers on flipcharts. Each flipchart should be numbered to reflect the question and flipchart number. (For example, 2–3 would denote question two and the third flipchart of responses to question 2.)

1. What do you know about <u>Team Leader</u>?

2. What would you like to know about <u>Team Leader?</u>

3. What concerns do you have about <u>Team Leader</u> taking this role at this time?

4. What would you like <u>Team Leader</u> to know about this team?

5. What else would you like to share with or ask of <u>Team Leader</u> that we have not covered?

For a team of 12, these questions should take somewhere between 1½ to 2 hours to go through. The facilitator may have to prompt thoughts without adding her own input to the group's thoughts. Once the input starts it will generally flow well and quickly. If the facilitator can put herself in the figurative place of the participants, she should be able to prompt the group along. Write legibly and in sufficient detail on the flipcharts so that the team leader can read and understand the point.

After the responses and input to the questions are fully exhausted you can ask the participants to depart and return in 30 minutes. They should wait outside the room before they come back in. At this time contact the team leader to return to the room.

Debrief

The team leader has now returned to the meeting room. Provide a high-level summary to the team leader in terms of your perspective on the tone and openness of the discussion. It would also be helpful if you have the time to synthesize for the team leader the three to five key themes that the team is feeling.

Then you should walk through each item on the flipcharts, beginning with the responses to question 1. During this presentation, it is your opportunity to explain the backstory, meaning, or intent behind each point or question. Although it is unacceptable to name who made the point or asked the question, it could be helpful to share how prevalent the question was. Be careful not to state that it was only one person as that might identify the source. The initial debrief should take about fifteen to twenty minutes. Then allow the leader some time to meander among the flipcharts to contemplate the method and manner of response.

Team Leader Discussion

The participants have now returned and are in the room. It is now the team leader's opportunity to respond to the points, questions, and concerns. The facilitator's role is to keep the conversation flowing and ensure the leader at least addresses all points and questions raised and recorded. The team leader can respond to each point individually or discuss and respond to themes surfaced. If the facilitator feels like a point was not sufficiently responded to, it is important to ask the participants if their question was answered.

At the conclusion the team leader should thank the participants for their time, interest, and candor. He or she should also thank the facilitator as well as anyone who assisted with logistics. In addition, the team leader should try to synthesize the input and discussion with their key learnings or takeaways and any immediate action items they are willing to share at this moment.

It would be helpful to take down the flipcharts and have them transcribed for the facilitator and team leader.

Team Celebration

As mentioned previously, some sort of social engagement with the team is a good way to conclude this type of event.

The Goals-Values Matrix: A Framework and Tool for Building Collaboration

Contributed by Ken Ideus

What Is Collaboration?

Though collaboration occurs through action, it isn't something you "do." Collaboration is a way of being. It is a way of working with and understanding others, even if they are our competitors. Our collaboration partners might be otherwise competing with us for resources, reputation, market share, or even political position. We may or may not be in the same organization. Internal competition can be equally fierce to external competition and sometimes even more so. Current trends show an increase in collaborative relationships, and this will continue. Joint ventures and alliances are the norm. Moves toward connectivity over fragmentation are becoming more of the norm. While collaboration can be complex and challenging, it can also be highly rewarding in terms of both results and personal growth on the part of individuals involved. A simple framework can help us guide our collaborative efforts forward through what can seem gray and complex territory.

Collaboration and Alignment

A central feature of collaboration is alignment. A not-so pleasant slant on the word collaboration has its roots in times of war. Collaborators were those who ideologically "aligned" with the enemy or invading force and supported their efforts. This was often done in secret and signified some form of betrayal. Today collaboration has moved into the positive territory of open and transparent partnership. What remains, regardless of context, is the central feature of alignment.

Collaboration and Competition

What is also true is that most humans operate in one or more competitive environments. Competition, as mentioned earlier, may be internal or external. In an external environment we may be competing with the companies in one context and choose to partner with them in another. Internal to our own organization we may be in competition as well. Departments, units, and divisions are in a continuous competition for finite resources, be they financial, material, or human. We may also be competing for reputation, performance, or the standing of our group from a political perspective. Whether competing internally or externally, collaboration is still called for and can yield exceptional results and powerful experiences.

Setting the Collaboration Context

To discuss alignment, we need to clarify the context and boundaries of our working relationship. This is particularly true when competitive firms are working together on a project or commercial activity. It is also true in the case of parties from different parts of the same organization. Setting the context and the boundaries allows us to focus and get clear on what we will work on together, and how. This done, we can start to explore alignment. I say "explore" versus "generate" as the first step is to find out where we are already aligned and where we are not! With this clear, we have a more transparent view of our collaborative landscape and potential.

The Axes of Alignment for Collaboration

To keep things simple, we look at alignment on two axes: alignment on *Goals* and alignment on *Values*. The *Goals-Values Matrix* illustrates these axes. *Goals* are simply what we are trying to achieve in this particular context. They are not yet "joint" *Goals*. They are the goals the parties have in hand, in this shared context, as they come to the table. With goals shared, we can move on to *values*. Once again, we need to simplify an often complex and emotionally charged topic. To simplify, I define a value as *What I hold as important when consciously taking a decision or action*. This simple definition of values is true for *all* conscious choices. The parties ask themselves, in this context, and related to their goals, what they hold important when taking decisions or actions. With the answers on the table, they can again look for existing alignment.

We might note that the process to this point is one of conversation and dialogue. Existing goals and values should be heard *without judgment*. Information is shared to help all assess current levels of alignment. Having put this information on the table and having built the groundwork for conversation and dialogue, we can now move into the shaping of joint *Goals* and the *Values* required to deliver them effectively. Only when alignment is high on both axes do we have true collaboration. In summary, the *Goals-Values Matrix* (Figure 14.1) shows:

- Cooperation Quadrant: Low alignment on *Values* with high alignment on *Goals* leads to Cooperation (we will work together to get the job done but forget about having lunch or dinner!).

- Affiliation Quadrant: Low alignment on *Goals* with high alignment on *Values* leads to affiliation (we enjoy hanging out, sharing professional stories and ideas but are not looking to deliver something together).

- Conflict Quadrant: Low alignment on both *Goals* and *Values* leads to conflict! (Remember we are working in the same competitive environment and context,)

- Collaboration Quadrant: High alignment on both *Goals* and *Values* leads to collaboration (we become generative, creative, and capable of high performance, working in a mutual direction).

Figure 14.1. Goals-Values Matrix.

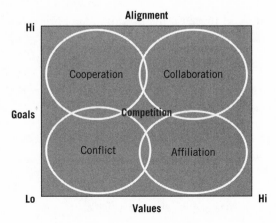

While it appears that full collaboration is the goal, it may also be the case that two groups agree only to "Cooperate" or "Affiliate." These can be legitimate choices given the particular context. Going into every circumstance with a pre-determined outcome of collaboration can lead to significant problems around expectations. Though full "Collaboration" may be the most productive way of working together, it may not always be realistic. Whatever the eventual choice, this can all be worked through a facilitative process, best done with a facilitator whose primary stake is in getting the various parties into conversation and dialogue leading to the best possible alignment on joint *Goals* and *Values*.

Facilitating a Collaboration Session

These five facilitation steps assume that very little pre-work has been done prior to the various parties coming together for a session. Pre-work can always be of value but is not always practical. This process also assumes that there are at least two parties present. In reality collaboration often involves several parties or sets of stakeholders. Note: It is important to have adequate easels or corkboards around the room to record and display the thoughts and ideas of the group.

Step 1—Establishing the Context and Boundaries for This Collaborative Effort

- Working around the room, ask the parties to identify what they understand to be the focus of their collaborative efforts, and, over what period of time.

   Record these on the boards. There are no right or wrong responses at this point as you are finding out what people came in with.

- Now ask the group to identify areas which they feel sit outside of the partnership. What's not included in the territory?

   Same as above, record these on the boards and simply clarify as there are no right or wrong responses here.

   Note: The above might be done with the parties meeting in their respective groups, then reporting back in a plenary.

- With the group, explore areas of alignment and facilitate a general agreement on context and boundaries. Follow the 80/20 rule as further clarity will emerge out of later conversations.

Step 2—Introduce the Collaboration Framework

- Share the collaboration framework with the group. Begin by pointing out that the group has just set the context and boundaries, in other words, they have defined "the box" in which they will be operating. (Being "in the box" is sometimes the best place to be!)

- Provide the group with the definitions of *Goals* and *Values* as defined above for the purposes of this framework.

- Ask the group to identify (in plenary or in their respective groups) their *Goals* for being involved in this project or activity. What do they hope to gain? What do they want out of it? Also ask them to identify some of the key *Values* that drive their actions and decisions in this arena.

  Note: These are not yet the specific Goals for the collaboration itself but the goals they brought to the table.

Record these responses so they are visible to all.

- Ask the group to note where they see alignment, where they see diversity, and where they see potential areas for conflict, if any.

  Record these responses so they are visible as well.

- Should areas of potential conflict or tension be identified, ask the group for ideas on how they might address conflict and tension as they arise in the future.

  If there are areas that appear to be "show stoppers," agree on a plan to address the key conflict areas and either do this in the moment or agree to conduct another session to address these points. If these are critical areas, it does not make sense to continue the rest of the session until they have been addressed.

- Having identified preexisting *Goals* and *Values,* ask the group to place themselves, as a whole, on the grid. Are they pleased with the placement? If not, where would they like to be? What ideas do they have on getting to that space?

Note: Going to the next step in the process is a good way of moving toward the upper-right-hand quadrant of the collaboration space.

Step 3—Setting the Joint Goals and Values for This Relationship

- Breaking into mixed groups, ask participants to identify a set of *Goals* for the relationship with a focus on the various results they would like to deliver and achieve. Share these out and record them, then work toward a basic consensus for this starter set of *Goals*.

- Now, with a starter set of *Goals* identified, have the group identify and discuss the *Values* they will need to incorporate and adhere to in order to reach their aspirations.

Step 4—Moving from Intention to Action Collaboration starts in earnest when action happens on the ground. At this stage the group is still working at an "intention" level. This next step moves things from intention to action.

- Now with an understanding of *Goals* and *Values,* ask the group to identify the key processes they will use—this includes how they will plan, communicate, track their performance against goals, manage changes, and so on.

- Second, what are the next steps they will take to put their collaborative efforts into action? Who will do these? By when? How are the actions being shared by the joint team?

Step 5—Sustaining the Collaborative Relationship Too easily, a group can fall into simply measuring progress against hard goals and not check in on the rest. With this in mind, ask the group for ideas on how they will continue to check and maintain their working relationship. Assure their commitment to a few key actions in this area.

Group Brainwriting and Electronic Brainstorming

A number of research studies have demonstrated that when groups attempt to engage in brainstorming they can encounter a number of factors that can limit the effectiveness of their efforts. One such obstacle involves the inevitable delays that occur as members are forced to wait for others to voice their ideas and have these ideas posted on the board. In addition, when working with larger groups, or groups characterized by particularly vocal or dominant participants, a high degree of general fatigue can set in halfway through the session.

Apart from these obstacles, some team members may find it intimidating to voice their ideas in front of others, even when the group has agreed to follow guidelines that all ideas are welcome and that members are to hold back from critiquing ideas until all ideas are generated. A related drawback is that while some individuals have no difficulty spontaneously generating ideas, others may require a few minutes to privately reflect on the topic under review—a requirement that is generally impeded by attempting to concentrate while the people around you are quickly voicing ideas.

Brainwriting provides one way to overcome these limitations. There are several versions of brainwriting, although most approaches generally start by having the facilitator clearly define the topic under review, and then provide group members with a few minutes to privately write down their own ideas for addressing the topic.

In one *Brainwriting* approach, the group is arranged in a circle. Every few minutes the facilitator calls for a pause, during which time participants pass their list of ideas to the person on their immediate right. As each person takes a list they see the ideas that the team member on their left has generated, and (with some thought to the ideas that they have just generated) use this information as a springboard to generate additional ideas. These ideas are added onto the list, and at the next pause these expanded lists are once again passed to the right.

Another version of *Brainwriting* involves participants privately writing down as many ideas as they can during a specified period of time, before putting their list in the middle of the table. When team members feel that they have reached a point where they are finding it difficult to generate additional ideas they can draw one of the lists from the center of the table and see if they can add to it. In either version the ideas are accumulated at the end of the session and, with redundancies eliminated, a final master list of ideas is generated for the team.

In a third version of *Brainwriting,* participants privately write down a list of their ideas, and when directed to pause by the facilitator, randomly pass their ideas on to another team member for expansion.

When facilitating very large groups it becomes difficult to have sufficient time to provide participants with a good vehicle for face-to-face brainstorming. Likewise, face-to-face brainstorming may be difficult when team members are separated by location, time zones, and business schedules. In such situations it is more realistic to look for ways to support asynchronous brainstorming options; that is, options that enable team members to individually contribute their ideas over the Internet or company intranet.

Electronic Brainstorming involves the use of computers with the standard guidelines that have been developed for brainstorming. Such approaches allow team members to see all of the ideas that have been posted by other team members and add their own ideas to the collective. Generally members submit their ideas anonymously to reduce concerns regarding personal bias and critical feedback. *Electronic Brainstorming* often takes an iterative form, with team members logging into the team site every so often to review the growing list and add or refine their own ideas. One advantage of electronic brainstorming is that it supports group memory by allowing members to type out their ideas in their own words (as opposed to have facilitators attempt to "capture" their ideas by reducing them to a few words on a flipchart), and by enabling the group to archive their results in a common online site.

Some of the criticisms regarding *Electronic Brainstorming* are that the process can feel rather depersonalized, and that it fails to create the type of rapport building that often occurs in face-to-face brainstorming encounters. One method for blending the advantages of both approaches is to use *Electronic Brainstorming* in advance of a team meeting for brainstorming process, while having participants use the team meeting to review the pool of generated ideas and select those for implementation.

Additional Reading

Mongeau, Paul A., and Morr, Mary Claire. (1999). Reconsidering Brainstorming. *Group Facilitation: A Research and Applications Journal,* *1*(1), 14–20.

Paulus, Paul B. (2006). Putting the Brain Back in Brainstorming. *Associations Now,* November, 2006. http://www.asaecenter.org/Resources/ANowDetail.cfm?Item Number=20824

Group Interaction Matix

One way to resolve team boundary disputes is by using the *Group Interaction Matrix.* The matrix can help you establish the relative importance of work issues by assigning team responsibilities to four different quadrants. Each quadrant, labeled A through D in the model, represents a different aspect of team performance, as outlined below:

- **A—Upper-Left Quadrant:** Work processes, ongoing responsibilities, and objectives that require a high degree of interdependent activity between your team and associated work groups and significantly affect the performance of other groups. These are important factors that warrant joint review.

- **B—Upper-Right Quadrant:** Processes and objectives that require the support of other work groups but affect only your team's performance. Conflicts in these areas usually have an impact on other, third-party, work groups, which means it is imperative to address them, particularly if the affected third parties are external customers or suppliers.

- **C—Lower-Left Quadrant:** Activities, work processes, and so on, that do not require much interdependent action (such as, can be performed almost exclusively by your work group without information, feedback, or assistance from the other team) but do affect the performance of other work groups. These actions usually involve services supplied directly by your team to other teams.

- **D—Lower-Right Quadrant:** Items that call for a low degree of interdependent action and do not affect the other team's performance. These processes and objectives aren't relevant for discussion with other work groups, since they are completely self-managed by your team and do not affect the performance of other work groups.

Follow these steps to apply the *Group Interaction Matrix* to inter-team conflicts:

1. Ask the members of your team to help you identify their most important team-based work processes, ongoing responsibilities, and objectives.

2. Write each item down on a separate index card.

3. Introduce the *Group Interaction Matrix* to your team. Explain that the four quadrants of the matrix represent the four ways of classifying team responsibilities in terms of their impact on other work groups in your company and the degree of interdependence or cooperative effort required from those groups to complete these activities. Describe the criteria for each quadrant as given above. It is important to note that the solutions to items placed in quadrants A and B often demand extensive negotiations on modifying jointly managed work processes and activities. Also explain that solutions to factors in quadrant C may require learning more about the other team's operations so you can adapt your activities to support its requirements; it may also be necessary to educate the other team on the rationale behind your own work operations.

4. Draw a copy of the matrix on the flipchart.

5. Have team members place each of their cards in one of the four quadrants shown on the flipchart.

6. Based on the results of the previous step, select the work activities, processes, or objectives that are most important for review and have the greatest overall impact on both teams' performance.

7. Meet with the other team to review the topics you've selected for discussion. Sometimes, it is useful to ask the other team to complete a Group Interaction Matrix before your meeting so that you can both bring in matrixes for review. This gives both teams the opportunity to provide feedback on how they view the relative interdependence and impact of different work functions.

8. During the joint meeting, explain to the other team how its performance may unintentionally be problematic for your own team. Teams are often unaware of how they may affect work groups that are downstream within a work process.

9. Encourage the other team to give concrete, detailed examples of how its performance or other work functions are being adversely affected by your team's performance.

10. Explore options for resolving team boundary issues as well as for jointly or individually resolving critical work challenges. Such solutions might include the following:

- Set up a subteam composed of representatives from both teams and authorize this subteam to make decisions affecting the work area in question.

- Have your teams agree on mutually acceptable decisions on a case-by-case basis. This allows both teams to assume direct ownership and accountability for their decisions.

- Establish definitive borders between your two teams by creating uniform boundary guidelines. This requires explicit and precise definitions of the functions and areas of responsibility of both teams.

- Select solutions that are acceptable to both teams and create a plan for testing these solutions. A test period assures the teams that they will not be prematurely locked into a solution and provides a method for jointly monitoring the success of the solutions.

11. Finally, be sure to follow up on the results. Conduct a joint team review approximately three to six months after the initial meeting. During this review, both teams should evaluate the success of the solutions they have tested and decide whether to establish them on a permanent basis.

Group Interaction Matrix

High Interdependence Responsibilities requiring a **high** degree of interdependence with other groups	Quadrant A	Quadrant B
Low Interdependence Responsibilities requiring a **low** degree of interdependence with other groups	Quadrant C	Quadrant D
	Major Impact Responsibilities that have a **major impact** on other groups	**No Impact** Responsibilities that have **no impact** on other groups

Guide for Balancing Team Participation

This *Guide for Balancing Team Participation* provides techniques for drawing out and reining in team members. To create maximum participation, this guide offers "when" and "how" to address each of these needs.

Draw out Team Members

When to draw out team members:

- When they appear intimidated or awed by the suggestions or comments of other more experienced or knowledgeable members

- When they seem to be censoring themselves or stop speaking before completing their thoughts

- When they are struggling to quickly formulate ideas

- When they cannot break past the commentary of dominant team members

- When they have been silent for an extended period of time

How to draw out team members:

- Call on them by name and ask them to share their ideas

- Break your team into subgroups assigned to different issues. Smaller groups provide a less intimidating setting for sharing ideas.

- Attend to nonverbal clues. "Jeff, I can tell from the way that you are shaking your head that you have some concerns about that idea. Tell us about it."

- Engage your team in silent idea generation through the use of tools, such as the *Nominal Group Technique, Group Brainwriting and Electronic Brainstorming,* or the *Gallery Technique.*

- If certain team members have difficulty "thinking on their feet," prior to the meeting e-mail your team members and ask for their input. During the meeting credit them for their ideas.

- Draw out quiet team members before the meeting or during breaks. Provide an opening for those members during the meeting by saying, for example, "During the break, Sara brought up a great idea for tackling our cost issue. Sara, would you mind sharing that idea with the rest of the team?"

Rein in Team Members

When to rein in team members:

- When they dominate the discussion
- When they appear to be intimidating others or pressuring them into adopting their decisions
- When they are not taking the time to carefully formulate ideas, and are moving too quickly on key decisions
- When they fail to pick up on subtle clues that others wish to be heard

How to rein in team members:

- Conduct a structured brainstorming session in which each person is asked to share only one idea for review as you go around the circle. Continue with additional passes around the circle until all ideas have been exhausted.
- At the beginning of the meeting, have the team generate ground rules for encouraging open discussion. When a team member violates the rules, pause and remind the entire team of the posted ground rules.
- Use a prompting phrase to alert team members that they need to step back and listen, such as, "Bill, could you hold that thought for a second? Mary has been trying to speak for a minute and I want to make sure that we capture her thoughts."
- Use nonverbal signals, such as a "time-out" sign, to alert dominant people that they need to give others a chance to speak.
- If these suggestions are not working, take a five-minute break and provide one-on-one coaching. Call the dominant team member to the side and say, "I can see that you are putting a number of good ideas on the table. My concerns is that a lot of other people are passively listening and not contributing their ideas. When we go back into the room, I would like you to help me draw others out into the discussion."

Guidelines and Questions for Engaging Dialogue
Contributed by Jim O'Neil

Dialogue is a process involving active listening as well as talking. It implies accepting and respecting the views of others and trying to understand where they are coming from. Diversity and division are openly addressed in this process.

Dialogue deepens understanding of our own and each other's positions, often leading to shared understanding and an enhancement of our ability to make informed decisions. It does this by shifting the focus from the stated positions that we so often argue over to the needs (often shared), which underlie them. We of Community Dialogue (see *About Contributors*) believe that if groups understand each other more deeply they would be better able to make informed decisions about starting, continuing, or ending conflict. If they step into the world of another group and see how these others came to hold their positions, feel their emotions, and choose their values, then, although the groups may often remain opposed to each other, they would be less likely to engage in violence. Some of the issues discussed could be highly emotive, but through the dialogue process people would learn more about the issues, deal with them in a less emotive way, and slowly begin to hear why other groups hold the positions they do. The process may:

- Lead to trust, respect, and the building of a shared future in which we all belong, or

- Clarify our disagreement and our need to follow separate paths to separate futures.

One of the most important outcomes of a dialogue is not what answers the participants have arrived at but what questions they will leave with.

Dialogues

In our dialogues we ask people to:

- Question their own positions and look at the needs underlying them.

- Question the positions of others and look at the needs underlying them.

- Explore how to meet those sometimes shared and sometimes conflicting underlying needs.

We encourage a reexamination of stated positions, based on the assumption that we all want something different and we are all unlikely to get what we want. We also ask:

- What do you want?

- What do you really need and why do you need it?

- What could you live with, given that the needs and hopes of others may differ from yours?

Our dialogue process involves engaging with individuals and groups from a wide variety of backgrounds and experiences. They could be single identity (people from one community), women's groups, men's groups, or people from an ethnic minority background such as refugees and asylum seekers.

The dialogues could either be one-off, part of an ongoing series, or involve a residential retreat where participants stay over either one or two nights to enable a deeper process. With some groups we may work through all three processes.

Importance of Ground Rules and Guidelines

In order to create a safe space for participants in this process, it is important to create a set of ground rules and guidelines for people to follow, which provide a tool for the facilitators to ensure that the dialogue runs smoothly. These are as follows:

Ground Rules for Dialogue

1. Treat what you hear in confidence.

2. Others have the right to believe and feel differently from you.

3. Others have the right to express their beliefs.

4. You do not have to respect beliefs that are wrong to you.

5. Treat others with the respect you expect yourself.

6. When others share do not interrupt, show respect, and wait until they finish.

7. Do not represent the views of a wider group, share your own views.

8. Do not pressure anyone into speaking.

9. All participants' views and ideas have value.

Guidelines for Dialogue

1. Dialogue is a two-way process; it involves balancing deep listening and open, honest sharing.

2. Everyone is encouraged to speak.

3. Risk trusting other people with your feelings and experience.

4. Share what feels comfortable for you—don't go beyond that.

5. You do not need a clear position or to be an expert; it is okay to be confused or to change your mind.

6. People who listen more than they speak often have more of value to share.

7. Try to be present for the full process, as absence can have a negative impact.

8. If you feel uncomfortable you may need to take time out, but let the facilitator know.

9. Take care to listen well.

10. Feel free to ask if you don't understand.

11. Dialogue is not about agreement; it is about deepening understanding.

12. Question what you hear and what you think.

13. Keep an open mind.

14. Help and support each other throughout the process.

15. The facilitator is there to support you.

Case Studies of Community Dialogue

This section summarizes eleven case studies of Community Dialogues' dialogue work within contexts of conflict. Conflict of itself is neither good nor bad; it is a natural, necessary, and inevitable consequence of life. It is how we use conflict that renders it good or bad, creative or destructive. This is where *dialogue* comes in as a tool that we can use to mold conflict into a creative, positive, and productive process. Community Dialogue has a long and successful track record of instigating and facilitating a whole series of dialogues with diverse groups and issues. We work closely with the group in question in the design planning stages. This ensures that the group feels ownership of the process and can identify with the aims and objectives and delivery styles chosen and be assured that these fit with the profile and needs of the participants involved.

Cases Between Communities The following case studies are of cross community results/impacts where various misconceptions about each other's community were dispelled and areas of commonality explored and celebrated to date.

> **Case 1.** The Crevagh Women's Group from Derry/Londonderry group consists of women who live in a predominantly nationalist/republican area of the city and the Families Beyond Borders group is from the Shankill in Belfast, a predominantly unionist/loyalist area of the city. These two groups' dialogues helped to dispel various myths and misconceptions, which contributed to a mutual change in outlook toward each other's community.

> **Case 2.** Dialogue between the Ard Carn Women's Group, from a unionist/loyalist housing estate, and Connswater Women's Group, from a nationalist/republican housing estate located in East Belfast, an area that has been blighted by sectarian attacks and tensions.

> **Case 3.** Dialogue between two previously polarized communities in Lurgan who, for the first time, crossed the religious divide to come together and listen to and explore each other's beliefs and cultures.

Cases Across Borders Results and impacts of dialogues taking place across borders, that is, between groups in Northern Ireland (part of the United Kingdom) and groups in the Republic of Ireland, have included:

Case 4. Dialogues involving Irish former service personnel who served on the Donegal border during the Northern Ireland conflict who were often ignored, or who had forgotten that the conflict also had an impact on border areas of the Republic of Ireland.

Case 5. Women in Search of Peace involving women from rural areas of County Cavan (Republic of Ireland) and County Fermanagh (Northern Ireland).

Case 6. Banner project involving women from Donegal (Republic of Ireland) and Tyrone (Northern Ireland) producing and sharing banners depicting their community's history and local heritage, which formed the basis of a series of conversations between the women exploring their heritage and culture.

Case of Attitudinal and Cultural Change

Case 6. Cartoons in Conflict Exhibition and Dialogue Series, which used international cartoons of political and ethnic conflict to stimulate dialogue. This process utilizes materials developed and donated to Community Dialogue by The Parents' Circle, Families Forum a group of bereaved Palestinian and Israeli families who wanted to highlight the futility of violence in the region. The cartoons served as a tool for dialogue to encourage participants to draw parallels from international conflicts with our own conflict here.

Cases Between and Among Groups These cases addressed issues of isolation, polarization, division, and prejudice between and among groups.

Case 7. Many of the men living in the Ard Carn estate in East Belfast (a predominantly unionist/loyalist area) faced a degree of isolation and polarization. Community Dialogue was the first organization to enable the group to articulate their views and concerns.

Case 8. Many refugees and asylum seekers felt isolated and marginalized living in Northern Ireland. Dialogue sessions with members of that community enabled them to articulate and explore these experiences, feelings, and needs and to plan responses to address them. Subsequent dialogues provided them with the opportunity to engage members of wider society on these issues.

Case 9. Women living in Lenadoon came together for a series of dialogue sessions which enabled them to articulate often desperate and traumatic experiences for the first time in a safe environment. The sessions involved the use of creative writing and song-writing workshops as mechanisms for the expression of difficult experiences in a healing manner.

Cases of Outreach These two cases illustrate our outreach dialogue work to minority ethnic communities and to those sectors of society that have until now been rendered voiceless by dominant discourses.

Case 10. Dialogues were facilitated with members of the Northern Ireland Community of Refugees and Asylum Seekers (NICRAS) to begin to explore the key problems and issues facing themselves and their families living in Belfast. The process met the participants' desperate need just to be listened to—with respect and with no agenda. A sense of belonging lies at the root of personal identity and being able to be with others in a spirit of fellowship and to share experiences in confidence while being treated with respect was hugely important to participants.

This communal gathering had reignited something that used to happen in the past. Therefore the sessions were clearly of particular value for members who live in hostels and for whom it represents some kind of return to family. This pilot was a valuable exercise in what it means to *really* listen—reflectively and reflexively.

Case 11. Lenadoon is a housing estate located in a nationalist/republican area of West Belfast. We were asked by local community workers to facilitate a series of dialogue sessions with a group of women who met informally on a weekly basis. Many of these women lacked self-confidence and motivation. Yet when given the opportunity to talk about their lives and the issues they faced, they proved to be extremely able and articulate.

Some of their issues were reflected through a song written by one of the facilitators and which is provided below. The women slowly developed the confidence to write their own songs. These women's songs can be accessed on Community Dialogue's website (www.communitydialogue.org).

Song writing proved to be an invaluable tool in this particular context, enabling women who felt that they had nothing important to share to uncover powerful truths about themselves and explore these with each other—a truly empowering process.

"One Small Step"

Absent fathers
Bitter kids
Broken promises
The will to live
Mr. Wonderful
Who walks away
Left to struggle
Day by day
Chorus
One small step
Is all it takes
One small step
Despite the pain
One small step
You're through the door
One small step
You're off the floor
If my kids are happy
I'm happy too
Yet it's so damn hard
To make it through
I need some space
Some time to be
To ease the worry
Some time for me
Chorus
Throughout our lives
Mistakes are made
That's how it goes
That's the price you pay
You learn to cope
By moving on
And through it all
You become more strong
Chorus

The Human Due Diligence Audit

Contributed by John Sturrock, QC

The Advantages of Conducting an Audit

When entering into a new business arrangement, whether it is a newly established team, a joint venture, specific project, merger, or other alliance, there is a real need for businesses and individuals to find ways to check that the project will work. Conventionally, they will carry out financial due diligence but often they will fail to undertake a similar exercise to ensure that the people and relationship issues are also addressed.

While the benefits of successful collaboration can be significant, the establishment of a new joint venture is far from risk free. Indeed, a high proportion of joint ventures fail to deliver the desired results, often because of a breakdown in relations between partners. This can present those investing money, time, and reputation in such a venture with serious and unwanted difficulties.

So often, new ventures fail or are handicapped because those involved find out, too late, that they do not share the same values or objectives—or have not considered the underlying concerns or interests that really motivate them. The pressure to do the deal can lead to the key players assuming that everything will be alright, often suppressing private fears or doubts. They do not build in mechanisms to deal with the difficult times.

We know that effective collaboration requires high levels of trust to realize its full potential. If an alliance is entered into without a full understanding of the real interests of each party, or is based on misunderstandings or misplaced assumptions, disappointment, disillusionment, and the eventual breakdown of trust can be the result.

Thus, up-front investment to help individuals to understand better their different interests and assumptions, hopes and fears, concerns and aspirations, expectations and objectives, will lay strong foundations for the personal relationships on which trust is based. These foundations will help ensure more productive, more effective, less costly alliances, which are less likely to break down.

What is needed is a structured, nonbinding process to allow potential partners to explore issues in complete confidence, probably using a combination of private and joint meetings.

Such a process can help build greater understanding of what each party wants to achieve through the business arrangement, what each brings to the collaboration, and where they have genuine shared interests. It can open up discussion of what each party really expects of the other and of the potential constraints that may frustrate expectations. Above all, it can get under the surface and identify those issues that may really worry potential collaborators.

Building on this exploration, the process can help partners identify options for addressing potential problems. As with other forms of due diligence, in some cases the concerns raised may result in a decision not to proceed. Although this may be disappointing, it is far better to discover this at an early stage than when the venture is up and running. More likely, the process will uncover the kind of concerns which can be addressed as part of the establishment of a well-founded platform for going ahead—and which will lead to more effective problem-solving and dispute management in the future.

It is suggested that working with a third-party independent facilitator will add real value to this human due diligence. Whether described as a mediator or facilitator, the third party can provide the structure or framework to give those involved the safety and confidence to address difficult issues. A good process will offer participants the opportunity to address these sorts of questions:

- What are your real objectives in this project?
- What do you really need to achieve out of this project?
- If you achieved this, what would that mean for you?
- What do you need to **do** today to achieve this?
- What do you need to **say** to the others to help you achieve this?
- What do you need to hear from the others to help you achieve this?
- What do you think that the others really need out of this?

- What are your main concerns at this stage?

- What do you think are the others' main concerns at this stage?

- What is the common ground?

- Where might there be misunderstandings?

- What do you think the others need to hear from you at this stage?

- If you are going to work together really well in the future, what needs to be done?

- What will be the consequences for you if this does not work out (a) now? (b) later?

- What will be the consequences for others if this does not work out (a) now? (b) later?

- If you can't find a mutually acceptable way to work together, what will happen?

- Reflecting on these questions, what protocols do you need to develop to help deal with any future problems?

- What are the options for moving forward?

These questions ensure not only (a) much reflection on a party's own circumstances but also (b) real consideration of the others' point of view—stepping at least partially into the others' shoes. As preparation for a subsequent meeting, that can be very powerful.

How to Complete the Audit

A questionnaire containing these questions can be issued and completed in advance and returned to the facilitator, or it can be used on the day of meetings, to inform the facilitator and/or by the parties themselves. One example is to set up a joint meeting, chaired by the facilitator, and invite each party to go through the responses one by one, listening carefully to the other's responses. The parties can alternate in answering, to achieve parity and a sense of fairness. This can be tremendously enlightening—and challenging. It is just the sort of thing that people find difficult to do by themselves.

The facilitator can follow the standard mediation approach of meeting with parties privately and/or together, as seems appropriate in the circumstances. Clearly it will be essential to set this in the most helpful context: using a comfortable venue, eating together to build rapport, setting the scene and laying down appropriate ground rules. Exploring and really understanding the underlying issues before looking at options for moving forward and coming to any conclusions is critical. Again, the facilitator can play a valuable role here.

Depending on the group dynamics, there may be opportunities to establish small working groups with specific tasks, to report back to the larger group. Perhaps key players can make presentations to decision makers or work collaboratively across parties to seek for different perspectives. There are many techniques for group work and insights that a skilled facilitator will bring.

There may be moments to take stock and ask questions such as:

- What has been achieved so far?
- What are the areas of common ground that have emerged?
- What have you learned that has surprised you?
- What new areas for discussion have emerged?
- What do you not understand?
- What areas need further exploration at this stage?
- What do you now need to say to the other party?
- What would you now like to hear from the other party?
- What are the key issues at this stage?
- How can these be taken forward now?
- What else can you do now, in this process, to help to map a way forward?
- What options are emerging?
- What do you really want to achieve now? What is your main priority?
- What should happen next?
- How can you best utilize the services of the facilitator as you go forward?

None of this is prescriptive. The questions are just illustrative. But the process is powerful. And it should be completed—after a day, or two days, or time for reflection—with an action plan, prepared by the parties. They need to invest in the outcome. What needs to be done, by whom, by when, and how? The parties may also be encouraged to formulate the "why": what is our vision, our mission, and/or our values?

Overall, the parties should leave with a clear view of what their real interests are, how they can work together most effectively, and how they will deal with differences in the future. Or, perhaps, why they have decided not to go ahead at all, or with a different or reduced scope.

Idea Rotation

Contributed by Jonas Janebrant and Johanna Steen
MiL Institute, Lund, Sweden

This *Idea Rotation* tool is an intervention that dates back to a collaboration between the MiL Institute and IKEA Corporation. Over time the name was changed to the *Completion Workshop*, to reflect the fact that this technique, amongst others, enabled IKEA leaders to successfully complete eleven burning business issues in one week's time.

Purpose

The purpose of this tool is to build shared responsibility and ownership among all team members, to make certain that participation is manageable and that all participants have an equal voice in presenting their views, and to help teams engage in concrete discussions when they have limited time to address key issues.

Intended Aims and Outcomes

- To secure many different perspectives
- To insure a swift and discernible movement forward on burning issues
- To overcome deadlocks thanks to alternative work methods
- To have solved or to have moved further ahead on different burning issues

Description of a Hypothetical Case

Let's say that you are working with a project group from the HR organization of a company. The group consists of six to nine representatives from different HR positions and functions in the company who have just identified the following three burning issues that need to be solved in the near future:

1. How to get a good internal communication between the HR at headquarters and the HR in the different regional divisions

2. How to transform HR to be seen as a strategic dimension of the overall business and not as a support function for business

3. How to find, and implement, a shared approach to recruitment

The following steps outline the opening facilitation process and instructions to participants:

1. Have the group select or self-nominate three representatives, who will take ownership of one question each. The "owner" of each question should be the one who has the formal responsibility for addressing the question, and/or the person with the greatest commitment to see the issue resolved.

2. Subsequently three equally large groups are formed (minimum a pair).

3. As facilitator, you then instruct the groups that they are going to spend the next 1.5 hours working on the three burning issues according to a fixed schedule.

4. Present a matrix, as modeled below, to illustrate how the three groups would allocate their time across the three issues. During the work the facilitator can observe the progress and support the groups by different interventions necessary.

	20 min.	20 min.	40 min.
Group 1	Q3	Q2	Q1
Group 2	Q1	Q3	Q2
Group 3	Q2	Q1	Q3

5. Give the following instructions:

   a. "Each burning issue has been assigned a separate room. There you will find a large worksheet to be used for the recording of ideas, questions, and proposed solutions. We want to make sure to get as many perspectives as possible and to take all aspects into consideration. Every group has a separate color of pens so that we all can recognize your group's specific contribution."

b. "You all have ownership of one important question. We are going to do three rotations and each group will end by working on their own question."

c. "Before the final rotation each group will have had the opportunity to give and receive important input on each question. However, you will only have 20 minutes to make a contribution to your colleagues' question before you rotate again, so make sure that you spend that time wisely."

d. "When you rotate and find yourself in front of a new worksheet, take time to read your colleagues' contributions. Then build on the work of the previous group by adding your comments to their suggestions before you record your own contribution."

e. "For the final rotation each group will have 40 minutes to compile the information, suggestions, and questions gathered by the other groups and to prepare a presentation on how they will move forward with the question for which they are responsible."

The session concludes by giving each group the opportunity to present the results from the exercise—concrete actions, ideas, suggestions—that they are willing to pursue. The facilitator then asks the entire group to reflect on what insights or lessons they have taken away with them, based on their involvement in this method of working. As a prompt the facilitator might ask:

- "In what way has this process been different from how you would normally work with these types of questions?"

- "Have you made greater progress by this method than if you would have, had you spent the last 1.5 hours within the usual structure of talking together as one big group?"

If the answers to these two questions indicate that participants felt that this approach offered unique advantages over their typical ways of interacting, help them reflect on the advantages that they might obtain from spicing up ordinary business meetings by looking for alternative ways to apply this method in their work settings.

Kill the Critic Exercise

This exercise provides a humorous and nonthreatening method for changing team communication habits that may be discouraging the free flow of ideas. Team members sometimes communicate in ways that inhibit their coworkers' creativity. Unfortunately, many behaviors such as sarcasm or hostile criticism become so ingrained that people are unaware of what they are doing.

To conduct this exercise, complete the following steps:

1. Before initiating this game, ask your team to select for review an existing problem or challenge that requires some creative thinking.

2. To start the game, write "Killer Behaviors" at the top of a piece of flipchart paper. Then ask your team the following questions: "Without giving specific examples, what are some of the 'killer behaviors'—behaviors that tend to discourage or censor good ideas—that you've observed in our own meetings or at other meetings in which you have participated?"

3. To get things started, offer the following examples:

   • Poking fun at strange ideas

   • Dismissing or contradicting ideas before the speaker has the opportunity to fully develop them

   • Continually harping on the constraints under which you're working

   • Dismissing new ideas because they have never been tried and therefore are not valid

   • Reminding new or junior-level team members that their ideas reflect their inexperience

4. Record these killer behaviors on the flipchart for later reference.

5. Next, distribute soft foam balls to your team members.

6. Tell your team that you will all begin to brainstorm ideas for addressing the current problem or challenge. Suggest that whenever someone engages in any of the killer behaviors the team listed, the other team members should throw balls at that person.

7. After you've concluded your meeting, take a few minutes to conduct a debriefing session and ask team members to go back to the flipchart list and circle behaviors that may be causing problems in your own team.

This technique may sound a bit bizarre, but team members never fail to respond with humor the first time someone lapses into the habit of making critical comments. More important, it also encourages them to relax their thinking and consider novel ideas and solutions. Finally, it serves as a direct prompt for controlling the behavior of dominant, negatively focused individuals who may not pick up on subtle corrective feedback.

Listening Post Chart

The *Listening Post Chart* tool enables your team to stay in touch with your customers' changing needs. However, it is important to develop more than one kind of approach to keeping track of your variety of customers. This simple exercise will guide your team as you brainstorm options that will best suit the needs of each customer.

A completed model of the *Listening Post Chart* is provided to help you create one with your team. The model is based a hypothetical Human Resources (HR) team. Actions representing potential listening posts are listed across the top of the six columns to the right. Complete the following steps:

1. Our Customers: In the left column of your chart, list customers currently served by your work team. The model HR team has identified four departmental customers.

2. Potential Listing Posts: Identify five to seven options (the model shows six) that might be used as your team's listening posts. Write these across the top, one in each column. Write the general idea of the actions or events, no need to specifically define them at this time.

3. Describe Ideas per Customer: Once the options are identified, discuss and fill in the columns next to each customer with specific descriptions of actions or events. As the model shows, an idea can be applied to more than one customer or to all customers.

4. Take Action: If your team identifies options that will be implemented at different time, highlight the ones you feel are particularly valuable. These should be the first actions your team takes to create your customer listening posts.

Listening Post Chart: Human Resources Team

Our Customers	Potential Listening Posts					
	1 Attend Their Meetings	**2 Have Them Attend Our Meetings**	**3 E-Mail and Company Intranet**	**4 Customer Social Events**	**5 Focus Groups**	**6 Meetings with Senior Managers**
Marketing			Create an HR newsletter on the company intranet alerting customers to upcoming changes and inviting questions and responses through e-mail	Volunteer to facilitate the yearly sales and marketing meeting		Meet with the SVP of marketing to discuss staffing impact of impending reorganization
Field Support	Attend quarterly market area meetings	Invite them to attend our meetings on a rotational basis				
IT	Attend monthly staff meetings					Call a meeting with the IT directors to identify their concerns regarding our benefits program
Finance					Conduct a finance focus group centering around problems they have been encountering with our recruiting process	

Microanalysis Technique

The *Microanalysis Technique* enables your team to address a challenge creatively by breaking it down into its components and then brainstorming selectively around each part. When you are directing a team through the microanalysis process, you may find it helpful to construct a review chart, such as the model shown. A chart encourages a team to explore all possible aspects of problem solving and provides a visual reference for rearranging components into unique combinations to generate unexpected solutions.

In the model, a hypothetical transportation team has found that some of its company's products are damaged when shipped by truck to customer sites. The model chart shows the array of solutions developed by this team. The solutions that were finally chosen by the team are in bold print.

Complete the technique by taking the following steps:

1. Divide the problem into possible categories of exploration. If the problem involves a product or service, divide the product or service into its component attributes.

2. Separate your team into subgroups, and ask the subgroups to explore solutions based on the particular categories to which they have been assigned.

3. Post all lists of partial solutions and determine how they could be creatively combined to form an effective composite solution.

Microanalysis Technique Applied to Problem of Product Damage During Transport

Solution Category	Alternative A	Alternative B	Alternative C	Alternative D
Transportation method	Ship by air instead of truck	Establish distribution center to reduce transport distance	**Change route to reduce damage caused by bad roads**	
Transport vehicle	Upgrade to new insulated trucks	Add foam covering and flooring to trucks	**Add upgraded suspension system to trucks**	Reduce stack height in trucks
Container supporting product	Use plastic reusable transport molds for bulk shipments	**Add insulating buffer sheet between columns of products**	Change current cardboard product container to foam container	
Product design	**Add layer of rubber insulation to base of product**	Redesign product housing to make it more impact resistance		

Mind Maps

Mind Maps are tools that help a team develop ideas and graphically represent ideas that relate to a central theme or topic.

The first step in creating a mind map is to have the team discuss and agree on a few words that capture the core concept that they are discussing. For example, imagine that a community action group is interested in identifying factors that are affecting the quality of education in local public schools. So, the central theme that might be captured is "Quality of CPE (community public education])." The facilitator writes the core discussion theme within the center of a large piece of flipchart or butcher paper and draws a circle around it.

Next, the facilitator invites participants to offer ideas that are related to the core theme. As each additional idea is offered the facilitator asks whether the idea is related to the first idea or is a totally new idea. In the education example, a participant identifies "student to teacher ratios" in schools as being one factor that can affect "quality of CPE," so this idea is a line extending from the core. Similarly, a second participant offers "availability of teacher assistants" and, when asked, suggests that it follows from the first idea rather than the core theme. A third participant mentions the degree to which parents are kept informed of changes to curricula in the local schools, and suggests that "changes to curricula" be represented as a separate line.

The process of presenting ideas and drawing relationship lines continues until all ideas are presented on the paper or board. At this point, ideas that appear to be closely related under a general theme should ideally be denoted by a single color. The result is the relationships of ideas and concepts visually illustrated through lines and color—a creative mind map that drives further considerations and actions.

Variations in Creating Mind Maps

Teams can use a version of the *Multivoting Technique* with sticky notes to identify key themes in the mind map. The facilitator provides each team member with five sticky dots each and asks them to place their dots on those factors listed on their mind map that they believe to be particularly important to the topic under discussion. This simple step is one way to obtain a quick graphic representation of factors that appear to be particularly important to the group.

Mind mapping can be structured or unstructured, as the situation requires. An example of structured mind mapping would be a team that is attempting to identify external factors (changes to the organization, industry, federal regulations, and so on) that could significantly affect the team's performance over the next few years. In this case, the facilitator might find it advantageous to impose some initial guidelines on the ideas submitted by posting the question: "What are some of the most important external factors, such as changes that are now under way—such as changes in our organization, product base, industry, customer expectations, and federal regulations—that could affect the performance of our team over the next two years?" Conversely, if the goal of mind mapping is to encourage creative, divergent thinking, the facilitator could simply place the core theme inside the central circle on the board and then ask participants to call out the first words that come to mind when they think about this theme. These words can simply be placed around the core theme, with arms connecting the core theme and supportive ideas. An example of such an unstructured approach would be a team that is attempting to arrive at a name that captures the essence of a new product. In this case the center hub would contain a brief description of the product, with team members calling out words that they associate with the major features and advantages of that product.

Another way to mind map is to draw a circle in the middle of the poster board, representing the central topic for discussion, and then pass out several note cards to each participant. Participants are given 15 minutes to write down their individual ideas related to the central theme, one per each card, and to post these on the board around the central circle as they are written. As team members see the ideas building on the board additional ideas may occur to them. At this point the team gathers around the cards to determine how they could best be grouped or organized to represent themes, and then draws lines to represent these relationships among the ideas. Although this approach can require a bit of patience to work through the relationships between the posted ideas, it offers the advantage of starting out the process with individual brainstorming unconstrained by any graphic structure.

One last way of using mind maps is to have different stakeholder groups meet together to identify the ideas that they want to post and then place these on the board with different colored lines used to denote different stakeholder groups. Additional connecting lines can be used to show relationships between ideas presented by each stakeholder group. This approach can be applied when working with a large number of group members, or where it might be useful to illustrate the different perspectives of different stakeholder groups.

As a final consideration, when facilitating the creation of mind maps with virtual teams explore the option of making use of one of the many mind-mapping software packages that are commercially available. All the resources listed below provide free downloadable trial demos:

- iMindmap5 by ThinkBuzan

  http://www.thinkbuzan.com/us/?utm_nooverride=1&gclid=CK6j3LvJpKkCFYVx5QodXCh0vA

- MindManager by Mindjet

  http://www.mindjet.com/mindmanager-uses/brainstorming

- PersonalBrain by The BrainTechnologies

  http://www.thebrain.com/products/personalbrain/

Mix and Max

Contributed by Mary Stall

Mix and Max is a method that can be used to help a group of people engage in a structured process of conversation or idea generation around a topic that matters to them. In doing so, they are able to maximize the collection of ideas and data. The process is designed to initiate discussion, build community, and engage those in the room in meaningful ways. It may be especially helpful when conflict is present, when consensus building is necessary in order to move forward, or when communication and information sharing between disparate groups is not present.

The *Mix and Max* process facilitates conversations in small-group settings, followed by larger group report-outs. Small discussion groups affect conversation in many ways. This format encourages participants to engage and to explore values and goals at a deeper level. Large-group report-outs ensure that each individual feels heard by the small and large groups and acknowledges all contributions to the conversation. The connections made through the sharing of knowledge, cocreated insights and careful listening to others encourages trust building, which leads to more effective communication and team building in the future. This engagement process helps to cement future commitment to the project.

Questions are designed in order to keep the conversations at a high level. This is done in order to maximize the amount of time usually devoted to the process, typically 1.5 to 2 hours. The harvested information is handed off to an idea committee team to streamline and turn into action steps. This committee may be a group of participants who indicated an interest in that particular idea or a defined group of people in the organization, depending on the reason the ideation and information gathering is taking place. Collecting large amounts of information supports the designated committee by tapping into the collective knowledge of the larger group—highlighting the thoughts and visions of all participants.

Preparation and Roles

To begin, preparation and organization are very important. Materials and station step-ups are required, two distinct facilitation roles are assigned, and aids to facilitate questioning should be available.

Small-Group Station Set-Up Create small-group stations. Stations should accommodate no more than six participants and one facilitator. Stations are set up around three walls of the room. The small-group station materials should include:

- Chairs—No more than six participant chairs
- Flip charts and easel—one set per small group
- Colored markers—several colors per group
- Painters tape to affix paper to the walls

Small-Group Facilitator The small-group facilitator's role is to ensure that everyone has the opportunity to participate, to record the ideas and thoughts of the group, and to ask clarifying and confirming questions to ensure the participant's perspective is clear. One person is assigned to facilitate the small-group discussion at each station (Figure 14.2).

Meeting Facilitator The meeting facilitator's role is to capture the top ideas, categorize them, and look for patterns in what is being reported out by the small groups. The meetings facilitator's station is set up on the fourth wall in the room, visible to small-group stations. His or her materials should include:

- Chair
- Flipchart paper
- Colored markers
- Assorted sizes of sticky notes from 3x3 to 6x8 inches

Aids to Facilitate Questioning To aid the facilitation process, clarifying and confirming questions may be posted on flipchart paper for everyone's reference. Ensure the writing is either large enough to be read across the room or post copies of these aids in multiple places in the room.

Figure 14.2. Small-Group Station and Facilitator.

Sample clarifying questions include:

- What do you mean by that?
- What does that look like to you?
- What does that sound like to you?
- Help me understand . . . [how that fits in, affects the process, why it is important].
- Can you be more specific?
- Can you share some examples?

Sample confirming questions include:

- If I understand correctly, you are saying that . . .

- You are claiming . . .

- You mean that . . .

- Your conclusion is . . .

Facilitation Process

The *Mix and Max* process is iterative. The following is an outline of the process that is discussed next. This outline assumes that the questions are selected, the welcoming message has occurred, and that small-group facilitators and participants are at their stations.

1. Small-Group Conversions (1 question)

2. Large-Group Report Out (1 question)

3. Meeting Facilitator's Synthesis (1 question)

4. Repeat Steps 1 through 3 with Next Question

5. Meeting Close

6. Post Meeting Activities

Step 1: Small-Group Conversation Each small-group facilitator poses the first question, sets a timer for the designated amount of time (fifteen to twenty minutes), and encourages the conversation. The small-groups' facilitators should enable the mood of the group to shift from quiet apprehension to cheerful engagement in the discussion. At the end of the timed session, each small-group facilitator, with the help of the group's participants, identifies the top three to four ideas, perspectives, or questions that were raised in the discussion.

Step 2: Large-Group Report-Out Going around the room, each small-group facilitator reports out the top three to four ideas discussed. If an idea has already been reported, the small-group facilitator may move to the next item on their list or if they have substantial information to add to the already reported idea, they may do so. The process is not to replicate but to add to the pool of information. During the large-group report-out, ideas are not challenged or questioned by others.

Step 3: Meeting Facilitator's Synthesis As the small-groups report out, the facilitator captures the top ideas, categorizes them, and looks for patterns in what is being reported (Figure 14.3). This may be done in one of two ways:

1. The meeting facilitator may work directly on the flipchart paper with markers, creating one category per piece of flipchart paper and then adding ideas to that category as the small-group or station report-outs continue; or

2. The meeting facilitator may capture the ideas on six-by-eight-inch sticky notes. The meeting facilitator should also begin to capture categories on the different colored sticky notes, grouping the ideas on flipchart paper—one category per piece of paper. One advantage of the sticky notes is that ideas may easily be moved from one category to another. An example is that an idea initially posted under Communication may later be transferred to the Technology category.

Figure 14.3. Meeting Facilitator Creating Patterns of Small-Group Reports.

Step 4: Repeat Steps 1 Through 3 The steps of small-group conversation, large-group report-out, and meeting facilitator's synthesis repeats itself until all the questions for discussion have been asked and answered. The station facilitator may refer to prior station conversations to add insight or context to the current conversation.

Step 5: Meeting Close After the large-group report-out is finalized, the meeting facilitator should review and summarize the top ideas under each category. Identified patterns should also be reviewed and debriefed (Figure 14.4). The final step of the session is to ask participants to sign up for the "idea committee" with which they choose to work. In an organizational setting, committee assignments may be assigned to participants based on the business need.

Step 6: Post Meeting The flipcharts generated by the small-group facilitators are given to the designated idea committee team to process. The flipchart notes from the stations may be transcribed and disseminated to the other teams as well. As the idea committee teams receive this information they are charged with

---

Figure 14.4. Meeting Facilitator Reporting Final Patterns.

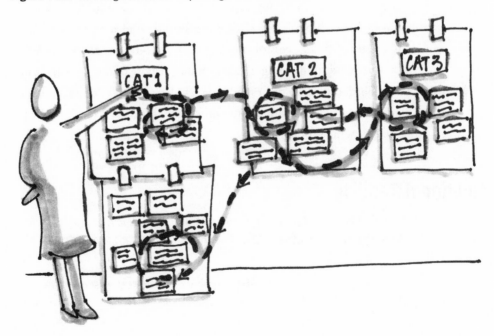

building on the ideas generated, in order to create structured processes with defined outcomes and/or project time lines.

Case

The *Mix and Max* process was recently used with a small, nonprofit agency charged with organizing and representing other nonprofit and for-profit entities on behalf of the city government. The umbrella organization had a fractured past due to a lack of leadership and direction. The city was experiencing rapid growth and the agency was charged with uniting the member organizations, creating a spirit of collaboration and community, as well as a sense of future direction.

During the initial discussion with the client agency, the identified outcomes were to: (a) create a shared vision for the community, (b) identify the initial steps to be taken in order to move toward the shared vision, and (c) address some immediate projects to establish communication between the member organizations. The organization had an existing board and I, as meeting facilitator, opted to ask the board members to act as the small-group facilitators. The board members were encouraged to focus on listening, clarifying, and confirming in this session as this would assist them in their future leadership role as a chair or cochair of an idea committee.

As a result of this successful *Mix and Max* session, the agency lobbied to affect future bond funds being directed to the purpose of the agency, created a shared community calendar, established a web presence, and has developed several additional relationships with community businesses to highlight the work of the member organizations.

Additional Reading

Strachan, Dorothy. (2006). *Making Questions Work: A Guide to How and What to Ask for Facilitators, Consultants, Managers, Coaches, and Educators.* San Francisco: Jossey-Bass.

Strachan, Dorothy, and Pitters, Marian. (2009). *Managing Facilitated Processes: A Guide for Facilitators, Managers, Consultants, Event Planners, Trainers and Educators.* San Francisco: Jossey-Bass.

Voigt, Eric, Brown, Jaunita, and Isaacs, David. (2003). *The Art of Powerful Questions: Catalyzing Insight, Innovation, and Action.* Mill Valley, CA: Whole Systems Associates. Publication available at http://www.theworldcafe.com/pdfs/aopq.pdf.

World Café: http://www.theworldcafe.com—The Mix and Max process was adapted from the World Café process to meet the specific needs of many of my clients. Having been involved in and graphically recorded many World Café discussions, I found a streamlined facilitation process was needed in certain contexts.

Multivoting Technique

The *Multivoting Technique* is very useful when, after several good ideas have been developed by your team, each member seems intent on defending his or her own position. Multivoting helps overcome this roadblock by encouraging individuals to consider the worth of others' ideas.

Follow these steps to complete the procedure:

1. List all ideas or solutions on a flipchart, and then number each idea for review.

2. Tell team members they may cast five votes each for any of the ideas listed on the flipchart. They may apply all five votes to a particular item or distribute their votes among several items; however, all individuals can give no more than three votes to his or her own idea.

3. Provide team members with markers and ask them to vote by placing hash marks next to the ideas or solutions they favor. Speed up the process by having several team members approach the flipchart at the same time.

4. Tally all votes and highlight the ideas that received the most. If two or more ideas receive almost the same number of votes, ask the team to continue discussing these until they know which solution they prefer.

Needs Checklists for Team Members and Team Leaders

The *Needs Checklists* are helpful for team members and team leaders. Sometimes team leaders and members find themselves in conflict because they don't understand the types of support and assistance that they need from each other. This situation is most likely to occur under the following three conditions: (a) a new leader has been placed in charge of the team, (b) the team has only recently been formed and mutual expectations have not yet been defined by the team and team leader, or (c) there are broader changers under way in the organization that are forcing team members and leaders to reevaluate their respective roles and the expectations they hold of each other. Faced with any of these situations a team can use the following tool to help team members and their leaders clearly describe what they need from each other in terms of support and assistance. This tool is comprised of two checklists, one to be completed by team leaders and the other by team members. A related tool for uncovering needs and concerns by the team and team leader is the tool "*Getting Naked" Session.*

Here are guidelines for applying this tool:

1. The column labeled "types of support needed" gives examples of the kinds of assistance that team members and leaders typically require from the other, while the right-hand column leaves room to write in specific examples. For instance, a team member might check off the need statement that says, "Providing needed resource support." That person could elaborate on this issue in the second column by describing a need such as the following:

   Currently only two members of our team have tablet computers. Given the long hours we're putting in on our work projects, if we all had tablets, we could work from home and perform document exchanges when we are on the road.

2. If you are a third-party team facilitator, then before scheduling a meeting to discuss the results of these checklists we recommend that you set aside a few days to personally review them. One way to do

this is to have someone collect the checklists (team members should have the option of remaining anonymous) and make copies for distribution to everyone on the team. This provides all team members with opportunities to reflect privately on their team's overall concerns, and to see whether the needs they have identified are shared by other team members. It is also advisable to meet personally with the team leader in advance of the session to discuss that person's responses to his or her own form.

3. At this point during your session ask the team leader to describe what he or she sees as recurring themes that have emerged from the team members' checklists? Ask: "As a group, what are the members of your team saying that they are looking for from you in terms of help and support?"

4. Invite the team leader to discuss steps that he or she is willing to take to address some of these concerns.

5. Continue the discussion, this time by asking the team to identify some of the key themes they have identified from their team leader's list. Once again, ask them what actions they could take as a group to support these needs and concerns

Needs Checklist for Team Members

Types of Support Needed	Examples
As team members, we are looking to you for the following kinds of support: Keeping us well informed of organizational changes Running interferences for our team with other work groups Representing our team to senior management Providing needed resource support Providing coaching or instruction on technical or administrative skills Providing developmental and training support Troubleshooting; taking the time to help us plan and test our ideas and spot the potential problems before they expand beyond our control Helping us resolve conflicts between certain team members Pitching in and helping us during times of peak workload Making our successes known to senior management Other needs: _____ _____	
As the team leader, I am looking to you for the following kinds of support: Committing to team decisions, even when you don't agree with them Maintaining a positive image when representing our team to other work groups, suppliers, or customers Being willing to take on extra work when we are struggling through peak workloads Providing help when it's needed by other team members Providing me or other team members with assistance in developing specialized technical skills Helping our team identify innovative opportunities for improvement Being my eyes and ears; keeping me informed of new developments or emerging problems Assisting me in some of my administrative leadership functions Challenging my ideas rather than rubber-stamping them Other needs: _____ _____	

Nominal Group Technique

With the *Nominal Group Technique*, team members anonymously write their ideas for resolving a problem on index cards. This technique is particularly useful when you encounter one of the following situations during the team-building session:

- Team members need additional time to sort through their thoughts. When people write down concerns or ideas, they tend to be less emotional and are able to carefully assess the issues at hand.

- Some team members may feel uneasy about openly expressing their ideas in front of other, more dominant, team members. This technique provides a means for anonymous data collection.

- Opposing parties may be reluctant to reveal their underlying concerns to you as the team leader and conflict facilitator. This technique provides an added measure of safety.

- It is particularly useful when you are working with teams characterized by power inequities (that is, when some team members are inhibited from speaking in front of more powerful organizational members).

As simple as it is, this technique addresses several needs. First, it gives team members time to cool off while they organize their thoughts on paper. Second, it helps rein in verbally dominant team members. Finally, once all ideas are anonymously on the flipchart, you remove pride of authorship; that is, team members discuss "an idea" with no personality attached.

Follow these steps to complete the process:

1. Provide team members with index cards to write their responses. Collect the cards.

2. Give the team a ten-minute break, while you summarize their ideas on a flipchart.

3. When they return, systematically review all posted ideas. No single idea should be evaluated until all have been summarized and are clearly understood.

One-to-Ten Technique

The *One-to-Ten Technique* can be used to gauge the initial commitment levels of participants for team decisions, and to determine what actions the team can take to address those concerns raised by uncommitted team members.

This technique involves going around the circle and asking each team member to give a number, from 1 to 10, that indicates their commitment level to the decision under review. A "1" means that the team member is totally against the idea, while a "5" means that the team member is somewhat neutral. A "10" means complete commitment with no reservations. Ask team members not to give any explanation for their answers, nor to comment on anyone else's responses, until everyone has given their scores. This guideline prevents team members from influencing others or engaging in extended debates on the issues.

After posting these numbers on the flipchart for review, invite members who expressed low levels of commitment to share their concerns. Next, ask them the following question: "What actions could we take that would enable you to raise your level of commitment?" Very often, their answers will involve very small actions on the part of the team that can dramatically ease their discomfort. These actions might include:

- Agreeing to pilot a solution on a small scale before undertaking a big change

- Assigning the hesitant team member to the subteam that will be monitoring the results of the improvement effort

- Conducting frequent check-ins with the entire team to assess progress on the improvement effort

- Making small refinements to the proposed improvement plan

Continue the discussion and then once again circle the group, asking members to present their commitment scores, in light of the discussion.

The powerful feature about this simple technique is that having participants voice their commitments to action is often enough to keep them from backsliding when they run into difficulties later. In addition, this approach allows team members to hear the full range of commitments among members before engaging in discussion.

Opportunities Assessment

When planning for a project, teams naturally tend to become so preoccupied with all things that could potentially go wrong that they miss out on opportunities for improving their chances for success. The *Opportunities Assessment* is an effective way to counter this preoccupation by capturing ideas for maximizing the success of a project, and for exploring ways to extend the benefits that could be derived from it.

The following example is an extension of the example used to illustrate the *Threats Analysis* tool. You may wish to review that tool to see how the two tools can be used in conjunction to address both threats and opportunities associated with a given project. Shown below is a model *Opportunities Assessment* that has been prepared by a cross-functional team that has been charged with planning the reorganization of its company's operation department.

A hypothetical team has used this assessment to identify the opportunities that could arise during Steps 1 and 5 of their project. The team has also used this chart to rate the relative probability of occurrence for each of these opportunities, as well as their potential impact. Note that both probability and impact are rated as High (H), Medium (M), or Low (L). In the final phase of the exercise, team members have identified what they can do to increase the likelihood of potential opportunities, and identify ways of exploiting these opportunities should they occur.

The following useful questions can be used to help your team consider ways to implement potential project opportunities:

1. Who, within or outside our team, is in the best position to bring about this opportunity?

2. Is there a critical time period within which we need to pursue this event?

3. What other steps can we take to improve the likelihood of this event?

Opportunities Assessment for Departmental Reorganization

Project Step	Potential Opportunities	Probability of Occurrence	Impact of Occurrence	How to Encourage This Event	How to Exploit This Event
Step 1: Identify new functional and business requirements	Ability to obtain internal benchmark date from other plants	M	H	Make inquiries to HR director of other plants, with push from our president	Use data to verify design assumptions and dramatically shorten time for planning reorganization
Step 5: Assess current bench strength against requirements	Can extract data from 360-degree competency study if completed sooner than expected	L	M	Explain how moving up completion date would benefit our project	Would provide data to independently support performance appraisal findings

4. How can we modify this opportunity to make it more useful for our project?

5. How can we use this opportunity to generate other positive outcomes for our team?

6. How can we apply this opportunity to other areas within our organization?

Opportunities/Threat Matrix

The *Opportunities/Threat Matrix* helps teams address the challenges they often face in comparing two or more options for action. In doing so, it is important for team members to arrive at a balanced discussion of both the potential threats that may be associated with a given course of action, as well as any opportunities for growth and development associated with that course of action.

Potential threats could be such factors as:

- Financial risks associated with pursuing a given option
- The fact the option in question is untested, with no clear history of success
- The difficulty involved in getting organizational support for the option
- The complexity of implementing the option
- That pursuing the option would require a firm commitment of the team's time and resources over an extended period of time.

Potential opportunities could involve such factors as:

- The option represents an opportunity to extend the team's organizational influence
- The option will enable team members to build new and exciting work skills
- The option will substantially raise the long-term performance capability of the team

Instructions

Let's review a completed model of the *Opportunities/Threats Matrix* to help you create one for your team. This model is based on a hypothetical small consulting team who used the tool to evaluate the comparative desirability of developing consulting proposals on two different projects. Because

Opportunities/Threats Matrix—Two Comparable Projects

NOTE: Option A yields a Comparative score of − 21 (Threat score of 49 subtracted from an Opportunity score of 28), whereas Option B yields a total score of 9 (Threat score of 36 subtracted from an Opportunity score of 45). Option B is therefore the best choice.

	Option A: Pursue Proposal with Company A	I	P	T	Option B: Pursue Proposal with Company B	I	P	T
Threats and Disadvantages	Customer has a history of extensive revisions to project plans that result in high costs and project delays.	4	4	16	Customer has history of delayed payments to other vendors, a key point if we were to continue to have a cash-flow problem.	5	4	20
	Distant location would mean a lot of travel time.	2	4	8	Extensive contractual requirements would place a large administrative burden on us.	4	4	16
	We could have to make a complete commitment to the entire program, which would represent a big drain on our cash flow.	5	5	25	Some initial up-front costs here might not be recouped if the contract were terminated in the initial stages.			
	Total Threat Score			*49*	*Total Threat Score*			*36*
Opportunities and Advantages	Huge opportunity for follow-on business with large long-term revenue opportunity.	4	4	16	Represents a highly profitable consulting opportunity.	5	5	25
	Customer would provide entry into a new market area.	3	4	12	Represents an industry in which we are highly experienced (no learning curve required).	4	5	20
	Total Opportunity Score			*28*	*Total Opportunity Score*			*45*
	COMPARATIVE SCORES			−21				9

developing a detailed proposal can involve a lot of time and money the team is interested in determining which of these potential projects is the best option to pursue.

1. The team begins by identifying all potential threats and opportunities that are associated with each of their two decision options. These have been listed on the *Matrix* for each option.

2. Each participant is then asked to rate each potential threat or opportunity on a 1 to 5 scale in terms of two factors: probability (P) and impact (I). In rating for probability, assigning a threat or opportunity the lowest score of "1" means that a participant believes that this threat/opportunity is highly unlikely to occur, while a rating of "5" means that it is highly likely to occur. In rating for impact, assigning an item a score of "1" means that a participant believes that should the threat or opportunity occur it will have minimal impact on the team's success, while a score of "5" means that the factor in question will have a high impact on the team's success.

3. After all participants' scores have been listed, the facilitator averages the score for each cell (averages are shown below). Multiplying the averaged probability (P) score times the averaged impact (I) score yields a total (T) score for each item.

4. Threat scores are then subtracted from Opportunity scores to yield a total for each option. The option with the higher score is the one favored by the team.

5. As a final caveat, we have found that instead of regarding this tool as a "voting" process from which conclusions are automatically drawn, use it as the initial starting point to help team members think through all potential positive and negative aspects associated with a given decision option.

Organizational Social Networking

Organizational Social Networking, customized or commercially available online systems that are designed to work within the firewalls of an organization enables team members to network on key issues and topics both with each other, and with other professionals across their organization. Many organizations have found that they can use social networks to accelerate learning and knowledge creation. Some organizations that are striving for intra-organizational collaboration and have strong concerns about privacy and the protection of intellectual property are opting to make use of enterprise or organizational social networking systems. These systems allow teams to build social networks based on areas of common interest, such as new product development or customer bases, and to reach out across the organization to solicit help and advice on work-related challenges.

Common Applications

Some of the most common applications of these systems include:

- Creating personal profiles that contain summaries of your expertise, unique knowledge areas, education, and training. Some systems make these profiles searchable so that anyone in an organization can locate other employees who have particular skill sets that are in high demand. An example would be an engineering firm looking for employees who have a background in nuclear engineering along with some knowledge of Mandarin, and who have worked in mainland China.

- Posting queries regarding such areas as customer segments, products, or new areas of research to some or all other work associates in the organization.

- Making such conversations searchable and archived, so that team members can track knowledge and expertise in the organization, and the organization can maintain future access to that information.

- Uploading or sharing documents.

- Supporting access to team discussions through mobile-enabled software, such as Skype or FaceTime.

- Facilitating the on-boarding process for new hires, and making these new team members feel that they are a part of the organization.

- Allowing senior managers and others to use weblogs to ensure message clarity and continuity (rather than having messages distorted by successive layers of management).

- Vetting potential decisions on new projects with organizational experts.

- Accelerating response time on urgent questions by being able to simultaneously reach out to others within the networked system.

If you would like to further explore the potential applications of social networking to your own organization, you might consider starting by taking a look at some of the more commonly used enterprise social systems. Among these are Yammer, IBM Connections, Socialcast, and Chatter by Salesforce.com.

Plus/Delta Technique

During team-building sessions participants sometimes become preoccupied with criticizing alternative solutions to team issues. This is due in part to human nature, given that we typically find it easier to identify the weaknesses in an idea than to discover its salvageable aspects. Team members may tend to focus on the negative if they view idea generation sessions as a competitive process ("My idea is better than yours"). This situation can result in wasted time as participants defend their own ideas while attacking those of their teammates. The *Plus/Delta Technique* is one way to overcome this tendency.

To complete this technique, follow these steps:

1. Provide team members with several index cards each, and ask them to use these cards to briefly summarize potential ideas to the issue or challenge at hand. They should limit themselves to one solution to a card.

2. Collect the cards and shuffle them.

3. Write each solution at the top of a flipchart page. We recommend doing this anonymously, without noting members' names.

4. Go back to the first flipchart page and draw a line down the middle of the rest of the page, separating it into two columns.

5. Label the left-hand column "Pluses" and the right-hand column "Deltas."

6. Go back to the first flipchart page. Read the solution aloud, and then turn to one of your team members. Ask this individual to identify one positive thing about the solution—for example, that it is easy to implement. Record this comment under the *Pluses* column.

7. Next, ask the same individual to think of one concern regarding the idea, such as that it would be costly to implement. Write this comment under the *Deltas* column. It's important to remember that whenever a team member presents a concern or criticism, that person must also add a comment to the pluses side of the sheet.

8. Take only one plus and one delta from this person; then move on to the second team member and continue the process.

9. Conduct multiple rotations around the room until team members have had several opportunities to share all of their pluses and deltas.

10. Repeat the exercise for the section idea that was listed (which should be written at the top of your second flipchart page). Continue until your team has evaluated all the ideas.

11. Post the ideas for review. Ask for suggestions on refining or building upon any of them.

12. Ask your team if any one idea stands out as being the strongest, based on having the largest number of pluses and very few deltas.

13. Propose that the team act on this idea.

14. Use any additional time to explore ways to address the concerns that were listed in the deltas column for this solution.

Preventive and Corrective Action Plans

One of the ways your team can avoid getting "painted into a corner" is to troubleshoot potential obstacles and explore ways to overcome them. The *Action Plans* charts below provide a method for performing this type of troubleshooting. Use the questions listed in the *Preventive Action Plan* section to help your team explore steps it can take to prevent the occurrence of problems. Write your answers in the space provided in the right column. In the same way, use the questions in the *Corrective Action Plan* section to identify team options for correcting difficult problems, should they occur.

Preventive Action Plan

Questions	Steps Our Team Will Take
1. What actions could we take to prevent this problem? How potent are these actions? 2. If several options are available, which would be most useful? 3. What is the most effective timing for these actions? If not, what steps are necessary to prepare for them (additional training, resources, information, and so on)? 4. Who. within or outside our team, will be responsible for implementing these actions, and how will they report back to our team?	

Corrective Action Plan

Questions	Steps Our Team Will Take
1. What actions could we take to minimize the impact of this problem or eliminate it once it occurs? 2. Of all available actions, which would be the most potent? Which could be implemented most quickly and have the most beneficial effect? 3. Are we currently capable of taking these actions? If not, what steps are necessary to prepare for them (additional training, resources, information, and so on)? 4. How quickly could we put these actions into effect? What could we do to shorten delivery time? 5. Who within or outside our team will be responsible for implementing these actions and how will they report back to our team?	

Process Check Sheet

Sometimes a team's performance-improvement efforts are not completely successful. When this happens, it is important to approach this situation as another opportunity to understand and solve a problem. The *Process Check Sheet* model below shows the five principal reasons for unsuccessful team improvement efforts, provides examples for each one, and outlines suggested actions to address them. Apply this analysis with your team the next time you encounter less than satisfactory results with your team problem-solving efforts.

Process Check Sheet

Reason for Failure	What to Do About It	Example
You have identified the wrong problem.	Go back to the drawing board and reevaluate your problem. Be very cautious about having a single member of your team interpret your team's problems, or having your team interpret the concerns of other work groups. Ask yourself what symptoms your team has ignored or overstated. Ask others outside your team for input on how they're being affected by your team's performance problems. Carefully consider the potential interactions of different team problems.	A corporate recruiting team knew it was having difficulties meeting the needs of internal customers, but defined the problem as excessive cost-per-hire. After taking several actions to reduce recruiting costs and then discussing these corrective actions with customers, the team discovered that its customers were far less concerned about cost-per-hire than they were about the time it took to fill a position.
You have identified the correct problem but the wrong underlying cause for the problem.	Solicit additional input on your team's performance directly from individuals and work groups outside your team. Try to obtain hard data to help substantiate the true cause of your team's performance problem. Ask yourself when the problem was first noticed and try to determine its trend line. Consider what changes might have been taking place within your team at the time. Explore what current factors may be contributing to the problem.	A cross-functional quality improvement team was set up to resolve recent complaints from a corporate customer. The team put together a detailed improvement plan, only to have it shot down by the customer's quality assurance manager. Later, the team discovered that this manager had long resented what he viewed as the "arrogant" behavior of one of the team members. Armed with this information, the team formulated a new action plan and resolved the underlying issues with the angry manager.

You've identified the correct problem and underlying cause but implemented the wrong improvement solution.	Seek the advice of others within or outside your company who have successfully tackled this problem. What solutions did they implement? Ask yourself if your team has covered the broadest range of solutions, or if they settled for the most convenient or routine solution. Consider performing a best-practices review to see how other companies have resolved similar problems. Try to determine whether your team chose an ineffective or unfeasible solution.	An HR team conducted an organizational effectiveness survey that showed widespread dissatisfaction among company associates regarding the lack of career opportunities. The team attacked this problem by putting months of effort into designing a career development program. When the program was presented, it met with a high degree of cynicism from many employees, who felt that while the program provided excellent skills training, its lack of a job posting process and formal career paths made it difficult for them to take advantage of career opportunities.
You have put the right improvement action in place but failed to effectively implement it.	Ask whether your team has allowed adequate time to review the solution. Many team problems cannot be fixed overnight. Ask if additional resources would make a difference in the success of the implementation plan. Consider whether this is the best time to implement the plan. Would it be better to wait until conditions change? Finally, ask yourself if you have the full support of your organizational stakeholders? Does everyone really want this solution to work?	In attempting to attack the problem of "lack of innovation," a marketing team performed a few limited best-practices studies within its own field to see how other, related companies were encouraging innovative performance. In retrospect, the team realized that it hadn't gone far enough in its review. The second time around, the team revised its study to go outside its industry and include input from some of the most creative companies in the United States.
Your team has encountered factors completely beyond its control that have reduced the effectiveness of the original improvement plan.	Leverage all possible support from senior management to eliminate these barriers. Consider putting a hold on your implementation plan until the situation stabilizes. Ask if there is a way to bolster your plan. Make every effort to anticipate future roadblocks.	A support team developed a reasonable action plan for establishing clearer direction over the next one to three years. Halfway through its efforts, a department-wide reorganization forced the team to rethink many of its original operating assumptions.

Provocative Questions for Encouraging Dialogue
Contributed by Jim O'Neil

One useful technique for building collaboration is to identify *Provocative Questions for Encouraging Dialogue* that can be distributed in leaflets or pamphlets to participants before a group discussion or a team-building session. These are the types of questions which are intended to (a) encourage participants to think carefully about the issue or topic that will be discussed, (b) think more carefully about all of the significant factors which influence the development and potential outcomes of this issue, and (c) more critically examine their own positions and concerns related to the topic in question.

Applications for Provocative Questions

Since its inception in Northern Ireland, the nonprofit agency Community Dialogue has had a constructive role in producing a series of leaflets and documents that have added to the general discourse of topics that were a key element of the political process. Additional information, including case studies, on Community Dialogue may be found under the tool *Guidelines and Questions for Engaging Dialogue*.

One of the earliest leaflets produced by Community Dialogue was the *Summary of the Belfast/Good Friday Agreement*, which was circulated to 9,000 people throughout Northern Ireland. The leaflet was circulated prior to a referendum on the Belfast/Good Friday Agreement and was designed to encourage people to think deeply about what they wanted, what they needed, and what they could live with in any future agreed settlement of the conflict. The leaflets often take the following form:

- Illustrates and explains how others see the issue under discussion
- Challenges the reader to question his or her position and concerns on the topic
- Questions each viewpoint

Special Note of Acknowledgment: This work would not have been possible without the support of several funding bodies over the years, most recently the *European Union Special Support Programme for Peace and Reconciliation*.

- Suggests a shift in thinking and understanding that is needed in order to build collaborative dialogue, and asks the reader—"will you make that shift?"

Some of the publications have attempted to pose often awkward and controversial questions, or have attempted to clarify key policy documents that have addressed governmental policy and strategy and simplify these documents into "lay terms" ("Unraveling the Jargon"). Key questions and issues that impact on local communities are also addressed such as alienation, gender equality, and sectarianism, among others. This involves the production of pamphlets and follow-up workshops to help the community at large understand the issues raised and assist them in making informed choices about their future. One example of an "Unraveling the Jargon" type of document was *The Consultative Group on the Past.* This document provided an aid to dialogue for people who were victims of the conflict, enabling them to gain a deeper insight into issues around truth recovery, and dealing with the past. The dialogues based on this document led to participants making an informed response to government policy proposals.

There are also a number of documents that posed questions about the past, present, and future in our society and invite people to have difficult conversations with each other on those issues. These often pose a series of "itchy" questions that are aimed at nationalists, unionists, republicans, loyalists, and the general public. One example of this type of document was *From Past to Future: The Saville Inquiry and Beyond.* This document posed the following types of provocative questions:

- Questions for Nationalists and Republicans: Republicans think they were fighting a just war but focus on holding British security forces accountable. Should Republicans be held accountable too?

- Questions for Unionists and Loyalists: Many Unionists and Loyalists want investigations into Republican killings. Are you as keen on looking into Loyalist and security force killings?

- Questions for All of Us: How does the way YOU focus on the past help young people to grow up free of the baggage of the past?

Real-Time Implementation Planning

One of the obstacles that teams face as they strive to improve their performance and strengthen their working relationships is the lack of a coherent "team memory." This means that it is not uncommon for team members to reach decisions and make commitments to complete improvement actions, only to find that days or weeks after their team session they have difficulty accurately recalling or following up on those commitments.

The *Real-Time Implementation Planning* tool addresses this need. This scenario is directly related to how team outputs (the decisions, actions, and commitments arising from the session) are typically captured during a team-building session. The standard approach is to have the team-building facilitator or a team member record these outputs on a series of flipcharts. Later these rough notes are typed up and distributed to team members. The problem here is twofold. First, quite often during the final hour or so of a team-building session participants quickly identify a number of follow-up actions that they wish to take. Only a small portion of this information is captured on the flipchart, leaving these summaries open to interpretation. Second, the time delay (often several days) that members encounter before they receive their typed summaries means that they experience some delays before they can begin implementing their plans, and by this time they may have different recollections of their agreements. The solution is to engage in real-time implementation planning. This technique is very simple, and the instructions are as follows:

In Advance of the Session:

1. The team should bring a laptop or tablet computer, projector, and screen to their team-building session.

2. The facilitator prepares an e-mail distribution list containing the e-mail addresses of all participants and preloads this list onto the laptop or tablet.

3. It is also helpful to conduct the session in a room that has an intranet connection to enable the outputs collected in the session to be immediately distributed to all members *before* the session is completed.

During the Session:

1. During the session, whenever participants pause to record their outputs ask one team member (we recommend rotating this responsibility) to volunteer to record everyone's commitments, decisions, and agreed-upon actions onto the tablet or laptop. This information should be simultaneously projected onto the screen for viewing by all participants.

2. In doing this, the person who is recording this data should never paraphrase but always attempt to use the actual wording provided by participants.

3. In addition, the facilitator should ask team members to confirm that what is projected on the screen is an accurate "capture" of their thoughts. If not, invite participants to make any needed changes there, on the spot. This represents their last chance to make changes to agreed-upon decisions and action items.

4. When all outputs have been captured these documents should be saved on the tablet or laptop, and immediately e-mailed to all participants through the prepared distribution list. If participants have their laptops or smartphones with them, ask them to immediately confirm the receipt of those documents.

5. This technique can also be extended to additional applications. For example, certain tools, such as the *Action Planning Chart*, *Stakeholder Analysis Chart*, or *Decision Matrix*, require the creation of forms or charts that are populated during the team-building session. If these tools are to be used in the session, they can be prepared in advance of the session and loaded onto the tablet or laptop, then projected to everyone in the room through the use of the LCD display. This approach saves time and provides participants with a clear graphic tool for later reference.

6. An alternative to a distribution e-mail would be to immediately load the team's outputs into a shared folder that participants can later individually access.

7. Prior to the team follow up session these documents can once again be e-mailed to participants to remind them of the team commitments that will be reviewed in the follow-up session.

One Final Note

This is a deceptively simple technique. Although easy to implement, it helps to build accountability among members by forcing them to confirm their agreements during the session, and to leave the session armed with a common list of agreed-upon outputs. In our experience this approach raises the overall energy level for the team and helps participants feel that they are being more proactive in taking action to support their joint success.

Reframing Technique

This *Reframing Technique* drives how participants in a team-building session and their facilitator frame the team's development and improvement needs—thus significantly influencing the direction and focus of the team-building process. How we envision and frame the basic questions that we use to structure team requirements establishes a certain *entry path* into this process. This in turn can have an important impact on the range and creativity of the ideas that a team generates for addressing an issue or opportunity.

Consider the following example. Years ago a group of tomato farmers was concerned about the degree of damage that their products sustained during shipping. At first, the group defined its problem in the following terms: "How can we ship our tomatoes in a way that will reduce damage in transport?" This way of seeing the problem led the farmers to consider a rather limited set of solutions, such as selecting alternate transportation routes or looking for ways to improve the packaging of tomatoes. It was only after the farmers had reframed their challenge as, "How can we make our tomatoes less susceptible to damage during transport?" that they came up with the innovative idea of selectively breeding tomatoes to produce a thicker-skinned variety that was less susceptible to damage.

The following steps can help you apply the reframing method to your own team-building need:

1. Begin by asking if one participant would be willing to suggest a single sentence that clearly describes the team-building need. Write this sentence on the flipchart.

2. Ask other participants to withhold all comments regarding this statement. Instead, challenge them to come up with two or three alternative ways of rethinking and rewording their team-building needs. For example, an initial statement might be, "How can we meet together more often to maintain our project schedules and keep each other alerted to potential problems?" An alternative way of framing this issue might be, "How can we each provide regular input on our project plans, despite the fact that we work on different schedules and out of different locations?"

3. Discuss the different lines of inquiry presented by each reframed statement. Ask, "What will this statement help us explore?" "What does the wording of this statement assume to be outside of our team's review?" In the example presented above, reframing the initial statement would help the team move beyond thinking only about solutions related to meetings, and might include such options as the use of groupware.

4. Once team requirements have been constructively framed, the facilitator needs to help team members assess the relative importance of different requirements. It is not uncommon for a team to create a list of five to ten important issues or opportunities for review, when in reality a single day might be required to fully explore a single issue. The *Team Building Assessment Questionnaire* tool is one way to help team members target their team-building needs and identify priorities for discussion. The *Online Facilitator's Guide* provides a downloadable version of this document that you can distribute to team members for their input.

Relationship Audit

There are many ways to obtain input from other work groups on your team's performance. You can conduct meetings involving both teams or representative members from each team, you can selectively interview members of the other team, or you can talk informally with the other team's leader. Unfortunately, because none of these approaches utilizes anonymous feedback, the other team may not be completely candid about its concerns. In addition, in group settings you will often find that a few dominant and extremely vocal team members end up speaking for everybody. Finally, such face-to-face methods don't provide a means of assessing changes in team relationships that are occurring over time.

One way to overcome these limitations is by using a simple questionnaire, the *Relationship Audit,* which invites other work groups to provide confidential feedback on their relationship with your team. The model is provided below. You will find that it is closely related to the *Customer Relationship Audit* tool.

The following instructions will guide you and your team through this audit process:

1. If you feel it is advisable to audit several work groups, we strongly recommend that you start by focusing on a single work group and avoid taking on too many improvement actions at one time. Instead, start with the one work group that you feel would benefit most from improved interteam relationships.

2. Before applying the *Relationship Audit,* clear it with the leader of the team you would like to survey. Explain your purpose in conducting the audit, the steps you will use to collect and apply the feedback you obtain, and how you intend to report the results of the survey to the other team. We also recommend that you draft a cover letter to accompany the audit and review this letter with the other team leader before you distribute it.

3. Strive for ensuring confidentiality. Identify a trustworthy, neutral third party such as an office coordinator or college intern to

distribute and collect the audit forms. These individuals should average the scores for each question and then transfer the averaged scores and all answers to open-ended questions onto a second sheet.

4. Discard the original audit forms to assure the other team that you are addressing concerns they might have regarding the anonymity of responses.

5. Caution your team that the audit is designed to obtain feedback on your team as a whole, and not on the performance of individual team members.

6. Don't conduct the audit during periods of intense organizational change, when broader concerns and issues may influence the survey responses you receive.

7. Give some consideration to your methods for reviewing the findings from your audit with those who completed it. My general recommendation is to conduct a very candid and informal review session with these individuals. Here are some additional suggestions:

   • Instead of presenting the audit as a team report card, it's more effective to discuss the major benefits you've extracted from it. One way to do this is summarize the areas that have been identified in the survey as a team's two greatest strengths as well as those that represent your team's two greatest performance improvement opportunities.

   • Share any suggestions from your team on how to strengthen team relationships. At the same time, solicit suggestions from the other team regarding additional improvement actions that can be undertaken by your team.

8. Toward the end of the discussion, don't hesitate to indicate actions the other team can take to help strength the relationship and resolve critical problems between the teams.

Relationship Audit

Relationship Factors	Team Ratings Low. . .Moderate. . .High
Accessibility You can reach us easily by phone or e-mail. We are readily available for face-to-face meetings. We take the initiative to arrange meetings with you.	1. . .2. . .3. . .4. . .5. . .6. . .7 1. . .2. . .3. . .4. . .5. . .6. . .7 1. . .2. . .3. . .4. . .5. . .6. . .7
Relationship Building We make an effort to understand your operation, work processes, and performance issues. We enlist your feedback before we take actions that could affect the performance of your work team. We have effective one-on-one relationships with your team members.	1. . .2. . .3. . .4. . .5. . .6. . .7 1. . .2. . .3. . .4. . .5. . .6. . .7 1. . .2. . .3. . .4. . .5. . .6. . .7
Listening Skills We give you our full attention during discussions. When you leave a discussion with us, you feel we clearly understand and have not misinterpreted what you have said. We present ourselves as open-minded and willing to listen to different points of view.	1. . .2. . .3. . .4. . .5. . .6. . .7 1. . .2. . .3. . .4. . .5. . .6. . .7 1. . .2. . .3. . .4. . .5. . .6. . .7
Information Sharing We freely share important Information with you (we are not reluctant to disclose information you need to perform your job). We provide timely information about changes that could affect your department. When sharing information, we communicate clearly and succinctly.	1. . .2. . .3. . .4. . .5. . .6. . .7 1. . .2. . .3. . .4. . .5. . .6. . .7 1. . .2. . .3. . .4. . .5. . .6. . .7
Conflict Resolution We make an effort to work harmoniously with you. We look for win-win solutions to problems. When involved in a conflict, we conduct ourselves professionally (polite, composed, and task-focused).	1. . .2. . .3. . .4. . .5. . .6. . .7 1. . .2. . .3. . .4. . .5. . .6. . .7 1. . .2. . .3. . .4. . .5. . .6. . .7

What one behavior should we continue, or improve upon, to strengthen relationships between our teams?
What one behavior do we need to change to strengthen relationships between our teams?
What is the most important work issue our teams need to resolve together?
What steps do you suggest we take to resolve this work issue?

Relationship Map

Sometimes, a simple graphic depicting a team's relationships with other internal work groups makes it easier to understand the factors that are driving interteam conflicts. This is the idea behind relationship mapping. A *Relationship Map* provides a simple graphic that serves as a good starting point for a team discussion on where members should focus their efforts in strengthening relationships with other organizational work groups.

The completed model below (Figure 14.5) shows a *Relationship Map* drawn by a hypothetical team that manages all training activities for one division of a large corporation. Relationships that are strong are represented by solid lines, with weaker relationships represented by broken lines. The training team in

Figure 14.5. A *Relationship Map* Model from a Divisional Training Team.

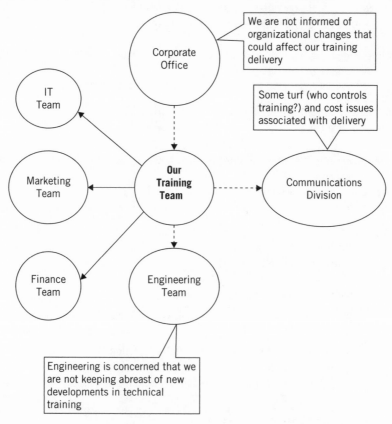

our example is having problems with the services and information it receives from its corporate office, while its two largest internal customers—the engineering department and the communications divisions—seem to be dissatisfied with the services they're getting. These three work groups, which the training team has indicated as especially important to its survival, are represented by large circles on the relationship map. On the other hand, the IT, marketing, and finance departments—less crucial to the functions of the training team, as shown by the smaller size of their circles—are relatively satisfied with the training team's services.

Follow these instructions to create your own *Relationship Map*:

1. Draw a circle in the middle of a flipchart to represent your team.

2. Now invite the members of your team to draw other circles around the central circle to represent those internal suppliers, customers, support groups, or any other stakeholder groups that influence your team's performance. Use bigger circles to represent groups that are especially important to the survival of your team.

3. Place other circles close to your circle if your team interacts frequently with those groups, and further from your team if interactions are infrequent.

4. Use arrows pointing outward to indicate services or products you provide to these other work groups, and arrows pointing inward to indicate services or products you obtain from these work groups.

5. Use solid, thick lines to indicate strong positive relationships, and dotted lines to indicate areas where concerns have arisen with other teams. (An option is to use green and red markers to represent strong and weak relationships.)

6. Use dialogue boxes to summarize some of the interteam issues that may be creating conflict between your team and affiliated work groups.

7. Invite selected individuals outside your team to review your team's relationship chart and offer their own commentary and feedback. Third-party representatives are often able to provide a team with

completely different perspectives on interteam conflicts. They may, for example, point out key stakeholders you have omitted from your chart, or challenge the relative importance of different stakeholders or the types of conflict issues identified by your team. They may also be in a position to share insights regarding factors that could exacerbate interteam conflicts.

Running the Gauntlet Technique

The *Running the Gauntlet Technique* can help your team evaluate its readiness for successfully pursuing different business objectives. With this tool, you will be able to test the robustness of your business objectives against three or four short-term business scenarios. This tool is an excellent next step from the *Scenario Forecast* tool that develops alternative change scenarios.

To better understand what we mean, consider an individual preparing for an extended camping trip. Someone planning for a narrow set of contingencies may take only a few bare essentials, such as a sleeping bag, tent, flashlight, and matches, whereas the person who develops a sturdier plan will bring along a variety of supplies—perhaps foul-weather gear, a cook stove, water purification tablet, a first aid kit—to cope with a wider range of environmental conditions. In the same way, when your team is establishing business objectives, team members can use this technique to determine how well your business plans incorporate the types of changes created by alternative change scenarios.

The model below shows how this application could be used with four scenarios developed by the hypothetical strategic planning team that serves as our hypothetical model within the *Scenario Forecast* tool. (Note: It is helpful to review the *Scenario Forecast* model before moving on to the following explanation.)

This hypothetical team has discovered that in undertaking its first objective, it is well prepared to handle any of the four potential business scenarios. Looking at this example from another perspective, we can see that the Export Express is the overall scenario for which this team is least prepared, whereas it is most prepared to deal with the Golden Window scenario.

Teams often incorporate into their plans a set of implicit assumptions—a Plan A—which is based on their conviction that a given scenario will occur, while at the same time, they ignore the need to plan for other contingencies. This tool drives teams to examine their operating assumptions and evaluate the overall strength of their plans.

Running the Gauntlet

Alternative Scenarios	Everyone Wins	Golden Window	Sharp Fall	Export Express
Objective 1	High	High	High	Moderate
Objective 2	Moderate	Moderate	Low	Low
Objective 3	Low	Moderate	Low	Low

Scenario Forecast

This *Scenario Forecast* tool encourages team members to think creatively by trying to anticipate a variety of large-scale changes that could affect their team, or broader organization. It goes beyond the simple, straight-line extrapolation of a company's projected performance to show how different factors can interact to produce powerful change scenarios. When performed correctly, this technique forces teams to develop business plans that can accommodate a variety of interacting change factors. It also provides a valuable tool for building alignment among team members on future opportunities and threats. Still another benefit is that scenario forecasting helps team members better understand how their disagreements on key issues are often based on very different assumptions about the future.

During the first three steps of this process, it is important to obtain input from those individuals outside your team who can expose your team to different assumptions and inputs. These individuals might include technical leaders who have a reputation for accurately tracking industry trends, industry leaders, and even key customers and vendors.

Follow these eight steps for conducting a *Scenario Forecast*. A model forecast from a hypothetical petrochemical company is provided.

1. Identify Influencing Factors. With your team, brainstorm a list of external factors that are likely to shape the business environment in which your company operates. For example (as is shown in the completed example below), a strategic planning team for a U.S.-based petrochemical company might include factors such as changes in environmental regulations pertaining to petrochemical removal, disposal, and transport; domestic gasoline consumption levels; and petrochemical production levels in other countries, including OPEC members.

2. Rate Influencing Factors. Rate each factor on a scale of 1 to 10 (with 10 being the highest) in terms of degree of impact and scope of change. "Degree of impact" refers to how intensely changes in this area may affect your company's performance. A score of 10 means this factor could have major impact on your business performance. "Scope of change" refers to the amount of change this factor is likely

to undergo over the next two years. A rating of 10 means that you believe a factor will change substantially over the next two years.

3. Identify Key Influencing Factors. Multiply each factor's rating for degree of impact with that for scope of change. You should have a scoring range that extends from 1 ($1 \times 1 = 1$) to 100 ($10 \times 10 = 100$). Select from your list the two factors with the highest overall score. These are your key influencing factors.

4. Create Alternative Scenarios. Describe two other possible scenarios for each factor. In the example that we have provided for our hypothetical petrochemical company, domestic gas consumption is a key influencing factor. As a result, one future scenario might be "increased business and leisure travel create a 15% increase in gasoline consumption over the next two years," while an alternative might be "domestic economic pressures cause a 20% reduction in business and leisure travel over the next two years." Create optimistic and pessimistic scenarios, but avoid highly improbable scenarios.

5. Combine Scenarios. Integrate your scenarios into a combined scenario matrix as shown in our example. Next, create a title that best describes the combined scenario represented in each cell of the matrix. In our example, the title "Golden Window" indicates the window of opportunity created for increased gasoline sales, given a strong increase in domestic gasoline consumption and a simultaneous decrease in worldwide production.

6. Describe Each Combined Scenario. Create a one- to two-page summary describing the details of the combined scenarios in the four cells, including the sequence of actions that would likely lead to each combined scenario.

7. Assess Probability. Use all available information to assess the relative probability for the occurrence of each combined scenario. In our example, there is an estimated probability of 16% that the Golden Window scenario will occur during the next two years.

8. Assess the Implications. Ask team members to jointly identify the implications of each four combined scenarios for your business strategy.

Scenario Forecast Matrix for Petrochemical Company

Scenarios Related to Worldwide Production	Scenarios Related to Domestic Consumption	
	20% increase in domestic consumption	15% decrease in domestic consumption
20% increase in worldwide petrochemical production	Everyone Wins (24%)	Sharp Fall (36%)
10% decrease in worldwide petrochemical production	Golden Window (16%)	Export Express (24%)

Illustration

One of the most potent applications of a *Scenario Forecast* is to help a team look far into the future to consider the implication of how different change scenarios might affect its performance. One such implication involves the types of competencies that will be required of a leadership team, given different business and organizational scenarios. After reviewing the eight steps for completing a scenario forecast, review the model *Scenario Forecast and Executive Competencies* provided below. This model shows how four different scenario forecasts could influence the types of competencies required of a leadership team.

Scenario Forecasts and Executives Competencies

Scenario Forecasts	Implications for Competency Requirements
We will undergo a major shift from the defense to the commercial market, with 70% of revenues coming from commercial sales in 5 years, compared to 30% today.	Less emphasis on importing executives who have had military backgrounds, or experience in marketing to the military. Need to import or develop marketing executives with strong skills in commercial marketing and sales.
Within the next 5- to 10-year period, more than 50% of our revenues will come from the development of new products.	Need executives with the ability to manage fast product development and design for manufacturing. Need executives who can perform effectively in marketing, production, and legal so we can shrink development times.

(Continued)

Scenario Forecasts and Executives Competencies

Scenario Forecasts	Implications for Competency Requirements
We anticipate streamlining our direct overhead expenses, with our entire field support and audit functions outsourced to external providers.	Require leadership competencies in negotiating and managing large outsourced work functions. Need organizational development executives who can help us plan a smooth transition from in-house to outsourced work functions.
We will open our first e-commerce site on the Internet next year, with the goal of having 20% of all sales coming through the Internet within the next 4 years.	Need IT executives who are able to identify appropriate e-commerce target markets and manage website design, including integration of inventory, tracking, credit, and billing.

Selection Matrix for Virtual Team Members

Virtual teams are a unique entity, and successful members of these teams possess certain competencies and personal qualities. This *Selection Matrix* (model shown below) provides an effective method for selecting members for your virtual team. Follow these steps to complete this matrix:

1. Begin the discussion by reviewing the member selection criteria shown in the chart.

2. Next, ask your team to contribute any additional selection critical that they want to add to the chart.

Selection Matrix for Virtual Team Members

Selection Criteria	Value	Candidate's Ratings			
		A	B	C	D
Evidence of self-management skills; able to follow through on assignments without repeated prodding, to manage own schedule, to be consistently on time for phone, e-mail, or videoconferences, and so on					
Excellent communication skills; has the ability to present information clearly or to probe for understanding when communicating virtually					
Experience in working as part of a virtual team, or (as a minimum requirement) experience in working with a team that was distributed across several work sites					
Experience with telecommuting or working from home, with limited contact with a field site or corporate office					
Is computer-literate; comfortable with using shared folders, and required software for electronic communications (such as Skype, Microsoft Project)					

3. When your team has completed its list, ask members to rate the relative importance of each selection criterion on a 1 to 5 scale (5 is highest). Place the team's averaged rating for each criterion in the Value column.

4. Assess each candidate with the same rating process. Spaces have been provided for four candidates (Candidates A through D).

5. Multiply Value scores by Candidate's Ratings scores for each criterion to calculate the total score for each candidate.

Stakeholder Analysis Chart

The *Stakeholder Analysis Chart* can be used to map out key stakeholders within your organization. To begin, let's discuss how to complete the chart using the model shown below. A blank chart is provided below for your use.

Background to the Model

Our completed model concerns a hypothetical cross-functional team that was asked to design changes to its company's performance appraisal process. Currently, the process operates in the following way:

- Managers obtain appraisal sign-offs only from immediate senior-level managers, resulting in unreliable ratings based on varying personal standards.

- In the last performance review, more than 50 percent of employees received "exceeds" and "greatly exceeds" ratings, producing a skewed evaluation system.

- There is little direct relationship between performance ratings and merit increases. Allocation of merit increases varies across functions.

The team will be proposing the following changes to the appraisal process:

- Prior to approval, all appraisals must be reviewed by the corporate HR director to ensure more equitable and consistent performance ratings.

- The company will utilize a "forced distribution" appraisal process in which no more than 20 percent of employees can be given ratings of "exceeds" or "greatly exceeds."

- Merit increase ranges will be established for each performance category. Managers will not be able to award increases outside these ranges.

With these projects' specifications in mind, the team leader has used the chart to identify those stakeholders who can be expected to *support* or *block* the proposed changes. Team members have also determined those points in the project schedule at which they are likely to encounter *support* or *resistance*. In addition, they have tried to identify the reasons why a given executive would support or attempt to block their project. Using this information, the team can develop proactive strategies to secure support or reduce resistance. The team has listed these actions in the last column of the chart.

When applying the *Stakeholder Analysis Chart* to your team, we recommend completing the following steps:

1. Select a team objective or major project to review. This objective or project should be one that will directly affect other functions in your organization. Our example focuses on the company's performance appraisal process.

2. Ask your team to list on a flipchart or whiteboard all the potential stakeholders for your objective or project. Before doing this, you might find it useful to discuss any guidelines for identifying potential stakeholders. Don't attempt to categorize stakeholders at this point—simply list them on the flipchart.

3. Now, review your list and identify stakeholders who are expected to be key supporters or blockers. Supporters are those leaders who are likely to provide your team with resources, help remove obstacles to project completion, or provide the influence needed to insure that the project is implemented. Blockers are those leaders who, for a variety of reasons, are more likely to take action to stop, delay, or impede your project or initiative. As we have done for our example, list these names in the appropriate rows of the *Stakeholder Analysis Chart*. If your team has identified a large number of stakeholders, you may find it easier to focus on the top five for the remainder of this exercise.

4. Determine when, in the course of pursuing your objective or project, your team is likely to encounter initial signs of support or resistance from each of these stakeholders. This information should go in the second column of your chart.

5. Discuss the reasons for each stakeholder's support or resistance. Although it may be a challenge, it is important to try to put

yourselves in the shoes of people you are reviewing. This information should be summarized in the third column of your chart.

6. Under the right-hand column, identify those actions your team could take to gain support or neutralize resistance.

7. Once your team has completed the chart, step back and highlight or circle the most important factors that emerge from this discussion.

8. Consider reviewing your analysis at a later point with your most trusted sponsor. Make certain that this person is politically savvy and understands the power network within your organization.

Stakeholder Analysis Chart for Performance Appraisal Project

Type of stakeholder	Who are these stakeholders?	When during our project are we most likely to first encounter them?	Why would they support or resist our project?	What action can we take to secure support or reduce resistance?
Supporters	Vice President of HR	Will provide sponsorship from the beginning if asked	Believes it would create a more equitable pay system	Use as sounding board and troubleshooter to ensure our recommendations are well considered
	Company president	Will officially launch project and personally support team's recommendations	Believes it will match rewards to performance and better identify high-potentials	Provide interim reviews; create better vehicle for tracking high-potentials
	U.S. Engineering staff	Will probably respond favorably to planned changes in system Believes it would create a more equitable pay system	Last employee survey indicated high voluntary termination rate due in part to frustration with performance appraisal system	Conduct focus groups to confirm employee support for changes; use groups to fine-tune progress

(Continued)

Stakeholder Analysis Chart for Performance Appraisal Project (Continued)

Blockers	Vice President of Sales	May attempt to discredit team's recommendations	New system forces him to give up some control over dispensing merit increases	Perform bench-marking study of other sales units that use similar systems to boost their performance
	President, Mexico	Has already made his concerns known to CEO	Is concerned that the team's proposed uniform performance standards won't be applicable to his employees	Check research for types of performance standards used in Mexico Conduct personal review of performance standards; consider creating a separate set of competencies for performance within this country

Stakeholder Analysis Chart

Name of Project or Business Initiative:

Type of stakeholder	Who are these stakeholders?	When during our project are we most likely to first encounter them?	Why would they support or resist our project?	What actions can we take to secure support or reduce resistance?
Supporters				
Blockers				

Stakeholder Hats

Contributed by Jonas Janebrant and Johanna Steen

MiL Institute, Lund, Sweden

Purpose

This intervention has been inspired of de Bono's Six Thinking Hats (for more information see Edward de Bono's book, *Serious Creativity*) and aims at securing a solid base for managing a fundamental company change. An example might involve the decision to centralize a function or service that previously was decentralized. This technique can help participants more effectively manage a change by securing stakeholders' perspectives, and more accurately assess stakeholder needs.

Intended Aims and Outcomes

- Create greater alignment concerning the coming change

- Think outside the box, break free from the internal perspective

- Expose and examine arguments against and in favour of change

- Clarify stakeholders' perspective and needs

- Clarify positions (arguments against and in favor of the change)

- Achieve greater alignment concerning the change

Description of a Hypothetical Case

Assume that you are working with a management group that is discussing a proposal by the top executive (managing director or CEO) to centralize the company's IT organization. The management group is divided into different camps, which have already begun to view this issue in terms of being a simple problem that can be solved with a "yes/no" solution, rather than a complex dilemma which requires the analysis of many different factors. To complicate things, this leadership group is made up of some executives who, by their disposition, jump at the possibility of change. Other members are habitually reluctant to make changes and tend to engage in extended debates regarding the "Why?" and "How?" issues. In short, there is a need to steer the group toward a constructive use of time, while surfacing the different viewpoints represented within this team.

Instructions—Part 1

Before meeting together the team should identify a group of stakeholders, for example customers, employees, the owner, the management group, the board, partners, and so on.

1. Ask the group to identify the three most important stakeholders.

2. State: "For the next 20 minutes you are all going to wear the "Customer Hat" and you are going to look at this change from the customer's perspective. In doing so we want you to list what you believe your customers would identify as representing the pros and cons of moving toward a centralized IT function. As you do, make sure to document your discussion."

3. The same procedure is followed with the next two categories of stakeholders. (Twenty minutes of discussion for each stakeholder.)

4. When the interests of the three different stakeholders have been mapped out, the group gets another twenty minutes to summarize the results of their discussions. One way to map out this information is to circle or highlight those pros and cons which are particularly important to each stakeholder group, with particular emphasis on those concerns that appear to be shared by all three stakeholders.

By the end of Part 1 participants will have a better understanding of the potential consequences of a change for each of the different stakeholders, and will gain a greater understanding of the arguments and of the positions held by other participants.

Instructions—Part 2

The group is now better prepared to make a more informed decision. However, in order to promote equality of opportunity regarding for example, gender differences, or other possible differences involving power within the management group we need to do one last thing:

1. Let the group organize itself into two subgroups, according to those who are pro or con regarding the proposed change. The subgroups do not have to be equal in number.

2. State: "We have now done the preliminary gathering of information concerning the question of a centralized IT organization. Now each side will get a final opportunity to make their arguments heard."

3. "With the help of a chess clock we are going to have a final debate in which you will be asked to represent your stakeholders' "pro" or "con" views regarding this proposed change. However, unlike many ordinary meetings, each side will have the same amount of time at their disposal. You will have 10 minutes each to represent the positions. The two positions are: "This change will fail because . . ." and "This change will work because . . ."

4. Give the groups 10 minutes to prepare and then let the debate start.

Conclusion

Through this intervention the decision regarding a proposed change will rest on a solid foundation in that important stakeholder perspectives will be accounted for, and different sides will have a greater understanding of each other's viewpoints.

Team Adaptation Diagram

Every large-scale change event drives individuals and teams to reevaluate the emphasis they place on competing priorities. The *Team Adaptation Diagram,* shown as a table below, helps a team evaluate major changes in terms of seven different types of trade-offs that must frequently be made to accommodate competing priorities. The table lists seven categories for analyses in two different situations—the past and the projection of the team's future. Take the following three steps to complete this process:

1. Change: Briefly describe, in the space provided at the top of the table, the large-scale change that is affecting your team.

2. Categories: Use the seven categories to help team members explore how the change is likely to affect your team's approach in the future.

   - Competencies: What competencies will become obsolete? What competencies will be regarded as state-of-the-art?

   - Customers: Given the anticipated change, which customers will become more tangential to your team's success? Which customers will assume a more central role?

   - Experience: What type of work experiences will become increasingly irrelevant? What work experiences will be more applicable to the new challenges your team is likely to face in dealing with the change?

   - Information: What information and resources (journals, Internet sites, conferences and seminars, technical knowledge, proprietary knowledge related to the workings of your company) will become outdated with the impending change? What information will be very opportune?

   - Issues: What work issues will decline in importance with the onset of change? What work issues will emerge as increasingly important?

   - Networks: What professional networks appear to be static, or less connected to the focus of change in your area? What professional networks are viewed as more dynamic, or closest to the center of action in your field?

- Requirements: Which aspects of your team's product/service performance will elicit only head nods from customers as these issues decline in importance? Which performance features will emerge as hot buttons as they develop greater value for your customers?

Your team may feel that some of these categories (such as customers) will change relatively little in the new scenario, whereas other factors (such as resources) will be dramatically affected. One of the benefits of this tool is the ability to sift through aspects of impending change to determine those that are likely to have the greatest influence on your team.

3. Use the information you have gathered to anticipate the types of trade-offs in staffing, resources, project priorities, and so forth, that will be required as a result of the impending change.

Team Adaptation Diagram

What large-scale change is our team facing?

Categories	Past Situation	Future Situation
Competencies	Obsolete:	State-of-the-art:
Customers	Tangential:	Central:
Experience	Irrelevant:	Applicable:
Information	Outdated:	Opportune:
Issues	Declining:	Emerging:
Networks	Static:	Dynamic:
Requirements	Head nods:	Hot buttons:

Team Alignment Pyramid

There are times when teams have difficulty determining how best to unravel and prioritize the many issues that they need to discuss. If you encounter this situation consider making use of the *Team Alignment Pyramid.*

There are two assumptions behind the pyramid (Figure 14.6). First, we believe that in order for teams to be successful, team members must gain alignment on the six key team performance elements that make up the pyramid. Second, these elements need to be tackled in a certain order, from those at the top (level 1) of the pyramid—obtaining clarity on the team's Mission (current charter) and Vision (desired envisioned future)—to those at the bottom of the pyramid. The assumption here is that higher-level elements shape and influence factors at successively lower levels. For example, it makes little sense for team members to look for ways to try to reach alignment among priorities (level 3) until they have first reached consensus in defining their long-term goals and success measures (level 2).

In looking at the pyramid, you can see that the top three levels (1 through 3) focus on *what* members should do as a team, and provide a team with elements that support their long-term efforts. The bottom three levels (4 through 6) deal with *how* the team goes about accomplishing

Figure 14.6. *Team Alignment Pyramid* Levels and Influences.

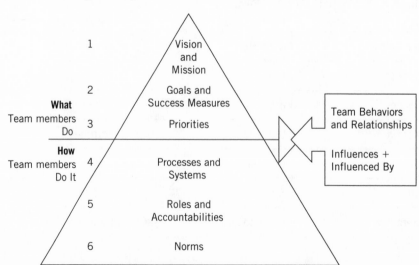

these things, and focuses on those supportive mechanisms that enable members to fulfill what it is that they are attempting to accomplish as a team. A critical factor to discuss is that the team's *behaviors and interrelationships* permeate all levels of the pyramid. This factor directly influences and is, in turn, influenced by the pyramid's levels.

The *Team Alignment Pyramid* provides a vehicle for helping participants determine where they do or do not have alignment on these six critical team performance elements. By the completion of the exercise participants arrive at a better understanding of the degree to which they share a common view of their team, and they are better able to identify those factors that should serve as a starting point for their discussions.

From the facilitator's perspective it is important to note that "gaining alignment" means that the team shares a common understanding of what is expected from each team member and of the team as a whole. Gaining this common understanding does not necessarily mean that team members have complete control in directing every element within the pyramid. As members move toward the top of the pyramid they begin to encounter elements that encompass a broader scope of impact. As a result, it becomes more likely that the team leader or the team's senior executives will need to take the lead in directing key decisions regarding how those elements are defined.

The six elements of the pyramid are as follows:

1. Vision and Mission: The degree to which we share a common vision of how we wish to grow and evolve as a team (achieve a shared sense of our desired future), and collectively define our overall mission and charter.

2. Goals and Success Measures: The extent to which we understand the goals we have set for ourselves as a team for the next twelve months, and the measures we will use to evaluate our success in meeting these goals.

3. Priorities: The relative priority that we assign to each of our large-scale projects and recurring responsibilities.

4. Processes and Systems: The extent to which we agree on how our work processes and systems *currently* operate, and how they should

ideally operate (desired changes in processes and systems) in order to perform in an optimal fashion.

5. Roles and Responsibilities: The extent to which we agree on how we can best organize ourselves to accomplish our goals and objectives, who on our team should take the lead in managing certain projects, and how responsibilities and related authority should be allocated within our team.

6. Norms: The degree to which we understand those "rules of conduct" by which we agree to abide as a team. Examples include how we handle conflicts, the process we use to make team decisions, and how we keep each other informed on critical issues.

There are five steps for implementing this tool. Plan for about ninety minutes to complete this technique with your team.

1. In advance of the workshop construct a model of the pyramid on a flipchart.

2. Introduce the purpose of the pyramid. The easiest way to do this is to provide members with a copy of this tool in advance of the workshop, and ask them to read through the overview and instructions.

3. Provide participants with green, yellow, and red sticky dots (six per person). [Note: The use of the dots is an adaptation of the *Traffic Light Technique*.] Explain the meaning of the colors:

   • Green: Placing a green dot next to an element means that they believe that their entire team is aligned on their understanding of that element.

   • Yellow: A yellow dot means that team members appear to hold different views.

   • Red: Placing a red dot means that the team lacks any a clear, shared understanding of that element. Red dots typically occur when teams haven't had the opportunity to openly discuss an element, or when that particular area of team functioning is quickly changing.

4. Ask participants to go to the flipchart and, *without discussion*, place only one dot of any color next to each element.

5. After all dots have been placed, the facilitator should ask for a volunteer to explain what meaning they extract from the array of dots. Build on this initial response and guide participants into agreement on how far up the pyramid they need to ascend to initiate their team alignment discussion.

Team Building Assessment Questionnaire

This *Team Building Assessment Questionnaire* identifies nine challenges typically faced by teams and twenty seven related opportunities for strengthening team performance. The assessment can be completed in advance of your team-building session, or during the first hour of your session. Have each team member individually rate the importance of each opportunity to their team's performance. Your team-building facilitator can then average all individual scores for each item, as well as generate an averaged score for each of the ten challenges.

This assessment does attempt to generate a total score or "report card" for your team. It does, however, help your team to identify unique strengths and those areas that you and the other members of your team would like to see strengthened. The assessment's rating scale is:

5 = This item represents a critical improvement opportunity for our team

4 = This item represents a significant improvement opportunity for our team

3 = This item represents a important improvement opportunity for our team

2 = This item represents a minor improvement opportunity for our team

1 = This improvement opportunity is not relevant to our team

Team Building Assessment Questionnaire

Team Challenge	Opportunities	Rating
Clarifying Future Direction	1. Getting aligned on our desired future as a team (how we would like to see ourselves perform and work together 12 months from now)	
	2. Obtaining a clearer picture of our long-term goals and priorities	
	3. Agreeing on priorities for action, when faced with competing projects and responsibilities	
	Average Score	

Team Challenge	Opportunities	Rating
Fostering Team Innovation	4. Generating innovative solutions to problems	
	5. Actively seeking out new opportunities for strengthening our performance as a team	
	6. Keeping current with new work methods and industry trends	
	Average Score	
Establishing Mutual Trust and Collaboration	7. Developing a team setting in which we can feel more comfortable to speak openly and honestly with each other	
	8. Finding constructive ways to address differences and prevent potential conflicts	
	9. Looking for ways to provide each other with needed help and support	
	Average Score	
Managing Change	10. Responding to change in a fast and effective manner	
	11. Keeping each other alerted to potential obstacles or opportunities	
	12. Determining the potential impact to our team of large-scale changes	
	Average Score	
Building Commitment	13. Having team members make clear, explicit commitments to accomplish goals and projects	
	14. Developing a better understanding of our respective roles as individual team members	
	15. Encouraging each other to be accountable for meeting team commitments	
	Average Score	
Managing Boundaries	16. Developing positive, mutually-supportive relationships with other work groups	
	17. Finding ways to strengthen our service quality to our internal customers	
	18. Developing clear guidelines for how we represent our team when dealing with other work groups	
	Average Score	

(Continued)

Team Building Assessment Questionnaire (Continued)

Team Challenge	Opportunities	Rating
Working Virtually	19. Setting up clear guidelines regarding how far we can go in taking action when working independently	
	20. Developing methods to keep each other informed of changes, project updates, and new information	
	21. Developing communication channels that support virtual team members	
	Average Score	
Managing Diversity	22. Discovering what unique advantages we can obtain from our diverse team composition	
	23. Showing mutual respect to all team members	
	24. Taking cultural differences into account when planning team communications and decision making	
	Average Score	
Overcoming Setbacks	25. Using performance setbacks as learning opportunities for future planning	
	26. Staying focused on the future rather than dwelling on the past	
	27. When faced with setbacks, avoiding finger-pointing and focusing on what we can do as a team to overcome these performance challenges	
	Average Score	

Team Commitment Audit

The *Team Commitment Audit* allows team members to provide anonymous feedback on their commitment to the solution they have jointly identified. By doing so this tool helps teams better understand those factors that are inhibiting their members from giving full support and commitment to a given project or change initiative. Note that the audit asks team members to rate their commitment in five areas:

- Criticality: How urgent is this problem?

- Solvability: How much of this problem can we solve ourselves?

- Scope: How difficult will it be to solve this problem?

- Accountability: How responsible do I feel personally for solving the problem?

- Solution Feasibility: Will the proposed solution effectively solve our team's problem?

To complete the *Team Commitment Audit*, take the following steps:

1. Ask each member of your team to complete the audit by circling the appropriate rating statement for each of the five areas.

2. Have a team member collect these forms. Then shuffle them, and, beginning with the topmost form, call out the score for each area. For example, under "Solvability," if the team member has circled the statement: "We are able to make minor improvements to this problem," then that area would receive a score of 3.

3. Ask team members to refrain from commenting on anyone's scores until all scores for all dimensions have been posted for review.

4. Using hatch marks, record all the scores on the blank *Team Commitment Audit Scoring Form* shown below. For ease of viewing it is useful to replicate this form on a whiteboard or flipchart and then record all scores as they are presented.

5. You may also wish to calculate your team's averaged scores for each area.

6. These scores can reveal your team's true level of commitment to the proposed solution. In addition, the audit can help you identify those areas that are perceived quite differently by team members. With this information, you are in a much better position to anticipate and address problems of commitment that might otherwise diminish the effectiveness of your problem-solving process.

7. A useful technique is to ask individuals who have given low scores for a given area a version of the following question: "Cindy, I noticed that you scored this project as a '3' under the category of solution feasibility. Tell a little bit about your concerns here and what it would take (the types of changes that would need to be made to the project plan or implementation process) to bring that score up to at least a '7'."

Team Commitment Audit

Scoring Range	1	2	3	4	5
Criticality	This challenge is not urgent. We can easily wait several weeks before acting on it.	This challenge requires a minor degree of attention over the new few weeks.	This challenge requires a moderate degree of attention over the next few weeks.	This challenge is important and requires us to quickly move on it.	This challenge is critical and requires our immediate attention.
Solvability	This challenge is completely beyond our ability to solve.	The only action we can take is to recommend improvements to management.	We are able to make minor improvements to this challenge.	We are able to make substantial improvements to this challenge.	We should be able to largely solve this challenge ourselves.
Scope	This challenge is "low-hanging fruit"—it's easy to solve.	This challenge will require some minor effort by our team over a few weeks.	This challenge will require a moderate degree of effort by our team over a few weeks.	This challenge will require significant amounts of effort by our team over the next few months.	This challenge will require an extensive amount of effort by our team over the next several months.

Scoring Range	1	2	3	4	5
Accountability	I don't view myself as being accountable for solving this challenge.	I view myself as having some minor responsibility for solving this challenge.	I view myself as being somewhat accountable for solving this challenge.	I view myself as being moderately accountable for solving this challenge.	I view myself as being fully accountable, with the other members of my team, for solving this challenge.
Solution Feasibility	The solution selected by our team will not work.	The solution selected by our team will have a minor positive impact on this challenge.	The solution selected by our team will have a moderate positive impact on this challenge.	The solution selected by our team will have a significant positive impact on this challenge.	The solution selected by our team will greatly improve this challenge.

Team Commitment Audit Scoring Form

Scoring Range	1	2	3	4	5
Criticality					
Solvability					
Scope					
Accountability					
Solution Feasibility					

Team Decision Style Chart

Balanced decision making is a crucial factor in effective member-leader relationships. The *Team Decision Style Chart* enables a team to compare its current decision-making process with its ideal decision-making process by asking team members and their leader to select among four alternative styles of team decision-making. The example below shows a *Team Decision Style Chart* that has been completed by a hypothetical work team. We have also included a blank chart for use by your own team and instructions for its use.

Instructions

1. In the *Work Areas* column, describe those work areas that you would like your team to review.

2. When filling out the area labeled *Decision-Making Options*, indicate how decisions are *currently* made with a "C," and indicate the option that is *desired* by your team with a "D." The four decision-making options are:

   - Leader Only: The team leader makes decisions without input from the team

   - Leader with Input: The team leader makes decisions after obtaining input from the team

   - Team Consensus: The team arrives at decisions through review and consensus

   - Individual Members: Decisions are made by individual team members

3. In our example, one of the work areas selected for review is "Preparing our annual budget." Team members feel that this decision is currently made by the team leader without input from members, but they would prefer to be included in the process before the budget is finalized.

4. You should also be aware that team members may not agree on how much influence they should have in certain key areas. This is natural and can be valuable in itself. One of the most important results of engaging in this activity is that team members may be able to reach

greater alignment on what constitutes an effective balance in the member-leader control continuum for specific decision-making areas.

5. Once your team has completed the *Team Decision Style Chart*, it may be useful to go back and summarize the need for change in each of the identified work areas, to remind yourselves of the rationale for making these changes. For example, given our hypothetical team's identified needs, the team might have made the following comments regarding their decision to shift the way that decisions will now be made on the annual budget:

> We have agreed that all of the members of our team will be able to provide input to our annual budget, as a means of helping our team leader anticipate situations in which additional resource requirements may be required, or resource support may be effectively reallocated, to support key project areas.

Team Decisions Style Chart

Work Areas	Decision-Making Options				Importance
	Leader Only	Leader with Input	Team Consensus	Individual Members	
Preparing our annual budget	C ▪▪▪▪▶	D			High
Selecting new team members	C ▪▪▪▪▪▪▪▪▪▶		D		Moderate
Making a commitment to customers on delivery dates			D ◀▪▪▪▪ C		High

Team Decisions Style Chart

Work Areas	Decision-Making Options				Importance
	Leader Only	Leader with Input	Team Consensus	Individual Members	

Team Leader Feedback Questionnaire

The *Team Leader Feedback Questionnaire* is designed to help team leaders understand how they are viewed by the rest of their team. This tool differs from the *Turnaround Feedback* tool, which outlines a method that can be used by team members to provide each other with honest feedback. In applying the *Team Leader Feedback Questionnaire* team members are asked to identify three performance areas in which they would like to receive additional help or support from their team leader, or changes to the leader's communication style.

In suggesting this tool to a team and their leader we recommend that you adhere to the following guidelines:

1. Give everyone a clear explanation of what they can gain from this questionnaire. It is most useful in the following conditions: (a) when new leaders are seeking initial feedback on how they are viewed by their teams, (b) when teams have recently undergone certain changes, such as staff reductions or tougher performance standards, that are requiring their leaders to evaluate the effectiveness of their current leadership styles, or (c) when leaders want to discover how they can leverage their performance by making changes to a few, key leadership behaviors.

2. This feedback mechanism will not be effective if the team leader is resistant to it, or views it as a "report card" on his or her performance. Explain that this tool is intended to help team leaders pinpoint opportunities for strengthening the team's overall performance by changing a few critical leadership behaviors.

3. Encourage team members to provide honest, candid feedback— what we refer to as a "warts-and-all" description of the leader's communication and management style. You can support candid feedback by suggesting that they anonymously submit their feedback to you, the team facilitator, for consolidation into a single report. Generate a consolidated report by simply tallying scores regarding the numbers of times that each of the twenty items is listed as being either a key strength (S) or a development area (D).

4. If you are both the team facilitator and team leader, ask another member of your team to collect and consolidate this information, or ask your organization's training or leadership development manager for help in consolidating these data.

5. It is often helpful for team leaders to complete the questionnaire as a self-assessment, as if they were viewing themselves through the eyes of their team. This self-report can then be compared to the team's averaged scores to identify blind spots (performance areas in which a leader's self-ratings differ significantly from those of the team). All answers to the two open-ended questions (21 and 22) should be consolidated on two separate sheets for review. Label one sheet as "Key Strengths" (question 21) and the other as "Important Development Needs" (question 22).

6. Some team members may claim their feedback isn't valid because they work with their leader on a limited basis, they are somewhat new to the team, or they are the most junior-level members of the team. Let them know that all feedback is valid—it is just as important for leaders to see how they come across to new members of their teams (first impressions are often very important) as it is to see how they are viewed by experienced team members.

7. Once you have obtained the team's averaged feedback, discuss this feedback one-on-one with the team leader before the start of the team session. This will alert you to potential blind spots or feedback that is confusing to the team leader and will require additional clarification by the team.

8. After presenting this feedback to the team leader, suggest that the team leader avoid walking into the team-building session armed with ready-made solutions for identified improvement areas. The purpose of this tool is to encourage an open dialogue between leaders and other team members. The most effective way to achieve this dialogue is for the leader to ask other members for their suggestions regarding leadership actions that could strengthen leader-member relationships and communication.

9. At the end of the session it is important for team leaders to thank the other participants for their input and their willingness to provide honest feedback.

10. For many team members, the true test of a leader's intentions will be whether the leader makes a sincere effort to follow up on any proposed improvement suggestions. For this reason, it is important to translate all suggestions into action plans, and to later follow up with team members to see if these actions have made a positive difference.

Listed in the following table are twenty leadership behaviors that are related to ten key dimensions of leadership style. Place an "S" next to those three behaviors that represent the strongest aspects of your leader's communication and management style, and a "D" next to those three areas that represent your leader's most important development needs. Questions 21 and 22 invite you to provide comments regarding your leader's overall communication and leadership style.

Team Dimension	Feedback Questions: To what extent does your team leader do the following?	S/D
Information Sharing	1. Pass on to your team important information provided by customers, senior managers, and other work groups?	
	2. Pass on to others the concerns, issues, and questions raised by team members?	
Direction	3. Provide clear direction on projects?	
	4. Provide clear feedback on work priorities?	
Team Building	5. Encourage open communication within the team?	
	6. Help the team build effective relationship within itself and with other work groups?	
Planning	7. Develop thorough project plans?	
	8. Seek out your input in the planning process?	
Empowerment	9. Give you a free hand in determining how you perform your work?	
	10. Solicit your input and feedback on key decisions?	

Conflict Resolution	11. Help resolve conflicts between team members?	
	12. Effectively manage conflicts between your team and other work groups?	
Resource Utilization	13. Make effective use of available resources?	
	14. Help overcome resource constraints?	
Feedback and Coaching	15. Provide clear and timely feedback on your performance?	
	16. Provide needed developmental coaching?	
Professional Development	17. Provide opportunities (training, seminars) for helping you build your skills?	
	18. Provide stretch assignments that test and develop your skills?	
Personal Growth	19. Remain open to feedback from the team on his/her performance?	
	20. Model professional development by continually attempting to strengthen his/her skills?	

21. What is the single most effective aspect of your leader's leadership style? What would you *not* want this person to change?

22. What one change could your leader make to his/her behavior that would help you perform even more effectively as a team?

Team Scoping Document
The Advantages of Creating a Scoping Document

A *Team Scoping Document* is a two- to four-page summary that defines those activities and responsibilities that a team considers to be either within, or out of, scope of responsibility for their team's mission and charter. This tool is particularly useful when the team in question is a cross-functional project team that has been brought together for a limited period of time to accomplish a set of objectives before disbanding. Examples would be process improvement teams, employee engagement teams, and product development teams. It is also a very useful tool for helping the members of virtual teams stay on task as they attempt to coordinate work efforts across time and space.

Scoping documents offer teams several benefits. These include ensuring that all team members are aligned on their purpose, goals, and intended outcomes, providing each team member with a deeper understanding of the organizational or business context leading to the formation of the team, and ensuring that the team is aligned on goals, outcomes, and success measures with its senior executive sponsors. As an example, a few years ago one of the authors (Robert) was a member of a customer service process improvement team. The team included functional representatives from across our company. As part of our team's launch we prepared a scoping document to make certain that we were aligned with our senior managers regarding the types of work processes that they felt should be included in this analysis of "customer service." For example:

- Would our team simply be expected to evaluate process deficiencies in current systems, or would we also be expected to import best practices methods from other organizations?

- Was our team expected to prepare recommendations relating to cutting-edge technology that might require massive system changes?

- Since customer interface points extended throughout the organization, which processes should be included in the findings (distribution, call center operations, and so forth)?

- Could we agree on how we define the end-points (inputs and outputs) for each of these processes?
- Would the team be responsible for simply generating a set of recommendations, or working through to final implementation and the review of return on investment?

How to Prepare a Team Scoping Document

1. Because project teams are often formed by senior executive sponsors, it is often helpful for the team leader to work with representative members of the team to prepare a preliminary scoping document in advance of the session, based upon the direction that they have been given by their senior sponsors. This document should include the following elements:

   a. Context: Factors or organizational challenges that have justified the need for the formation of this team

   b. Outcomes: The final deliverables that the team should generate, such as written data analysis, return on investment (ROI) analysis, performing an assessment of the root causes of underlying problems related to a business process, comparative reviews of potential suppliers, recommended actions for addressing an issue

   c. Success Measures: How the team's success will be defined and evaluated by senior stakeholders

   d. Project Scope: Those areas the team is authorized to review, analyze, or develop recommendations as part of the project

   e. Team Membership and Time Obligations: A list of those individuals who have been designated to be part of the core team, and the amount of time over the course of the project that these individuals should be prepared to dedicate to the project

   f. Completion Deadline: The date on which the project is expected to be completed. In addition, some scoping documents go further to cover the following components (in some organizations these elements are included in a separate project plan)

g. Costs and Resources: Any costs (such as travel to team meetings or to best practice site locations, or the purchase of required project software or groupware) that will need to be covered out of a central budget allocated to the team

h. Review Process: Who will be involved in the final review process and what form this review will take (submission of a written document to the senior team, review of the final recommendations by the team leader, or a team review to a group of senior sponsors) Whether the team will be expected to complete formal "gate" reviews with project sponsors to evaluate the completion of key milestones. Which senior executive has been designated as the team's senior sponsor?

2. We recommend that well in advance of the team-building session the team leader send the scoping document to the senior sponsor for review, and then follow up in a few days with a one-on-one meeting to confirm all points in the document. During this discussion it is not uncommon for team leaders to negotiate the fine points of the document with the senior sponsor. An example would be making sure that the team members have a reasonable amount of time to allocate to the project, given the final deadline and expected goals and outcomes.

3. With Step 2 complete, the team leader should e-mail all team members a copy of the scoping document in advance of the team-building session, asking them to identify concerns, opportunities, and suggestions they might have for making their project a success.

4. It is often a good idea to have the senior sponsor kick off the teambuilding session by reaffirming the importance of the project and why team members were selected for it. This is also the team's opportunity to ask questions so that they have an in-depth understanding of their project.

5. Once the senior sponsor departs the team should proceed to engage in a further discussion of the scoping document, with the goal of making certain that all participants leave the session with a clear understanding of their respective roles and accountabilities.

Team Sponsor Evaluation Form

We recommend that the members of your team complete this form before representatives from your team meet with your potential sponsor, in order to help you think through the types of support that you are seeking from your sponsor. The form summarizes five key roles typically filled by project sponsors: coach, troubleshooter, seer, political adviser, and guard. Use the right column to record the names of team sponsors who could assume each of these roles.

Team Sponsor Evaluation Form

Sponsorship Role	Description	Appropriate Sponsors
Coach	Provides suggestions and coaching on how to move more effectively through a given phase of your project	
Troubleshooter	Reviews your project plan to uncover weaknesses and to provide recommendations for improvement	
Seer	Helps you scan the horizon to identify emerging changes that could affect the outcome of your project	
Political adviser	Provides advice regarding others in your company who are likely to support or block your efforts	
Guard	Runs interference to remove obstacles to project success, such as resource constraints or lack of organizational support	

Team Sponsor Identification Form

This *Team Sponsor Identification Form* can be used to select appropriate team sponsors. As you glance over the list of desirable characteristics for an executive sponsor, you will develop a better understanding of the challenges involved in locating such an adviser and guide. Your search mission is critical because good sponsors are in high demand. While you are searching for sponsorship, your peers are also trying to locate reliable supporters for their own projects. As you will soon discover, the reputations of the best team sponsors precede them, meaning that the person that you are seeking may already be committed to other projects and objectives.

To complete this form, take the following steps:

1. Identify a major project or business initiative for your team.

2. Ask your team to suggest executives who would be good candidates for sponsors of this project or initiative, and list the names of these candidates at the top of the form.

3. Review with your team the list of selection criteria shown on the chart.

4. Using a 1 to 5 scale (5 is highest), evaluate each managerial candidate in terms of the selection criteria.

5. Your team should use this process to select not only the ideal sponsor, but also several back-up sponsors, in the case that your first choice is not available.

6. This evaluation can also be used to identify problems you might need to address in working with your selected sponsor.

Team Sponsor Identification Form

Selection Criteria	Managers Who Might Make Good Sponsors			
Knowledgeable about designated area or objective under review				
Aggressive change advocate				
Strongly committed to the success of your project				
Flexible; open to alternative ideas and opinions				
Willing and able to invest time in coaching and advising your team				
Tenacious; willing to push an agenda and maintain commitment over time				
Trustworthy; can keep a confidence				
Possesses sound business judgment				
In touch with the "heartbeat" of your company				
Good communication skills				
Has a solid, positive relationship with the members of your team				

Team Support Chart

The *Team Support Chart* is a means of specifying and recording team actions for improving mutual support within your team. The completed example shown describes possible action items for a team that is planning to improve its members' proficiency with a software training program. The support action plan provides information on six factors:

1. What actions will be carried out

2. Which team members will receive this support or assistance

3. Which team members will be responsible for ensuring that this assistance is provided

4. When the process will begin

5. When the process will be completed

6. The date for a follow-up discussion with the team

Team Support Chart—Plan for Learning New Software

Support to Be Provided	Team Member(s) Receiving Support	Team Member(s) Providing Support	Start Date of Process	Completion Date of Process	Date for Follow-Up Discussion
Attend training program offered by community college	Bob B. Carlos G. Sally T.	Rex T.	9/15	10/27	11/19
Attend after-hours coaching sessions on system	Bob B. Linda H.	Julie S.	11/4	11/18	11/19

Team Vision Summary

A *Team Vision Summary* is a detailed, one-page statement of how the team hopes to evolve and develop over time. A summary is written from a careful analysis of changing patterns in the team's industry, customer base, competitors, and value-added products and services. Of special note here is the word "competitor." If your work team directly supports other departments within your company, you may feel you have no competitors. In actuality, a competitor is any group or team within or outside your organization (an existing group or one that might form after a reorganization) that could assume your team's normal functions. Your internal customers may even become your competitors by deciding they could provide your team's services in-house. A vision summary also addresses the team's view of its evolving role within the organization. In this section, we will introduce a structured process for crafting a *team vision summary* that addresses both of these components.

Constructing a Team Vision Summary

There are five steps involved in constructing your vision summary. This section begins with the list of steps, and then walks you through the details of each with supporting examples.

1. Assess probable changes in customer base and market, competitors, and/or your field and industry (three worksheets)

2. Anticipated changes in your team's organizational role

3. Summarize into team vision

4. Identify key team performance gaps

5. Test feasibility and robustness of vision

Step-by Step Process

1. Describe anticipated changes in your customer base and market, competitors, and industry. These are not the changes that you *hope* will occur, but rather those you feel will most *probably* occur, given present trends. The first table provided, Assessing Changes in Customer Base and Market, can be used to help your team members

think through potential changes to these two areas. Two additional worksheets have been provided, Assessing Changes in Competitors and Assessing Changes in Your Field and Industry. We recommend that before conducting your team-building session you ask the members of your team to individually complete these three worksheets; and, before the upcoming session combine their views into a consolidated summary of anticipated future events. Typically this approach helps to push the thinking of participants and encourages them to engage in an in-depth review of these vision components.

Assessing Probable Changes in Customer Base and Market

Questions You Need to Answer	Your Team's Responses
What additional customers might your team be serving over the next 3–5 years? Which of these customer segments are likely to assume far greater importance for your team? Which of your current customer groups are likely to become less important or will cease to be served by your team? What changes do you anticipate in your customer's requirements? How will their expectations of your team change over time? What products and services do your customers want that your team isn't currently providing and will need to provide in the future?	

Assessing Probable Changes in Competitors

Questions You Need to Answer	Your Team's Responses
Currently, who are your team's primary internal and external competitors? What new competitors are likely to emerge over the next 3–5 years? What product or services gaps could these competitors fill (customer needs not currently being addressed by your team)? What distinct cost, service delivery, or relationship advantages could these competitors provide that might place your team at a serious competitive disadvantage? What activities could your team undertake over the next few years to meet the potential challenges posed by your competitors (strengthen lines of communication with customers, improve service delivery, and so on)?	

Assessing Probable Changes in Your Field and Industry

Questions You Need to Answer	Your Team's Responses
What new technological developments will dramatically alter the shape of your field over the next 3–5 years? What new technical and functional competencies are being sought by managers in your field? What competencies are likely to be in short supply over the next 3–5 years? What existing technical and functional competencies are becoming far less important? How is the role of your work function changing in other organizations? (Example: HR teams are gradually taking on the role HR business partners, in functioning as internal consultants to other departments) What major changes are occurring within your industry that could dramatically affect the demands on your team over the next few years?	

■ ■ ■

2. Describe anticipated changes in your team's future organizational role. Once again, at this point, you're being asked to describe how organizational and business pressures are likely to shape the structure of your team. A worksheet is provided below for gathering structured input from your team on this topic. The worksheet also asks for a description of your team's *desired* organizational role, or the role your team would like to play in the future, as well as any changes you foresee in the types of products and services that you currently provide to your internal and external customers.

Anticipated Changes in Your Team's Organizational Role

Questions You Need to Answer	Your Team's Responses
What likely changes in your company's business arena over the next 3–5 years could affect its expectations of your work teams? What changes are likely to occur in your company's organizational structure over the next 3–5 years? How will these changes affect your work team?	

(Continued)

Anticipated Changes in Your Team's Organizational Role (Continued)

Questions You Need to Answer	Your Team's Responses
How are your company's expectations for your team likely to change over the next few years? (Example: Do you foresee a severe tightening in quality performance standards? Are you likely to encounter severe cost pressures?) Over the next few years, how is your team's organizational role likely to change? Ideally, how would you like to see your team's organizational role evolve over the next 3–5 years? What new functions or responsibilities do you want to manage? What changes do you want to see in your team's service delivery over time?	

■ ■ ■

3. Summarize all the information gathered in the first two steps into a one-page vision summary that describes your team's desired future direction. The following example shows a vision summary crafted for a hypothetical training team.

Vision Summary for Training Team

Our overall vision is to help raise the performance capability of our organization and to become the benchmark for state-of-the art performance delivery systems among our competitors.

Our team intends to expand our service delivery function over the next 3–5 years to cover not only our internal customer base but our external customers as well. At the same time, we will evolve from a cost center to a discrete profit-and-loss center, with the goal of generating a net profit on all training activities undertaken by our team. With these changes, our team will develop from a domestic training team into a truly international one. Currently, we provide only limited and sporadic service to our international employees and customers. Our goal over the next five years is to shift at least 30% of our base training activities toward this international market in order to support our company's goal of becoming the premier international provider of corporate financial and investment services.

We realize that to accomplish these aims we must invest heavily in online learning management systems. We are just beginning to pilot in this area but have set the goal of having at least 25% of all training programs available through online delivery over the next five years. With regard to our executive development efforts, our intention is to build a seamless executive assessment and development system that will provide our executives and managers with a clear understanding of their respective leadership strengths and weaknesses, and will direct them through a program of development activities tied directly to identified performance improvement areas. To achieve this aim, we intend to introduce our managers and executives to the concept of 360-degree profiling. Within 12 months, we will create our first corporation-wide roll-up of executive competencies and development gaps and will match this data against the organizational requirements spelled out in our corporate strategic plan. We also intend to assume the role of development coach by extending executive activities beyond the classroom to include structured development assignments, third-party coaching by one of our staff, the creation of a formalized mentoring program, and a fast-track program for identified high-potential talent.

■ ■ ■

4. Identify key team performance gaps (for example, team competencies, knowledge, team structure) and any organizational obstacles (for example, current reputation of your team, lacking the support of key senior managers) that must be surmounted before your team can fulfill its desired vision. The following example is a continuation based on the hypothetical training team.

Performance Gap Summary for Training Team

Identified Performance Gaps	Current Situation	Desired Future Situations
What technical or functional skill gaps must be closed before your team can pursue its vision?	We're relying on an outside consultant to guide us in the design and delivery of our Web-based training pilots.	We will hire a manager of online development and two technical support people to direct this function. We will also invest approximately $100K in technical start-up costs.
What knowledge gaps will your team need to close to pursue its visions?	We don't have the expertise to decide when online training provides advantages over classroom training and have only limited, anecdotal information on our customers' requirements. We don't understand cultural factors that could affect training delivery in our new Pacific Rim ventures.	We will conduct best practice reviews and use our new manager's expertise with online development to make these decisions. We will incorporate questions on training requirements into our annual customer service audit and will develop cultural familiarity through partnerships with our international marketing team.

(Continued)

Performance Gap Summary for Training Team (Continued)

In what ways must your team's structure and composition change?	All training design and delivery activities are currently performed by a single team of trainers. Only one person is allocated to the area of executive assessment and design.	We may need to break out a special design team devoted entirely to online development, or consider the viability of purchasing off-the-shelf content from a major vendor. We believe that executive assessment and development will require two additional team members within the next two years.
What organizational obstacles will you need to overcome? What steps could you take to overcome them?	Our senior executive is uncertain about the potential applications of online training. In addition, our senior vice president of customer support is concerned about our ability to support training delivery to our external customers.	We will perform a best practice review in the area of online training within our industry. We will also suggest to our customer service executive that external customer training be comanaged by a member of his staff.

5. Test the feasibility and robustness of your *Team Vision Summary* by inviting reactions to it from a few leaders who are familiar with your team's operation, and whose judgment you respect. With the help of these objective observers answer the following questions:

- Does your team's summary represent the unique strengths of your team, and the unique challenges facing it? If the summary is so vague and generalized that it could pertain to any team, it needs to be rewritten.

- Have you taken into account all of the broader organizational and industry-related changes that are likely to occur over the next few years? (Here is where your outside observers can be of great help.)

- Has your team accurately assessed the probable effect of these changes on your work team?

- Is your vision summary exciting? Does it capture the commitment of your work team?

- Is your vision summary wrapped in fancy jargon and obscure language, or is it something that can be understood easily by team members and internal customers?

- Does your vision summary enhance your team's understanding of the types of choices or trade-offs involved in meeting the needs of various customers?

- Does your vision summary paint a clear and vivid picture of your team's desired future?

Telecommuting Check Sheet

The *Telecommuting Check Sheet* is used to determine whether telecommuting is suitable for yourself or other members of your team. The following twelve questions are designed as a check sheet for discussion. The check sheet can help you determine the feasibility of this work method, and the actions required to make an effective transition to telecommuting.

Telecommuting Check Sheet

Questions for Consideration / Discussion	Checked
1. What aspects of my work can I accomplish through telecommuting? Which aspects of my work require face-to-face interaction and need to be performed onsite?	
2. Under our telecommuting agreement, will I maintain my job title, employee status, pay grade, insurance benefits, and other compensation, or will I be classified as a contract worker?	
3. Which of the following costs will my company cover, and which of these costs will I be expected to cover myself? a. Lease or purchase my home office equipment and materials (tablet, laptop, desktop, fax/modem, answering machine, printer, scanner, copy machine, paper supplies, and so on) b. Additional space required for home office operation and file storage c. Installation of dedicated phone line(s) for data and business calls d. Monthly charges for phone/data services e. Insurance for theft or damage protection for office equipment f. Utility costs for operating all office equipment at home	
4. What guidelines can I establish with my manager and organization regarding communications (for example, should I expect that other members of our team might feel free to contact me late in the evening or on weekends)?	
5. For what types of emergencies should we plan? (Example: Can we establish a shared folder that will enable my team leader and coworkers to directly access needed computer files if I am unavailable?)	
6. How often will I be expected to visit the office?	
7. What is the best way to stay informed on organizational meetings and events that I might miss, and to determine those I need to attend?	
8. Will there be an empty office or cubicle available for me during my visits into the office?	
9. Will telecommuting keep me from attending in-house training programs?	
10. How often, and by what means, will my team leader provide me with performance feedback?	
11. At what point can we perform a joint review of this arrangement to see if it meets both my needs and the needs of our team?	
12. If I feel that the arrangement is not working, do I have the option of returning to the office?	

ThoughtOffice™

The biggest difficulty that most people face in generating and evaluating creative solutions to work challenges is not in just coming up with good answers, it is in determining the *best questions* to pose to *fully* explore the challenge under review. Good questions help you test the implicit assumptions that underlie your thinking and can push you to explore totally new avenues for meeting challenges. A team brainstorming session's advantage is the inclusion of other people who can help you explore a wide variety of options and test the viability of your own ideas. However, how can you replicate this kind of troubleshooter and devil's advocate role when you are trying to generate creative ideas by yourself?

One option lies in making use of electronic brainstorming software packages, such as ThoughtOffice™, which are designed to help push your thinking when you are faced with unique problems or opportunities. ThoughtOffice is a commercially available software program that is derived from an earlier program, IdeaFisher™, which has been tested for many years. This software is available both for Mac and PC systems and works by providing prompts that force you to more clearly define your problem or challenge. The software then provides thousands of questions (13,000+) that can help you explore different aspects of that problem. These questions have been developed by hundreds of contributing thought-leaders in the field of business and other areas, so the questions represent a wide range of perspectives. In addition, the questions are compartmentalized within sixteen problem categories to support a faster drill-down in problem analysis.

The software also provides connections to thousands of references, such as quotations, synonyms, images, and word associations, which are intended to push creative idea generation, as well as a presentation template for structuring captured ideas. Finally, ThoughtOffice provides a vehicle for helping you organize "idea fragments" into consolidated ideas. The software is web enabled, which means that the questions and sources it contains are updated weekly. It also contains alternative options, such as outlines or storyboards, for helping you explore alternatives for sharing and communicating your ideas to others.

For more information on this product, go to http://www.thoughtrod.com/.

Threats Analysis

When a team is troubleshooting any major team activity, such as the completion of a key project, it is easy to feel overwhelmed by the sheer complexity of the many challenges that they could encounter. One means of helping team members maintain their focus on the most important aspects of a change event is to guide them through a systematic review of potential threats and opportunities. The *Threats Analysis* tool can help you perform this assessment.

A completed model of a *Threats Analysis* is provided based on a hypothetical cross-functional team charged with planning the reorganization of their company's operations department. Note that the team has chosen to perform this analysis for each step of the reorganization project.

First, the team outlined the steps for their organization plan. For simplicity, the model shows only three of their project steps: 1, 5, and 8. Second, within the first column under each step, they identified "Potential Threats" that could interfere with the successful completion of that step. Third, in the next two columns, the team evaluated (as high, medium, or low) each potential threat in relation to the "Probability of Occurrence" (the relative likelihood that a given problem might actually occur) and the "Impact of Occurrence." A high rating indicated that a potential threat was viewed as extremely risky to the success of the project. Next, in the "Trigger" column, the team then identified events that will serve as early warning signs for these problems.

Based on this model, the single most important potential threat for the team is that of "identifying changing functional and business requirements," which has been rated "high" on the dimensions of probability and impact. The team has now determined that it will encounter its most important threat to the success of the project during the completion of their first project step. As the final analysis step in the last two columns, the team identified those "Preventive Actions" they will take to minimize the probability that a noted threat will occur and those "Corrective Actions" they will take to manage these threats, should they occur.

Threats Analysis for Departmental Reorganization

Potential Threats	Probability of Occurrence	Impact of Occurrence	Trigger	Corrective Actions	Preventive Actions
Step 1: Identify changing functional and business requirements					
Invalid requirements caused by inaccurate business forecast	M	H	Requirements don't match fourth-quarter business forecast	Recalibrate and adjust structure at midyear	Obtain rough forecast from strategic planning department
Step 5: Assess current bench strength against new requirements					
Incomplete assessment due to lack of data	H	M	Lack of execu-tive alignment on compe-tencies of incumbents	Mid-year recalibration of structure	Update all performance apprais-als and use assessment center to indepen-dently assess skills
Step 8: Notify redundant staff of transfer or termination options and establish time frames for personnel decisions					
Staff could contest decisions	L	M	Anger, resent-ment, and confusion at time of notification	Meet with selected staff to review options (timetable for actions) that might increase acceptance	Consult legal department on severance and transfer agreements, test approach on employee focus group

The Traffic Light Technique

Occasionally a team or group is faced with the task of sorting through a potentially overwhelming array of opportunities, concerns, or options, making it difficult for them to reach decisions and agree upon a clear course of action. This situation is most likely to arise when decision making takes place under any of the following conditions:

- The team includes a large number of participants.

- The topic under review is very complex and requires participants to process a large amount of information.

- Team members hold very different views regarding the relative importance of competing concerns, opportunities, or options that are under discussion.

Given any of these situations, one of the first things that a team needs to do before reaching a decision is to first develop a clear picture of how everyone views the current situation. For the facilitator, the challenge here is to provide a vehicle for helping the team achieve this awareness, while working with large numbers of people who are attempting to mentally process a variety of competing options. The *Traffic Light Technique* offers one option for addressing this challenge, by helping teams construct a simple graphic that reveals their collective perspectives.

Applying the Technique

We recommend that you follow these steps when implementing this technique:

1. Prior to the workshop, purchase packages of green, yellow, and red sticky dots from a local office supply store. Because sticky dots come in a variety of sizes we recommend that you purchase dots that are about an inch in diameter. Larger dots take up too much space on your flipcharts, and smaller dots will be difficult for participants to see from the back of the room. You should purchase enough dots so that each participant receives five dots of each color.

2. Prior to the start of the workshop create a flipchart that summarizes that information that you wish to review. The manner in which you do this will be influenced by the team's topic of discussion. Here are some examples from the authors' experiences:

a. *Process Improvement Team:* To help them identify inefficiencies in a complex work process, a cross-functional work team created a process flow map describing the sequential and interrelated steps of the process under review, in advance of the session. The *Traffic Light Technique* was then used to help the team flag the most critical (red) process points for further discussion.

b. *Training Teams:* Four companies within a large corporation were attempting to determine the degree to which their company's call center representatives were adequately skilled on over forty different competencies. In this case the flipchart modeled below was divided into two columns, with required competencies listed in the larger left-hand column and the right-hand column left blank. *Traffic Light Technique* was then used to rate the relative importance of each competency.

Required Competencies	Rating
Can access the medical database to pull up customer information	
Responds in a calm manner when dealing with irate customers	

c. *Directing Boards:* A large (3,000+ members) nonprofit professional association was administered by two different directing boards, each of which was responsible for providing oversight to a different agency within the association. Both boards reported up to the same board of trustees. Prior to the start of the session an organizational chart showing the entire breakdown of current accountabilities (labeled by position, not incumbent) was posted on the whiteboard. During a team-building session, representatives from the trustees, directing boards, and operating staff used the *Traffic Light Technique* to determine how each participant viewed the degree to which staff and volunteer responsibilities were appropriately allocated among personnel.

3. Explain to participants that the challenge they face is determining how to jointly review a large amount of data. To address this challenge, you will introduce participants to a technique that provides them with a graphic of how they collectively view all of the concerns, opportunities, or options under discussion. Also explain that the *Traffic Light Technique* is not a voting process, in that no decisions are finalized as a result of this exercise. It merely provides a starting point for identifying those areas where participants are in strong agreement.

4. Explain to participants what each color dot represents. Here are some examples of how the three different colors can be applied:

   a. For the process improvement team, green dots represented process steps that they felt were operating effectively, yellow dots represented process steps that were felt to exhibit minor difficulties (bottlenecks errors, redundancies, process inconsistencies, and so forth), and red dots represented process steps that were considered to exhibit severe difficulties.

   b. For the training team, green dots represented competencies on which call center representatives (as a whole) were believed to be highly skilled, yellow dots represented competencies on which representatives were believed to be moderately skilled, and red dots represented competencies in which huge skill deficiencies were frequently noted among representatives.

   c. For the directing boards, green dots represented those accountabilities that were currently being effectively managed, and also being managed by the most appropriate group (the six categories being the board of trustees, the two directing boards, full-time staff, volunteers, and outside consultants). Yellow dots represented responsibilities that were being effectively managed, but not by the appropriate group. Red dots represented responsibilities that were not being effectively managed.

5. Provide participants with guidelines for placing their dots:

   a. Each participant places his or her own dots.

   b. Only one dot can be placed on each item (a participant cannot, for example, opt to place all five green dots on a single item).

   c. Participants should place their dots silently, without discussion. The intent here is to give everyone an equal voice, without participants feeling that others are attempting to influence others' choices.

   d. When working with a large team, consider giving participants a fifteen-minute break, during which they can place their dots while they are getting refreshments. Note: It's not uncommon to find a large number of participants clustered around the flipchart at any one time.

6. After all dots have been placed on the flipchart you will usually see a few strong patterns begin to emerge. Rather than attempt to interpret these patterns, it is far more effective to ask participants to share their views regarding what they see. Those items covered by green dots tend to be viewed as being relatively effective, with red dots representing problematic areas. A patchwork of colors reveals items on which participants hold diverse views.

7. Ask participants whether they would like to use the patterns that they see emerging in the data to select a few critical areas for discussion, or to identify areas in which they are largely in agreement and which therefore require little discussion. In the example of the training team noted earlier, the group quickly identified competencies that were covered in red dots, which required immediate attention. They also agreed that those competencies that were largely covered in green dots required little attention. The teams also recognized multicolored items as those that required additional discussion, as team members held widely different views regarding the skill levels displayed by customer service representatives on those competencies.

Additional Thoughts

The *Traffic Light Technique* provides a simple method that team members can use to review a large amount of data. By observing the color patterns that emerge participants can determine where to proceed (green dots), where to slow down for discussion (patchwork of colors), and where to focus attention on addressing significant concerns (red dots). This approach also allows individual team members to recognize situations in which their own choices represent outlier views that are not aligned with the majority of team members. In such cases, the purpose of the team is not to inhibit discussion, but rather to help team members understand the degree to which their individual perspectives are aligned with the overall views of their teams.

Turnaround Feedback
Identifying Behaviors That Block and Support Team Process
Contributed by Kenneth Cloke and Joan Goldsmith

> *Man will become better only when you make him see what he is like.*
> —Anton Chekhov

Feedback is pivotal to learning, development, and growth. Without feedback, teams become stuck and soon begin to stagnate. The question is therefore not *whether* to give and receive feedback, but *how* to do so. We are not born with this knowledge or skill, and need to learn how to separate what is useful in feedback from what is not, how to reveal kernels of truth that lay hidden beneath layers of self-interest, and how to receive painful feedback without becoming angry, hurt, and defensive.

In delivering feedback, we can play it safe and adopt an "I'll scratch your back if you scratch mine" approach, or we can take a risk and adopt an "I'll be deeply honest with you if you'll be equally honest with me" attitude. By playing it safe and reducing the level of honesty, we temporarily avoid having to change anything important. However, for feedback to wake people up and motivate them to change, honesty in the *content* of what is communicated and empathy in the *process* of delivering it, are extremely important.

Inauthentic feedback can be distinguished from turnaround feedback by the degree of risk attached to it, and the combination of honesty and empathy, precision and kindness, openness and gentleness with which it is delivered. Turnaround feedback ultimately stems from a desire to help others improve—not just because they are behaving badly toward others, but because of the discomfort and unhappiness they are creating for *themselves.*

Turnaround feedback is therefore a manifestation of "tough love," because it does not shrink from pointing out what is not working. It separates the person from their behavior, extending loving acceptance to the first and unyielding honesty to the second. It encourages integrity and ethical, value-based behavior. It is most effective when the person delivering it is deeply nonjudgmental, yet honest and clear, and when it is:

- Opened with a self-assessment by the person giving it

- Offered after getting permission from the person receiving it

- Assumed that constructive intent is present in the person delivering it

- Delivered with "I" statements so it is clear that the speaker owns the perceptions being offered

- Focused on communication and acts rather than on personalities or personal characteristics

- Presented as from a peer, even if it emanates from a different level in the organizational hierarchy

- Offered constructively, with practical suggestions and concrete ideas for improvement

- Specific and detailed, so the person receiving it is clear about the problem and can identify the solution

- Balanced and fair, so the person receiving it sees the whole picture, understands that their positive qualities are appreciated, and is able to place the criticism in a context of learning and improvement

- Communicated in real time without waiting until the event is long over

- Delivered without anger or judgment, so that the personal feelings of the deliverer are acknowledged or removed from the communication

- Oriented toward learning, growth, and change

- Clear about the consequences and results of not changing the behavior

- Accepted with sincere gratitude by the person who received it, so that at the end of the process it can be successfully implemented without injured feelings, anger, or resistance

Ten Reasons for Communicating Honestly

In spite of these risks, the greatest danger in delivering feedback does not arise from inaccuracy or subjectivity, but from a reluctance to be honest about what is true. Some people have no difficulty delivering honest feedback, whereas others are more committed to politeness than to honesty. Some people are timid, quiet, or insecure, or have to be encouraged to say what they think, or have learned that it's safer to keep their mouths shut. Some say: "Yes, things are great," when they are actually suffering or have severe problems that could be cured through feedback and critical insight. Some are simply afraid of communicating honestly. Honest feedback is risky, because it possibly means we will be disliked, and most of us want to be liked more than we want to be honest. Many also lack the skills, empathy, and relational intimacy needed to deliver critical information without triggering defensiveness and resistance in others.

Here are ten reasons people commonly cite for *not* delivering honest feedback:

1. We don't want to hurt their feelings.

2. They will misinterpret what we say.

3. They won't be receptive.

4. It will put our friendship at risk.

5. We will be open to retaliation or counterattack.

6. There's nothing in it for us.

7. It could backfire and the problem could get worse.

8. It could escalate and we don't like conflict.

9. We'll be out on a limb and won't be supported.

10. Nothing will change anyway.

Each of these reasons undermines integrity, saps self-confidence, and lessens our commitment to improvement and making a difference. Each reduces respect for the maturity and intelligence of the people with whom we are trying to communicate and renders feedback useless. Each of these ten reasons can be countered as follows:

1. It is possible to communicate honestly without hurting anyone's feelings.

2. We can communicate accurately so there is no misinterpretation.

3. They can't be receptive unless we try.

4. Without honesty, we can't have a genuine friendship.

5. If we act collaboratively, they won't respond defensively.

6. We increase self-esteem and opportunities for change through honest communication.

7. The problem will get worse if we don't communicate honestly. If we succeed, we won't have to be bothered by it anymore.

8. If it escalates, we can use conflict resolution techniques to minimize and resolve the conflict.

9. If we risk being honest, others may take that risk also.

10. Things change when people communicate honestly with each other.

When we retreat from honest feedback, water it down, or make it useless, we cheat others out of any possibility of learning, turning their lives around, and becoming more skillful and successful. What is at stake in honest feedback is *their* opportunity to become better at what they do, and *our* opportunity to act with integrity.

The Risks of Feedback

There are other risks in delivering honest feedback, which can be countered by addressing them openly and adopting countermeasures, as indicated below:

- *The risk of arrogance.* Giving someone feedback with the assumption that we know how they should behave can be offset by negotiating with them as peers for more effective behaviors.

- *The risk of apathy.* A reluctance to give feedback because we do not care enough about the other person's growth and improvement can be countered by being curious about who they are and stimulating their interest through challenging learning opportunities.

- *The risk of judgment.* Judgments about who we are and what we have done can be shifted by listening more deeply, actively examining our assumptions, and asking questions about what we think we know.

- *The risk of creating a conspiracy of silence.* Adopting a conspiracy of silence, or tacit agreement to forgo being honest, can be broken by initiating open and honest communication.

- *The risk of triviality.* Keeping communications superficial and never addressing the real issues can be challenged by converting trivial interactions into deeper discussions, taking time, paying attention to larger issues, and focusing on the learning process.

- *The risk of focusing exclusively on the past.* Fixation on the past can be altered by focusing on the present or the future.

- *The risk of false objectivity.* An unwillingness to closely examine our biases can be countered by self-scrutiny and personal responsibility for creating more accurate perceptions of reality.

- *The risk of generality.* Depriving each other of specific examples of what was not successful reduces the possibility of learning, and can be opposed by citing specifics, details, and data for self-discovery.

- *The risk of unilateral action.* Feedback imposed without permission is an exercise of power over others and a kind of tyranny that can be shifted by creating a two-way process so people are more willing to participate.

- *The risk of excessive kindness.* Being excessively kind can be an act of cruelty, preventing someone from understanding how their actions affect others. This can be cured by honestly and empathetically communicating painful information, citing real examples and insisting on change.

How to Give Team Feedback

Petty frictions, miscommunications, misunderstandings, and dysfunctions can cause teams to experience drag and turbulence and lose their synergy, trust, and morale. Insignificant conflicts can accumulate to the point that emotions escalate beyond control and work grinds to a halt. For these reasons, it is useful to periodically clear the air of issues that have simmered beneath the surface through a process in which team members give feedback to each other.

In conducting these sessions, we often use the following feedback instruments: *Supporting Team Behavior* and *Blocking Team Behavior.* We start by asking participants to record any of their own behaviors or those of others that either support or undermine the team process. Like all frameworks, these follow a prototype that can easily be revised to reflect a team's unique circumstances.

Supporting Team Behaviors

Please score yourself and others on the following behaviors, ranking each from 1 to 5:
1 = Never; 2 = Rarely; 3 = Sometimes; 4 = Often; 5 = Always.

Supporting Behaviors	Self	Others
1. Volunteering for roles		
2. Encouraging others		
3. Speaking honestly		
4. Asking for feedback		
5. Supporting the agenda		
6. Bringing team back to the agenda		
7. Monitoring time limits		
8. Inviting others to speak		
9. Summarizing results		
10. Acknowledging others		
11. Being on time		
12. Bringing materials or refreshments		
13. Mediating conflicts		
14. Requesting clarification		
15. Being open to others ideas		
16. Inviting others into discussion		
17. Suggesting positive processes		
18. Sharing real thoughts and feelings		
19. Sharing information		
20. Encouraging fun		

Blocking Team Behaviors

Please score yourself and others on the following behaviors, ranking each from 1 to 5:
1 = Never; 2 = Rarely; 3 = Sometimes; 4 = Often; 5 = Always.

Supporting Behaviors	Self	Others
1. Interrupting discussion		
2. Starting side conversations		
3. Making sarcastic comments		
4. Building negative attitude		
5. Ignoring others' comments		
6. Being argumentative		
7. Making negative facial gestures		
8. Dominating discussion		
9. Withdrawing from discussion		
10. Making tangential remarks		
11. Manipulating for personal agenda		
12. Resisting consensus		
13. Forming divisions within the team		
14. Downplaying others' contributions		
15. Sitting apart		
16. Arriving late		
17. Leaving early		
18. Being unwilling to clarify		
19. Being defensive		
20. Rejecting feedback		

After completing these assessments, we ask team members to identify any insights they had while filling them out. We then ask the team leader to identify any of *her* behaviors that support or block the team-building process. The team leader then asks other team members to give her feedback on these observations. If the leader is tough on herself the team will come to her defense. If she lets herself off the hook or does not mention behaviors that undermine the team process, the team will identify them for her. After everyone finishes giving feedback to the team leader it becomes the next person's turn, and so on until everyone is finished. Afterward, everyone evaluates the process, discusses how to model transparency and openness in future communications, and acknowledges each other for their openness and honesty.

Feedback is ultimately a set of questions we each need to answer for ourselves. More simply, it is a way of waking ourselves up and cultivating awareness and authenticity at work. It not only increases our ability to see ourselves as others see us, but to discover and *be* who we actually are.

Visual Explorer™
A Tool for Enabling Creative Conversations
Contributed by David Magellan Horth and Charles J. Palus

Visual Explorer™ Defined

Visual Explorer™ (VE) is a tool for creating dialogue and producing insights in all kinds of contexts, by putting a set of images "in the middle" of the conversation and starting with one or more framing questions. The 216 images are deliberately diverse and global in subject, context, and aesthetics, and range from food to space travel, from birth to death, from organization to complexity and chaos. The images invite examination—they are visually interesting. The images invite connections—they provide metaphors and thus carry ideas and insights. VE helps conversations (Figure 14.7) within

Figure 14.7. Dialogue with Visual Explorer™.

and among teams become more collaborative and creative. VE supports team leadership by helping to create and maintain shared direction, alignment, and commitment among team members and stakeholders.

The audience for VE is global and diverse. Essentially the audience is everyone. We have found that a single set of images can speak to this diversity, including audiences in business organizations, teams of all kinds, youth initiatives, coaching, self-development, and social change, in every country and culture. VE transcends languages and cultures; the images themselves comprise a kind of cross-cultural visual language. Humanity is, after all, a single species with a huge common ground in how we experience work, love, play, survival, art, nature, and each other. Images have the potential to reinforce our commonalities while engaging our differences.

VE helps teams to:

- Surface and explore a variety of perspectives
- Provoke new questions
- Elicit stories
- Create metaphors
- Tap into personal experiences and passions
- Articulate what has been unspoken or "undiscussable"
- Relate with others through dialogue
- Define a shared vision
- Seek patterns in complex issues and make new connections
- Explore and discover solutions to problems and challenges
- Evaluate themselves and their work in a nonjudgmental way

Examples of VE Applications

A consultant-trainer at a large insurance and financial institution frequently uses *Visual Explorer* for team building. The tool's images support conversations about team identity, strengths, and purpose, building trust and alignment among and between teams. "It's not unusual for individuals in a work group, even those that have been together for a long time, to be ill at ease with each other," she told us. "Using photos and images brings safety. You're not talking about me. Instead, you're talking about a picture. That's safer and inspires confidence."

Another example: In planning a retreat at a global consumer products company, a team leader decided to feature storytelling. She wanted to share the rich history of the team that the newer members didn't know much about. She also wanted the team to tell stories about where it was going and what its future might look like. She began the retreat using *Visual Explorer*, asking each person to select three images: one connected to the past, one to the present, and one to the future of this team. She also asked each person to pick among a set of images that had been turned facedown, but not to look at the image. She saved those pictures until later, when members turned them over and asked themselves—while referring to these fresh images— "How might we get blindsided?" Figure 14.8 show a small sample of *Visual Explorer* images.

Figure 14.8. A Sample of Visual Explorer™ Images.

Conducting a Visual Explorer Session

Five steps constitute a typical session. A minimum of sixty minutes is usually required:

1. *Frame.* The first step is to identify the topic of the conversation and to focus it for the group through the use of one or more framing questions. Required Time: variable.

2. *Browse.* Participants browse through all the images and choose one for each framing question. Required Time: ten minutes.

3. *Reflect.* Participants quietly observe and think about the images and consider their responses to the question(s). Required Time: ten minutes.

4. *Share.* Participants share their images, one at a time, and converse about the framing questions in connection with the images they have selected. Participants respond to each other's images. Required Time: at least five minutes per person.

5. *Extend.* After a *Visual Explorer* session there is often momentum for continuing the dialogue and doing something more with the insights. Groups often cascade the conversation to other stakeholders inside and outside the organization, using the selected images for further communications. Required Time: variable.

Case: *Visual Explorer*™ in Afghan National Army Leadership Development

VE can be a useful tool when working across cultures in non-Western settings. The following link summarized a case in which Visual Explorer was used for and leadership development with a cadre of officers in the Afghan National Army, onsite in Kabul in March of 2009. See http://www.cclex plorer.org/2009/visualexplorer/visual-explorer%E2%84%A2-in-afghanistan

As pre-work the officers were asked to interview their peers and U.S. mentors about their approaches to leadership. At the beginning of the workshop, the facilitator engaged them in a conversation about the leadership of General Ahmad Shah Massoud, "Lion of Panjshir," the martyred military and spiritual leader credited with driving the Soviets from Afghanistan. Participants were pleasantly surprised that they were being *asked* rather than *told* about leadership.

With this initial preparation, they were then introduced to *Visual Explorer.* The images were vetted in advance by the local Muslim imam (the image of Lady Godiva did not make the cut but the rest were approved). Each participant was asked to choose an image that represented his own definition of effective leadership, and then to share and discuss the images and definitions with their table groups. A lively conversation ensued. The impact of the conversation was extended by the creation of a collage of all the selected images (Figure 14.9).

Visual Explorer was thus instrumental in a key goal of the program, which was to build respect, trust, and loyalty among the leaders and mentors using an adult learning approach of dialogue, reflection, teamwork, and shared inquiry.

Figure 14.9. A Collage of the Images Participants Used to Define Leadership, from Their Own Perspectives.

Additional Reading

Palus, C. J., and Horth, D. M. (2007). Visual Explorer. In Holman, P., Devane, T., & Cady, S. (Eds.). *The Change Handbook: The Definitive Resource on Today's Best Methods for Engaging Whole Systems.* San Francisco: Berrett-Koehler.

Palus, C. J., and Horth, D. M. (2002). *The Leader's Edge: Six Creative Competencies for Navigating Complex Challenges.* San Francisco: Jossey-Bass.

Palus, C. J., and Drath, W. H. (2001). Putting something in the middle: An approach to dialogue. *Reflections 3*(2), 28–39.

The support blog for VE is at www.cclexplorer.org/visualexplorer. VE may be purchased at www.ccl.org/ve.

Index

Page references followed by *fig* indicate an illustrated figure; followed by *t* indicate a table.

A

Accelerating Your Development as a Leader (Barner), 105

Accountability: building commitment barrier of vague, 134; clarify cross-cultural team members' roles and, 230; effective boundary management as promoting, 157; establish ground rules for virtual team members, 189–191; *Real-Time Implementation Planning* tool to build, 35, 366–368; team action plan clarifying areas of, 35; *Team Alignment Pyramid* tool to build, 55

Action planning: *Action Planning Chart* tool for, 35; description of, 13, 32; five steps for process of, 33, 35–36; follow-up meeting questions regarding process of, 37; how to facilitate, 32–33; matching team-building tool for, 42*t*; *Preventive and*

Corrective Action Plans tool for, 122, 361; tools available for, 35; understanding differences between intention and action, 34*t*. *See also* Team action plans

Action Planning Chart tool: description of, 244; instructions and example of, 244–245; used with *Real-Time Implementation Planning*, 367; suggestions for when to use, 35

Actions: regaining momentum, 212–216; supporting building commitment, 139–149; supporting cross-cultural teaming, 234–238; supporting future vision, 57–61; supporting mutual trust and collaboration, 91–105; supporting team innovation, 72–77; supporting working virtually, 181–198; supportive of overcoming setbacks, 207–216